Studies in Interactional Sociolinguistics 2

Language and social identity

Companion to this volume

Discourse strategies John J. Gumperz

Language and social identity

Edited by JOHN J. GUMPERZ
Professor of Anthropology,
University of California, Berkeley

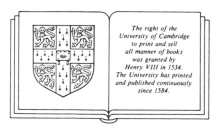

The right of the
University of Cambridge
to print and sell
all manner of books
was granted by
Henry VIII in 1534.
The University has printed
and published continuously
since 1584.

Cambridge University Press

Cambridge
New York   New Rochelle
Melbourne   Sydney

Published by the Press Syndicate of the University of Cambridge
The Pitt Building, Trumpington Street, Cambridge CB2 1RP
32 East 57th Street, New York, NY 10022, USA
10 Stamford Road, Oakleigh, Melbourne 3166, Australia

First published 1982
Reprinted 1983, 1985, 1987, 1988

Printed in the United States of America

Library of Congress catalogue card number: 82-4331

British Library Cataloguing in Publication Data
Gumperz, John J.
Language and social identity.–
(Studies in interactional sociolinguistics)
1. Communication – Social aspects – Case studies
I. Title II. Series
302.2'0722 (expanded)   HM258
ISBN 0 521 24692 X hard covers
ISBN 0 521 28897 5 paperback

Contents

Preface

This volume is the product of several years of cooperative field research. The initial goal was to seek comparative data to document and test the claim that interpretive analysis of conversational exchanges in key, naturally organized situations can yield significant insights into the communicative processes that underlie categorization, intergroup stereotyping, evaluation of verbal performance and access to public resources in modern societies. Ethnographic information and tape recordings of individuals of differing social and ethnic backgrounds interacting in such settings as counselling encounters, business and committee meetings, courtroom interrogations, public debates and family situations in North America and Britain were collected and subjected to comparative analysis. Most of the contributors were members of the research group directed by the Editor, and drew on a common pool of data. Heller, Maltz and Borker, and Tannen report on studies of their own that follow a similar perspective.

As the book developed, it became apparent that additional discussion was necessary to show how detailed analyses of conversational exchanges can contribute to an understanding of broader social issues. The introduction was therefore expanded to include a general discussion of basic communicative characteristics of modern industrial societies and their relation to ethnic and social distinction, and to the evaluation of verbal performance. The final chapter by Jupp, Roberts, and Cook-Gumperz reverts to this broader theme in discussing industrial communication in Britain, with special reference to the socioeconomic position of workers and professionals of Asian background.

Acknowledgments

Several of the chapters in this book appeared in preliminary form elsewhere. Earlier versions of Tannen's chapter appeared as 'Ethnicity as conversational style,' Working Paper in Sociolinguistics No. 55, Austin, Texas: Southwest Educational Development Laboratory (1979) and as 'Indirectness in discourse: ethnicity as conversational style,' *Discourse Processes* 4:3 (1981). An earlier version of Heller's chapter appeared in *Proceedings of the Berkeley Linguistic Society (BLS)* 4 (1978). Bennett, as well as Hansel and Seabrook Ajirotutu, published earlier versions in *BLS* 5 (1979), and earlier versions of Mishra's and Young's chapters appeared in *BLS* 6 (1980).

This book would not have been possible without the active cooperation of many organizations and individuals. Research in England was carried out in cooperation with the National Institute of Industrial Language Training and the Pathway Further Education Centre, Southall, Middlesex, England. We are grateful to David Bonamy, Evelyn Davies, Denise Gubbay, Tom Jupp, Elizabeth Laird, Celia Roberts, and Jaswinder Singh Sidhu for contributing both data and crucial ethnographic insights. Niyi Akinnaso, Gurinder Aulakh, Adrian Bennett, Richard Bonte, Kelsey Clark, James Collins, Sarah Freeman, Mark Hansell, Hannah Kaltman, Arpita Mishra, Cheryl Seabrook Ajirotutu, Deborah Tannen, and Robert Van Valin served as research assistants during various phases of the American portion of the project, and all contributed to the development of analytic techniques. Andrew Conrad acted as editor for a number of the individual field studies.

The following individuals contributed to particular chapters: Marilyn Silver commented on Chapter 3; Celia Roberts contributed data for Chapter 4; Morton Marks contributed to data collection for Chapter 5; Frederick Erickson commented on Chapter 6; Louis Chase assisted with Chapter 9; Alton S. Becker, Douglas Campbell, James Collins, William Geoghegan and Paz Naylor all made important contributions to Chapter 10. Monica Heller would like to thank the staff of the Outpatient Department of the hospital where fieldwork was carried out. Deborah Tannen acknowledges assistance from the following: Wallace Chafe, Jenny Cook-Gumperz, Pam Fahlund, Jim Garofallou, David Gordon, Dee Holisky, Dell Hymes, Kostas Lazazis, Mathilde Peterakis, Bambi

Schieffelin, Georgette Stratos, Theoni Velli-Spyropoulos and Cynthia Wallat. Tom Jupp, Celia Roberts, and Jenny Cook-Gumperz wish to acknowledge that in writing Chapter 13 they have drawn upon the ideas and practical experience of many Industrial Language Training staff, and that they owe a special debt to David Bonamy, Denise Gubbay, and Jaswinder Singh Sidhu. They are also most grateful to John Gumperz for his ideas, encouragement, and practical help. In preparing Chapter 11, Daniel Maltz and Ruth Borker acknowledge contributions from Niyi Akinnaso, Kitty Julien, and Ron Macaulay. They would like to add, further, the following acknowledgment: during the course of writing and rewriting this article we have benefited from the thoughts and suggestions of more people than it is possible to acknowledge individually. Our primary debts are to John Gumperz for our general approach to the anthropological study of communication and miscommunication and to Sally McConnell-Ginet, who first introduced us to the field of women and language, and inspired us in the courses on language and sex roles we audited from or co-taught with her at Cornell. Since many of the basic ideas in this paper were developed in conversations with Sally, it is nearly impossible to separate her ideas from our own. Our many thoughts on differences between men's and women's speech were solidified into a single argument comparing cross-sex conversation with interethnic ones as a result of a course entitled 'Culture and miscommunication' which Ruth taught at San Francisco State during the summer of 1979, and we thank the students in that course for their key role in contributing to the development of our argument. For encouraging us to turn our argument into a formal paper, we thank the various people associated with Pitzer College who arranged for us to give a formal presentation at their Linguistics Colloquium and provided additional encouragement in their response to our presentation, especially Roger Abrahams, Don Brenneis, Bette Clark, Ron Macaulay, and Fred Myers. We would also like to thank John Gumperz and Willett Kempton for arranging for us to present the paper to sociolinguistics classes at UC Berkeley and to Mario Davila and Loki Pandey for arranging for us to present the paper to an anthropology colloquium at UC Santa Cruz. Other helpful comments followed presentation of the paper at Lewis and Clark College, Georgetown University, Duke Uni-

versity and the University of California at Davis Medical School.
Next, we offer thanks to those specialists in the study of sex roles
and language who provided bibliographic or other assistance and
critical comments in response to earlier versions of the paper,
including Linda Coleman, Susan Ervin-Tripp, Candy Goodwin,
Hannah Kaltman, Mary Parlee, Bambi Schieffelin, and Candy
West, and thank Grace Buzaljko for her excellent editorial assistance. Finally, we must acknowledge the fact that almost everyone
we have talked to during the past two years has heard some
informal version of this paper and has contributed some of her or
his own insights and experiences as a native informant on male and
female speech in America. We assume that the many friends with
whom we have discussed these ideas know who they are and will
regard this as a group acknowledgement of their assistance. Our
argument on the relation between gender differences in the social
organization of children's play and adult rules for conversation is
developed further in a second paper (Maltz and Borker 1980), still
being prepared for publication.

The basic methods of data analysis, the design of the research
and the overall conceptualization of the book are the responsibility
of the Editor. The research was made possible by a grant from the
National Institute of Mental Health (NIMH/MH26831). The
writing was completed while the Editor was a visiting member of
the Institute for Advanced Study, Princeton, New Jersey, under a
grant from the National Endowment for the Humanities.

June 1982   John J. Gumperz

A note on conventions

Prosodic notation

Prosodic notation is included in the example texts only where and
only to the extent necessary for a full understanding; otherwise the
prosody is explained in the discussion.

/	minor, nonfinal phrase boundary marker
//	major, final phrase boundary marker
ˎ	low fall tone
ˋ	high fall tone
ˏ	low rise tone
´	high rise tone
˅	fall rise tone
˄	rise fall tone
‾	sustained tone
ˌ	low secondary stress
ˈ	high secondary stress
⌐	pitch register shift, upwards
∟	pitch register shift, lowered
acc	accelerated tempo
dec	decelerated tempo
l	lenis enunciation
stacc	staccato enunciation
⌈⌊	conversation overlap
..	speech pause
...	long speech pause
( )	unintelligible word

1

Introduction: language and the communication of social identity

JOHN J. GUMPERZ AND JENNY COOK-GUMPERZ

In this volume we present a series of case studies exploring situations of intergroup communication in modern industrial society. These studies are instances out of which we seek to develop interpretive sociolinguistic approaches to human interaction which account for the role that communicative phenomena play in the exercise of power and control and in the production and reproduction of social identity. Our basic premise is that social processes are symbolic processes but that symbols have meaning only in relation to the forces which control the utilization and allocation of environmental resources. We customarily take gender, ethnicity, and class as given parameters and boundaries within which we create our own social identities. The study of language as interactional discourse demonstrates that these parameters are not constants that can be taken for granted but are communicatively produced. Therefore to understand issues of identity and how they affect and are affected by social, political, and ethnic divisions we need to gain insights into the communicative processes by which they arise.

However, communication cannot be studied in isolation; it must be analyzed in terms of its effect on people's lives. We must focus on what communication does: how it constrains evaluation and decision making, not merely how it is structured. We therefore begin with materials or texts collected in strategic research sites which exemplify the problems we seek to deal with. Rather than concentrating on ethnography, grammar, semantics, or linguistic variation alone, we want to find ways of analyzing situated talk that brings together social, sociocognitive, and linguistic constructs, and to develop relevant analytic methods that build on the perspective of sociolinguistic theory outlined in the previous work on discourse strategies (Gumperz 1982). We are attempting to provide for the integration of individual consciousness, face-to-face processes of social activity, and situated group communication processes within contexts selected for their importance in the life space of the people studied.

These goals raise a further basic question. What is it about modern bureaucratic industrial society that increases the importance of communication processes? Perhaps the most important characteristic of the social environments in which we live is their unprecedented cultural and ethnic diversity. Social conflict during the last decades has increasingly come to be characterized as ethnic, class, or religious conflict. But cultural pluralism is not new. Why is it that social distinctions which in other times were taken for granted and accepted as intrinsic to social order have suddenly become points of contention? What distinguishes today's urban situation is that the modes of interaction among subgroups and the ways in which individuals of different backgrounds must relate to each other and to the system by which they are governed have changed. The old forms of plural society in which families lived in island-like communities, surrounded and supported by others of similar ethnic or class background, are no longer typical.

In our daily lives we have become increasingly dependent on public services and on cooperation with others who may not share our culture. Yet unforeseen difficulties tend to arise when individuals of different cultural backgrounds communicate in public speech events such as committee meetings, interviews, employment situations, and similar types of goal-directed verbal interaction. This can be true, even in cases where we find no overt conflict of values and goals. We all know that it is much easier to get things done when participants share the same background. When backgrounds differ, meetings can be plagued by misunderstandings, mutual misrepresentations of events and misevaluations. It seems that, in intergroup encounters, judgments of performance and of ability that on the whole are quite reliable when people share the same background may tend to break down. Interactions that are normally seen as routine often meet with unforeseen problems. Accepted strategies of persuasion and argumentation may no longer be successful. Furthermore, the difficulties occurring in such situations do not disappear with the increasing intensity of intergroup contact. On the contrary, they seem to increase and often become most acute after the groups involved have been in contact for several years and initial grammatical difficulties have disappeared. When this situation persists over time, what starts as isolated situation-bound communication differences at the individual level may harden into ideological distinctions that then become value laden, so that every time problems of understanding arise they serve to create further differences in the symbolization of identity.

One might argue that some urban residents acquire styles of speaking that serve them well in home and peer group situations but are likely to be misunderstood in intergroup settings, while others of different backgrounds do not have these problems. This would suggest that once linguistic sources of misunderstanding are isolated and situated norms of language usage specified, appropriate behavior can be taught. Yet the issue cannot be as simple as this because talk itself is constitutive of social reality. Where communicative conventions and symbols of social identity differ, the social reality itself becomes subject to question. On the other hand, however, both talk and social reality are part of and serve to maintain an ideology which takes on a historical life of its own. However, this is not a completely deterministic argument. We do not intend to claim that ideology shapes language and that since language shapes social reality there is no way out. Our main goal in this book is to show how ideology enters into face-to-face speaking practices to create an interactional space in which the subconscious and automatic sociolinguistic processes of interpretation and inference can generate a variety of outcomes and make interpretations subject to question. Thus we are not separating meaning and actions in their abstract analytical form, but we are looking at how they are realized in practices and how this process of realization can influence seemingly value-free assessments. To that end we begin with a more detailed discussion of institutional and socioecological forces that affect communication.

The social relevance of communicative processes

Post-industrial society in the urbanized regions of both Western and non-Western countries is characterized by the bureaucratization of public institutions and by the increasingly pervasive penetration of these institutions into the day-to-day lives of individuals. These phenomena produce certain characteristics that serve to differentiate present-day communicative environments from those of the past. What we are referring to here is a major historical change in the relationship of the individual to public institutions. This change has created a context where the public life of society members is materially affected by public agencies like educational and industrial institutions, union organizations, social welfare, or health services.

Technological specialization of function complicates life in many ways, but what is of special interest here is the communicative maze society erects as part of the process of producing demonstrably public rationality of decision making. In job selection, for example, replacing a practical demonstration of the applicant's ability to do a particular job are elaborate procedures involving complex verbal tasks. From the filling out of application forms, the career counselling session, the job interview, and the salary negotiation, assumptions about how information is to be conveyed are critical and these are assumptions which may vary widely even within the same socioeconomic group in the same community. Objective tests replace personal discretion. Hence candidates who do well may or may not be as competent to do the job as the non-successful test-taker. Finally, personnel judgments, and many other societal evaluations, are grounded on the individual's ability to talk well and to make a good presentation of him/herself, as well as the ability to pass tests. Many situations may only be entered by way of a written demonstration of verbal and mathematical skills, but, once demonstrated, these written skills must be reinforced orally, in interviews. In other words, what counts is the ability to conform to the principles of rhetoric by which performance is judged in bureaucratic systems.

The role communicative skills play has thus been radically altered in our society. The ability to manage or adapt to diverse communicative situations has become essential and the ability to interact with people with whom one has no personal acquaintance is crucial to acquiring even a small measure of personal and social control. We have to talk in order to establish our rights and entitlements. When we are at work we often rely on interactive and persuasive skills to get things done. Communicative resources thus form an integral part of an individual's symbolic and social capital, and in our society this form of capital can be every bit as essential as real property resources were once considered to be (Bourdieu 1973).

The conditions we have described have brought about major changes in the nature and significance of ethnic and social boundaries. The term 'ethnicity' has traditionally been used to refer to relationships based on the linkage of similar people, whose social identity was formed by influences from outside the society in which they now live; but increasingly it has come to indicate relationships based on differences distinguishing one, new, indigenous group from another (Glazer and Moynihan 1975). We shall refer to these two concepts as the *old* and the *new* ethnicity, respectively. The old ethnicity was supported both regionally and interpersonally through reinforced social networks which joined people through clusters of occupational, neighborhood, familial, and political ties. People of the same ethnicity often lived near each other and supported each other within their work and their political groups. Marriage and families continued these network linkages. In the large urban centers of the industrial world, the consciousness of immigrant groups' separate historical past was reinforced in the present by physical-geographic, friendship, and occupational ties.

The new ethnicity depends less upon geographic proximity and shared occupations and more upon the highlighting of key differences separating one group from another. Michael Hechter (1978), in developing a general theory of ethnicity that accounts for changes in the modern urban world, has referred to the dual basis of modern urban concepts of ethnicity as (1) *interactive* group formation, whereby one group is distinguished from another by its similarities and overlapping networks; and (2) *reactive* group formation whereby an ethnic group reasserts its historically established distinctions from other groups within a common national polity. The new ethnicity is more a product of the second process, because this ethnic identity is defined more as a need for political and social support in the pursuit of common interest than as regional similarity or sharedness of occupational ties.

Individuals build upon residual elements of shared culture to revive a common sentiment upon which to found ethnically based interest groups. Ethnic identity thus becomes a means of eliciting political and social support in the pursuit of goals which are defined within the terms of reference established by the society at large. Because of the complex communicative environment in which individuals must exist, the cohesiveness of the new ethnic groups cannot rest on co-residence in geographically bounded or internally homogenous communities. Even established immigrant communities are no longer able to survive in communicatively isolated separate islands. Inner-city ethnic neighborhoods may limit residents' access to public resources, but they no longer insulate.

The old ethnic ties found their linguistic expression in loyalty to a language other than that of the major society. The new ethnic identities rely on linguistic symbols to establish speech conventions that are significantly different. These symbols are much more than mere markers of identity. Increasing participation in public affairs leads to the introduction of terminologies and discourse patterns modelled on those of the community at large which come to exist and be used alongside more established forms. New communicative strategies are created based on the juxtaposition of the two sets of forms which symbolize not only group membership but adherence to a set of values. These communicative conventions are largely independent of the actual language, i.e., they may be used whether the minority or the majority language is spoken. Even where the original native language is lost the new discourse conventions tend to persist and to be taken over into the group's use of the majority language. In fact these conventions come to reflect the identity of the group itself and can act as powerful instruments of persuasion in everyday communicative situations for participants who share its values (Gumperz 1982, chapter 2).

For example, in the United States, American English is the primary language of the indigenous population but this common language hides an underlying diversity in values and discourse conventions. These differences were for a long time dismissed as nonstandard language practices that detracted from the potential effectiveness of the group as communicators, even though the first language of the group was English. But the fact that these linguistic and discourse differences seem to persist in the face of pressure for standardization has forced a reevaluation of their social and communicative significance.

The discussion of sex differences in language in Chapter 11 provides some initial insights into the question of how social processes function to create new linguistic symbols. Maltz and Borker show that participation in different small group structures gives rise to different discourse conventions even where individuals are reared in the same or similar family environments. Like the ethnic distinctions discussed in other chapters, these conventions can cause misunderstandings and lead to perpetuation of social distance. Gender distinctions thus have at least some, though of course not all, the characteristics of ethnic distinctions: Tannen's work in Chapter 12 suggests that the signalling of ethnic identity in modern society can be seen as part of the broader problem of social identity.

It is in these ways that we can see how the social and political conditions of modern life favor the creation of new linguistic symbols which can serve as the rallying point for interest group sharing. This reliance on in-group symbols, however, conflicts with the equally strong need for control of the rhetorical strategies of the bureaucratically accepted modes of communication. The bureaucratic system can thus be seen as a major structural source of the communicative complexity we have been discussing. Bureaucracy relies on the existence of what are seen as uniform meritocratic criteria of evaluation to control access to scarce resources. Meritocratic standards must be independent of the evaluator's individual preference. In theory at least, they must stand above ethnic and cultural variation. Such standards must ultimately be defensible in a public arena where courts and public hearings are the final arbiters of legitimacy.

Without an increasingly ethnically diverse population, bureaucracy might be far less of an issue than it is. A common ethnicity that includes a common communicative history would insure the transmission of strategies of negotiation which would be shared by most. But pluralism complicates the problem immeasurably.

The key point of our argument in this book is that social identity and ethnicity are in large part established and maintained through language. Yet it is because of the historical character of the process through which groups are formed and the symbols of identity created that we have the particular characteristics of the ways of speaking that we will be analyzing. This argument therefore serves to attenuate the explanatory relationship between language, ideology, and speaking practices. Only by understanding the specific historical roots of language divergence can we adequately account for the specific character of the communicative practices and monitor ongoing processes of social change.

The data for the analyses in this book consist of verbal interaction sequences where speakers of differing social and ethnic backgrounds unconsciously employ distinct language usage and rhetorical strategies. Where this occurs, differences in the interpretation of such strategies can be seen to affect the outcome of an encounter. Although professional personnel, local government officials, and especially minority group members active in community work in metropolitan areas tend to be aware of such communication difficulties, subtle cues are involved which are not easy to perceive in the course of the interaction itself where there is pressure to get things done. Even an odd word or turn of phrase, or a misunderstood tone of voice, can seriously affect trust among participants. But to isolate clear instances of how this happens is difficult. Some people have strategies for successfully overcoming these difficulties, or can adapt to the differences, or some members of ethnic minority groups do not speak their own variety of English and therefore can switch to the majority variety because this does not symbolize ethnic differences per se. However, many individuals from both the majority and the minority ethnic groups do not cope well in stressful situations of interethnic communication and then, as they do not recognize the reasons, have various ways of blaming each other. Since we are dealing with transitory oral phenomena, causes are hard to determine. Only through a social and linguistic theory which locates these phenomena in historical and contemporary space can we learn to know where to look.

The empirical basis: creating situations and texts
The first step in attacking these problems, which by their very nature are difficult to document and to analyze in detail, is to gain qualitative insights. Our analysis therefore seeks to emphasize interpretive methods of in-depth study, rather than relying on survey techniques to enumerate behaviors or compiling self-reports. What we need to do is find typical instances of key situations or

speech events which are critical given our analysis of the social and ethnographic background.

In terms familiar from recent work in ethnography of communication, we would argue that the developments of our recent past, perhaps as recent a past as the last few decades, have created, or at least brought to central importance, new *kinds* of speech events. Some of these new events are (1) interviews (job, counselling, psychiatric, governmental), (2) committee negotiations, (3) courtroom interrogations and formal hearings, (4) public debates and discussions.

While different in detail, such events share certain important features. Although on the surface an air of equality, mutuality, and cordiality prevails, participant roles, i.e., the right to speak and the obligation to answer, are predetermined, or at least strictly constrained. In interviews the interviewer chooses questions, initiates topics of discussions, and evaluates responses. The interviewees respond, i.e., they answer. Often they are expected to volunteer information but what it is they can say is strictly constrained by expectations which are rarely made explicit. When they venture into the interviewers' territory, interviewers may comment: *"I'm interviewing you , not vice versa."* In committee meetings and to some extent in debates and discussions, tacitly understood rules of preference, unspoken conventions as to what counts as valid and what information may or may not be introduced prevail. The participant structure of such events thus reflects a real power asymmetry underneath the surface equality, a serious problem when the lesser communicator does not know the rules. The issue is compounded by the fact that what is evaluated appears to be neutral. Evaluators tend to concentrate on presentation of facts and information, or problem solving and reasoning abilities, so that underlying sources of ambiguity are not ordinarily discovered.

Although evaluation may ultimately be subjective, whatever judgments are made must be made relative to explicit meritocratic and demonstrably objective standards of ability and achievement where decisions are appealable. Hence standards must, in theory at least, be publicly available. Judgments must be defensible in the public arena. But since appeals require rhetorical sophistication, including acquaintance with often unstated assumptions specific to the dominant culture or to the organization doing the judging, the weaker participant, who lacks the requisite verbal knowledge, is always at a disadvantage.

The initial task in the analysis is basically an ethnographic one of collecting actual instances of interactive situations containing all the internal evidence to document outcomes. Recordings of public meetings or on-the-spot public broadcasts provide a good first source of materials. Since it is often impossible to collect the background information necessary for further stages of analysis, field work is also required.

Yet ethnographic work in modern urban settings involves a great deal of time. Individuals involved in interethnic relations are often quite ready to be interviewed and to talk about communication problems. However, the structural conditions of the situations we need to explore make it impossible for them to be too closely involved in the research without changing the very nature of the social context. And besides, interviews alone, apart from the information they yield about attitudes, cannot provide the data we need.

In order to understand and evaluate a situation from a member's perspective, the researchers need to be fully involved in the everyday affairs of the organization. They need to know what participants' aims and expectations are in addition to observing what happens. Ethnographers of communication have the difficult task of experiencing in order to uncover the practical strategies of others while at the same time becoming so involved that they themselves become one of the main focuses of their own inquiries. What involvement does is create the practical knowledge which enables us to know which situations are best exemplars of the practices we need to analyze. But the ethnographers' presence in the situation is not necessarily a sufficient trigger to lead to the critical situations that reveal the relevant social and environmental forces coming together at the same time.

One successful strategy in fact is illustrated by Jupp, Roberts, and Cook-Gumperz (this volume, Chapter 13) who rely on direct involvement with persons in an institution whose workings they have become familiar with over time, and on enlisting the cooperation of participants who have become convinced that they can gain by insights into their own selection and evaluation processes. Given this type of cooperation, it is usually relatively easy to obtain suitable material recorded in situ for analysis. Where, for ethical reasons, direct recording is not possible, actual situations can be recreated through play to gain an insight into the subconscious communicative phenomena. Experience with a wide range of natural situations can serve as the basis for recreating socially realistic experimental conditions where individuals are asked to reenact events such as job interviews with which they have become familiar in everyday life. If these naturalistic situations are skillfully constructed and not too carefully predetermined, rhetorical strategies will emerge automatically without conscious planning, as such strategies are so deeply embedded in the participants' practices. Since it is these rhetorical devices that we want to analyze, eliciting such constructed texts does not necessarily entail a loss of validity.

Our goal in presenting the case studies is to show how information on intergroup communication problems can be collected and to illustrate a promising means of analyzing what are real social problems. Studies in this book, therefore, are guided by an orientation and a theoretical approach to issues in the everyday social world which are defined as problems by participants themselves.

The analysis of cultural expectations
The speech situations that we deal with in the following chapters, though diverse, share common characteristics. They are goal oriented in the sense that each aims to *get* something done, i.e., to reach an agreement, to evaluate abilities, or to get advice. These goals are a defining characteristic of the situation in question. The fact that these overall goals exist and are shared by the participants provides us with a participants' viewpoint for judging when something goes wrong. Thus as a first step in the analysis, by simply looking at the content of what transpires, it is possible to judge to what extent communication has succeeded or failed.

No two events of course are perfectly comparable. One way of dealing with this is to abstract from time bound sequences to certain recurring activities and communicative tasks, such as: (1) narrating, (2) explaining, (3) arguing, (4) emphasizing, (5) instructing, (6) directing.

'Communicative task' is an abstract semantic concept defined in terms of semantic ties among component utterances. Inferences about what these ties are underlie interpretations of what is going on, what is intended, and what is being accomplished (Gumperz 1982, chapter 7). The list of tasks we have given is in large part universal in that all natural activities can be seen as consisting of these tasks or various combinations thereof. By identifying these tasks, we reach a level of abstraction which, like the linguists' abstraction to grammar, is independent of content and of particular situations.

Although the pragmatic conditions of communicative tasks are theoretically taken to be universal, the realizations of these tasks as social practices are culturally variable. This variation can be analyzed from several different perspectives, all of which of course co-occur in the actual practices.

(1)   Different cultural assumptions about the situation and about appropriate behavior and intentions within it.
(2)   Different ways of structuring information or an argument in a conversation.
(3)   Different ways of speaking: the use of a different set of unconscious linguistic conventions (such as tone of voice) to emphasize, to signal logical connections and to indicate the significance of what is being said in terms of overall meaning and attitudes.

By "different cultural assumptions" we refer to the fact that, even though people in situations such as we study agree on the overall purpose of the interaction, there are often radical differences as to what expectations and rights are involved at any one time. This is perhaps most vividly illustrated in Chapter 4 by Young where differences in the politeness norms which govern what information is emphasized and what is left tacit may result in miscommunications. Chapter 9 by Cook-Gumperz and Gumperz on committee negotiations shows how different cultural assumptions about what is required in making a convincing argument in a bureaucratic context, or even differences about what counts as evidence, can lead to misunderstanding. Heller (Chapter 7) demonstrates that sociopolitical change and especially shifts in power relationships can cause basic shifts in language usage norms so that, in spite of clear efforts at being polite and accommodating, some individuals are unable to overcome interpersonal distance.

The second perspective, "ways of structuring," relates to issues traditionally covered in rhetorical analysis and deals with such phenomena as sequencing of arguments and with decisions about what needs to be stated and what must be conveyed indirectly. Both Mishra and Young (Chapters 3 and 4) demonstrate systematic differences between Asians and Westerners in the structuring of information in such common tasks as giving explanations or directions. Mishra goes on to show how often unnoticed rhythmic and other discourse cues serve to control this structuring process. Tannen (Chapter 12) focuses on problems of interpretation of intent which result when two individuals have different ideas of how much directness is appropriate in a particular situation. Bennett (Chapter 6) demonstrates the power of yes–no questions in channelling interpretation.

By "ways of speaking" we refer to the actual linguistic cues used through which information relevant to the other two perspectives is signalled. This level includes grammar and lexicon as well as prosody, pausing, idioms, and other formulaic utterances. Our basic assumption is that in conversation we simultaneously interpret and communicate at several levels of generality, i.e., we simultaneously signal both content and about content. The linguistic signalling mechanisms involved here, particularly the interplay between such discourse cues as prosody, code switching, and formulaic speech, on the one hand, and syntax and semantics, on the other, are explained in some detail in Chapter 2. The application of the method is illustrated through several brief examples. Chapters 3 by Mishra and 5 by Hansell and Seabrook Ajirotutu both illustrate how some of these cues work, and provide startling evidence that what is involved here are differences in perception of what constitute communicatively significant cues. In interactions among lower-class blacks and middle-class whites who believe they understand each other such minor cuing differences can be compounded into widely divergent inferential chains.

What these studies show is that the linguistic conventions signalling communicative tasks, particularly the interplay of contextualizing and content signs, are much more sensitive to the ethnic and class backgrounds of the participants than one might expect. Speakers may have similar life styles, speak closely related dialects of the same language, and yet regularly fail to communicate.

More importantly, the nature of the interactive situations that our society mandates, and the evaluative criteria employed, stand in direct conflict with the subtleties of conversational interpretation and the inability of people to be aware of the fact that, as Bennett shows in Chapter 6, speakers who produce grammatical sentences in English can nevertheless show systematic differences in rhetorical strategies.

Sociolinguistic methods in the study of face-to-face interaction
It has often been assumed that ethnically different speakers are not able to handle the formal criteria for giving information or producing contextually relevant talk in situations with which they have little direct experience, such as job interviews, public debates, or discussions. Much of the discussion has proceeded as if speaking appropriately required the learning of a different script, and a different set of semantic and lexical options. The real problem is that whatever the situation, whether a formal interview or an informal meeting, the need in all communication for all people who are relative strangers to each other is to achieve a *communicative flexibility*, an ability to adapt strategies to the audience and to the signs, both direct and indirect, so that the participants are able to monitor and understand at least some of each other's meaning. Meaning in any face-to-face encounter is always negotiable; it is discovering *the grounds* for negotiation that requires the participants' skills. Many of the meanings and understandings, at the level of ongoing processes of interpretation of speaker's intent, depend upon culturally specific conventions, so that much of the meaning in any encounter is indirect and implicit. The ability to expose enough of the implicit meaning to make for a satisfactory encounter between strangers or culturally different speakers requires communicative flexibility.

Some initial insights into how we can study the achievement of communicative flexibility come from work on nonverbal communication. Through frame-by-frame microanalysis of film it can be shown that communication depends upon usually unnoticed behavioral cues and postures which have interactional, i.e., social, significance. Birdwhistell (1970) and Hall (1959) have demonstrated that (1) taken-for-granted and subconsciously given nonverbal signs play an integral part in signalling of attitudes and intent in nonverbal communication, and (2) misunderstandings can arise in cross-cultural communication when the relevant signalling conventions differ. Considerable systematic analysis in this area has concentrated on isolating the actual physical behaviors that could potentially play a communicative role. A distinction was made between three basic kinds of signals: (1) microsignals, such as eye blinks or the contraction of facial muscles, which often go unnoticed, (2) proxemic signals such as gaze direction, posture, and body orientation, and (3) complexes of signs that carry meanings in isolation, emblems such as winking, handshakes, and nods (Ekman and Friesen 1969). A second research approach has explored the role that these often subconscious signals play in conversational coordination (Kendon 1970). It has been demonstrated that all natural conversations are characterized by interspeaker coordination of signals. There is further evidence that nonverbal signs are rhythmically coordinated with verbal signs, both at the micro level of syllables and at the macro level of utterances (Condon and Ogsten 1969).

The usefulness of this nonverbal work is that it suggests behavioral ways of studying what Goffman (1961) calls conversational involvement and what we refer to as communicative flexibility. It enables us to tell, by looking only at actual performance features and without knowing the content, whether two speakers are actively communicating.

Erickson in his studies of counselling sessions (Erickson and Schultz 1982) has demonstrated that (a) the ability to establish rhythmic coordination of nonverbal signals was partially a function of participants' ethnic background, and (b) interviews characterized by rhythmic coordination were most successful in terms of the information interviewees received from the session. Even where sentence level meaning and grammar are shared therefore, failure to communicate is not just a matter of individual ability or willingness to make the effort. Apart from grammar proper there seems to be a second, equally automatic, level of interactive signs and conventions which must be shared if communication is to take place.

Little in linguistic research on syntax, grammar, or discourse deals explicitly with the question of what these discourse signals are and how they are acquired. Although psycholinguists and applied linguists concerned with problems of bilingualism have done considerable work on second language acquisition (Ervin-Tripp 1970), and on problems of the phenomena of interference – i.e., the tendency of second language learners to transfer patterns from their first language to the second language – research in this area concentrates on the phonology and grammar of isolated sentences. Phoneticians have done a great deal of work on the phonology of intonation, rhythm, and stress. But they tend to look at these suprasegmental features of language as channels for expression of emotion which add to but are separate from the main information-carrying functions of language (Crystal 1975). Work by dialecto-logists on Afro-American and other minority dialects of English has similarly concentrated on describing differences. To the extent that communication problems are discussed in this literature, they are seen in purely referential terms as failure to understand words or sentences (Shuy 1974) at the level of phonology, grammar, and lexicon.

In yet another area, considerable work has been done during the last ten years on phenomena of discourse. Story structures, the nature of narratives (Propp 1958; Labov 1973), and the linguistic signs that mark the relationships between sentences in longer passages (Halliday and Hasan 1976) have been investigated in some detail. The main concern here has been to demonstrate that there are systematic features of language that go beyond the sentence, i.e., that stories can be analyzed as having rule-governed grammars (Van Dijk 1977). The effort has been to describe and analyze structure, rather than to deal with the question of what makes communication effective.

These studies have moved linguistic inquiry in directions that are of great value for the study of face-to-face communication. But a sociolinguistic approach to communication must show how these features of discourse contribute to participants' interpretations of each other's motives and intents and show how these features are employed in maintaining conversational involvement.

The theoretical tradition in modern linguistics that has most explicitly dealt with processes of interpretation of intent and attitude in language use is that work in linguistic pragmatics which, building on philosophy of language, has concentrated on investigat-ing speech acts and on Grice's definition of meaning as intention (Cole and Morgan 1975). Although linguistic pragmatics is explicitly concerned with presuppositions in the interpretations of intent, the data analyses are based on situations where presuppositions are shared. Analysis moreover is largely sentence-based. While it is concerned with the logical structure of communicative events, it does not attempt to deal with the role of language in interactive processes.

The notion of intent is crucial and has carried us far beyond the older, purely abstract, structural approaches to language, to enable us to show how people build upon social knowledge in interaction. The concept of intent itself, however, if it is to be adapted to our goals, needs some modification. In dealing with conversational exchanges we do not and need not treat the psychological issue of what an individual has in mind, but rather we focus on how intent is interpreted by ordinary listeners in a particular context. We assume such interpretation is a function of (a) listeners' linguistic knowledge, (b) contextual presuppositions informed by certain cues, and (c) background information brought to bear on the interpretation. Our main concern is with systematic or patterned differences in interpretation that can be traced to socially determined differences in contextual presuppositions as they relate to particular conversational conventions. When we talk about intent therefore, we mean the socially recognized communicative intent that is implied in particular kinds of social activities signalled in discourse. Our guiding problematic is to discover what is necessary for the maintenance of conversational cooperation.

Conversational cooperation is commonly understood to refer to the assumptions that conversationalists must make about each other's contributions and to the conversational principles on which they rely. Cooperation, however, involves not only communication through the use of words in their literal meanings, but construction across time of negotiated and situationally specific conventions for the interpretation of discourse tasks as well as the speaker's and listener's knowledge of how to conduct and interpret live performances. The features previously referred to as paralinguistic, intonation, stress, rhythm, and contrastive shifts of phonetic values are all ways of conveying meaning that add to or alter the significance of semantic choices. To the extent that we can talk about conversations being governed and controlled by shared expectations, we must assume that these expectations are signalled, and sharedness is negotiated as part of the interaction itself. We refer to those signalling cues that are seen to operate systematically within specific communicative traditions and to the communicative strategies to which they give rise as *contextualization conventions*.

One way in which contextualization conventions function is to serve as guide posts for monitoring the progress of conversational interaction. We use our knowledge of grammar and lexicon, along with contextualization conventions and whatever background information we have about settings and participants, to decide what discourse task is being performed and what activity is being signalled, and this provides information about likely communicative goals and outcome. We then build on these predictions to identify the communicative intent that underlies particular utterances. Contextualization conventions *channel* interpretations in one direction or another. The basic assumption is that something is being communicated. What is at issue is *how it is to be interpreted*. The judgments made at any one time are contingent judgments; they are either confirmed or disproved by what happens subsequently. If they are confirmed, our expectations are reinforced; if they are disconfirmed we try to recode what we have heard and change our expectations of goals, outcomes or speakers' intent.

Contextualization conventions are acquired as a result of a speaker's actual interactive experience, i.e., as a result of an individual's participation in particular networks of relationship (Gumperz 1982, chapter 2). Like grammatical knowledge, they operate below the level of conscious choice. Where these networks differ, as they do in ethnically mixed settings, conventions differ and communication can break down. The relevant differences in conventions may not present serious problems when individuals are at ease or in routine situations, but when the situation is stressful, i.e., when much depends on the outcome as in a job interview or in a formal negotiation, they are quite likely to affect communication. This is a largely unrecognized type of communicative problem and most people, therefore, interpret the other person's way of speaking according to their own conventions. This means that a person may draw totally incorrect inferences about someone else. For example s/he may conclude that someone is being rude, irrelevant, boring, or not talking sense at all. Or often hearers become lost in a maze of words or ideas that do not seem to cohere. They also lack the means to sort out the difficulties which will inevitably occur. So the strategies necessary for solving the misunderstanding which we ordinarily rely on to remedy and reevaluate communicative situations do not convey the necessary information. Our discussion of contextualization implies that to the extent that communicative breakdowns and miscommunications are the result of linguistic factors they can be attributed to the operation of processes which work below the level of awareness, and are no more available to the casual observer than are the eye blinks and facial cues discovered through microanalysis of nonverbal signs.

In our analysis, spoken language episodes are simultaneously examined from three perspectives. (1) Language usage: examination of speakers' actual verbal practices focusing on recurrent speech and accentuation patterns that can be shown to reflect relevant aspects of communicative history. (2) Inferencing: the interactive mechanisms through which speakers and listeners jointly negotiate and arrive at interpretations. Mismatch in these mechanisms is a sign of possible communication breakdown. (3) Evaluation: determination of how participants reflexively address the social activity that is being constituted by their ongoing talk. This can be done indirectly in the course of the interaction through formulating utterances, narrative evaluations, topic shifting or ways of marking context. Another form of evaluation is derived from the responses obtained by playing back part of a sequence and eliciting comments (Chapters 2, 4, 8).

Rather than writing rules or attempting to set standards of appropriateness, we look for fit among the three types of analysis, i.e., we seek to determine how expectations generated at the evaluative level are confirmed or disconfirmed by what happens at the other two. This is perhaps best illustrated in Chapters 3 and 9 where initial conflicts between evaluations and inferences from lower level signals led to reexamination of assumptions of what the significant signalling mechanisms were. This reexamination resulted in new analyses which are both internally more consistent and more defensible in terms of speakers' communicative background.

Chapters 2–7 of this book are more specifically concerned with establishing the procedures for uncovering discourse cues through which social and ethnic identity is communicated. Chapter 2 uses data from the English of South Asian natives residing in Great Britain to show how thematic cohesions are perceived. It presents a detailed discussion of those features of grammar which when carried over into the second language are most likely to affect interpretation. There follow five more chapters all dealing with elements of thematic structure and progression in different social settings. Chapter 3 draws on a counselling session with a South Asian teacher and a native English speaking counsellor in Britain. Chapter 4 deals with discussion in English among Chinese professionals in Hong Kong and in the United States and shows how these are evaluated by other bilingual Chinese and by Americans. Chapters 5 and 6 analyze rhetorical strategies and social background in the United States. In the first of these two chapters the focus is on phonetic and formulaic discourse cues. The second, Chapter 6, analyzes public debate between two highly articulate political leaders and show how rhetorical strategies and ethnic background combine to set off automatic reactions which ultimately affect the evaluation that is accomplished. Chapter 7 describes the speech situation in Montreal where sociopolitical developments have radically altered accepted standards of behavior and shows how this is revealed through code switching.

Chapters 8–13 present detailed case studies illustrating what we referred to in this chapter as the new speech events typical of modern bureaucratic settings. Analysis here concentrates on the event as a whole and deals with speech as it affects social outcome rather than concentrating on contextualization cues. In these last chapters we can perhaps best see the interaction of what we have described as different levels of interpretation. The job interview in Chapter 8 involved black women being trained for secretarial positions in public agencies and industry. Chapter 9 describes the board meeting of a London youth club where a West Indian social worker was attempting to negotiate for additional staff positions with the education authorities. In Chapter 10 a US Navy doctor of Filipino origin is accused of perjury for statements made in connection with an emergency room case.

In the last three chapters our viewpoint of social identity created through language practices is expanded beyond the issues of ethnic identity examined in the first four case studies to include social identity as gender and social class in interaction with ethnicity.

Chapters 11 and 12 apply the perspective developed in preceding studies to the more general issue of male–female communication. Maltz and Borker, using published sources, discuss how differences in gender identity shape conversational strategies. Tannen shows how gender and ethnicity interact in husband–wife communication. The concluding chapter explores the consequences of the coming together of ethnicity and social class in contemporary Britain. Ethnographic observations are used to show how, in a class-differentiated environment, the new immigrant populations are able neither to maintain the old ethnic solidarity nor yet to build a new ethnic consciousness. This results in a hidden disadvantage for ethnic minority members seeking to change the position imposed upon them by reason of their position within the occupational structure.

2

Thematic structure and progression in discourse

JOHN J. GUMPERZ, GURINDER AULAKH, AND
HANNAH KALTMAN

It has been customary to deal with cross-cultural differences in language behavior either in terms of correlations between interference (i.e., the mapping of grammatical and phonological patterns from one system to the other) and independently determined cultural presuppositions or in terms of social norms. The aim of this chapter is to show how these phenomena interact at the level of discourse so that, in spite of surface similarities, some styles of English used by many South Asians are even more pervasively divergent from Western styles of English, and are systematically different not only in the social knowledge their speakers use as bases for conversational strategies, but also in the conventions and principles that guide how a given conversational intention will be signalled in speech.

The bulk of our data derives from recordings of natural conversations of Indian and Pakistani residents of Great Britain who know English well and use it regularly in the course of their daily affairs. We will refer to the style of speaking they employ in the examples we cite as Indian English and we will contrast it with Western English, i.e., the conversational style or styles used by educated residents of England and the United States.

We begin with some illustrative examples. First of all, Indian English *sounds odd* to Western ears because it has systematically different conventions at the sentence level governing lexicalization, syntax, and, as we have shown in Gumperz (1982), prosody. The following single Indian English sentences are extracted from natural conversational data.

1. Because there is shortage of houses.

2.   Father and daughter normally no problem, but father and son, bit difficult.

3.   Because mortgage meaning to borrow the money.

4.   Building societies and the council have got no objection, doesn't mean if a council house, council mortgage, you can still sell it.

In these examples we can observe oddities in the use of articles (example 1), the copula (examples 2 and 4), and adverbial phrases (3 and 4). Generally when we examine transcribed sentences in isolation these may not present problems for comprehension. It seems easy to insert articles where they are deleted, or for example to reinterpret "meaning" in example 3 as "means." Example 4, however, presents a slightly different problem. The most straightforward propositional interpretation is that one cannot sell a council house, although this makes it difficult to see the connection with the first part of the utterance. When examined in the light of the discourse which preceded it, example 4 clearly means the opposite, that one is free to sell a council house, i.e., "doesn't mean" bears no surface syntactic relation to the succeeding clause. It serves instead to mark the entire utterance as a refutation of something else, namely assumptions expressed in preceding dialogue.

The point of this example is that Indian English diverges from standard Western English in ways that, at the sentence level, at least, make it seem odd but only occasionally incomprehensible. Severe problems may surface when oddities represent stylistic choices crucial in signalling *the connections the speaker intends to convey between utterances*. Thus (1) problems become more apparent when we look at longer stretches of speech, and (2) the cumulative result is the frequent observation by Westerners that Indian English discourse appears to them to be disconnected and is hard to follow.

We examine what is odd or deviant from standard and at the same time consider what involvement in discourse continuity these oddities might have, doing so from two points of view: (1) what problems of understanding these oddities might present and (2) what we can infer about the speaker's intentions, to which these might be related, by looking at longer examples.

These examples come from a recorded discussion about mortgages in an Adult Education class for Indian immigrants in a London industrial suburb. The students are mainly Asians from Uganda and East Africa who have used English all their lives. The goal of the class is to encourage the habitual use of English for conversation and at the same time to provide necessary information about the problems students encounter in settling in a new environment, dealing with local government agencies, getting jobs and houses, etc. The examples are from the speech of the instructor, an ethnically Indian social worker born in Malaysia and employed by the local council, who has lived in London for most of her life. We concentrate on her speech because she can speak with a wide stylistic range. Much of what she says does not significantly differ from ordinary native English usage. When talking to Western English speakers, her style, apart from minor features of accent, is indistinguishable from that of many other educated middle-class London residents. But on this occasion her speech takes on typical characteristics of Indian English. These characteristics can thus not be attributed to a lack of knowledge or command of English. As we shall see, these stylistic shifts are related to her effectiveness in the teaching situation.

Consider the following.

5.   So therefore / normally / most of the young people /
      who are / getting married / newly / they have got no families /
      meaning no children / or single people / professional people /
      if they want to buy a house / they go to / a building society //
      Not even bank //

Comprehension difficulties here relate to the use of anaphoric pronouns, relative clauses, and conjunctions. The first half of the utterance, until "or," seems to be leading toward some consideration directly related to childlessness. "Or single people" thus comes rather abruptly. It becomes difficult to see how the last two phrases relate to the entire previous argument, i.e., which is the main subject, and which are the qualifying clauses. Does "they" mean single, professional people, or does it include all the people mentioned? Apparently, single and professional people are to be added to young newlyweds as subjects of the entire utterance. But prosodic cues make this connection hard to follow. First of all, we would expect "or" to be stressed, which it is not. Then "they" *is* stressed, which by Western conventions serves to single out contrastively the most recently mentioned subject, i.e., single professional people. But if this were the case, we would expect some explicit signal or reason given that the young marrieds could be ignored.

This passage in isolation would appear to be an answer to a general question something like, "Where do young single etc. people go when they need a mortgage?" In the full text, however, it clearly has a different focus, and is a response to something like, "Who are the usual clients of building societies?" As with example 4, the use of the adverbial "normally," is concerned with marking the entire utterance in relation to previous discourse, rather than with making overt syntactic connections. Thus "*normally*" does not mean here that the succeeding predicate is normally true of the subject, although this is of course true, but more generally that the entire situation being described is the normal one, and therefore the subject of the utterance is the normal one for that predicate.

6.   Mortgages. If you are to buy a house. Who can get and who cannot get. What assumptions we made, what? If you work. If you don't work, can you get a mortgage?

7.   OK, that's that. Building society. So what happens, you are young and you're just getting married or you're single like your sister you see, go to the building society because you've got account with them ( ) Say you're buying, your sister, she's buying a house for ten thousand . . how much you think she'll require to pay . . if she's single . . first of all will she get a mortgage, or a single man or a single woman . . what are the chances?

As with the previous example, the difficulties here are in following the connections that are being made, and consequently in understanding the intention of the final questions. Example 6 starts with a string of noun phrases that appear to announce the intended topics. Is the final question intended to elicit a review of the 'assumptions' made at another time, or is it the commencement of discussion of the topic of 'who can get and who cannot get' a mortgage? In example 7, again, the topic is announced at the start: building societies. Then the teacher builds up a situation with a series of descriptions, asks one question, expands and clarifies the description, and then asks another question. This final question asks, in effect, "What are the chances of a single person getting a mortgage on a ten thousand pound house from a building society, remembering that he or she will have to make a down payment?" In other words, each topic mentioned figures in the hypothetical situation, although exactly *how* it ties into the present discourse is not overtly lexicalized. A question may refer to a particular aspect, but judging in part from the responses of the class, the social worker seems in these cases to be concerned less with pursuing particular questions than with the situations themselves, or, rather, with conveying that the situations are determined by the considerations the questions reveal.

We have claimed that these phenomena are stylistically consistent signals of communicative intention. How do we know? The data from which these examples were taken provide us with one kind of internal evidence. We have said that the social worker demonstrated a wide stylistic range; the odd constructions like the examples above occur only when she is speaking what we may call didactically, i.e., when the instructor is introducing new material on an overall topic and when she is seeking evidence that the students have assimilated this new material. When side issues come up, in brief anecdotal comments about herself, or when asking questions to seek information or clarification, her speech differs markedly from the above examples.

In the following example she is addressing herself to one student, who has raised a side issue, rather than to the class as a whole:

8.   The problem with that sort of thing is that you may not be able to have enough money to pay back your mortgage. If you . . . if you borrow so much more than you are able to return it back you can be in trouble.

Apart from one extraneous "it" and an odd two-part verb construction ("return back") these are two entirely grammatical complex sentences, with relativization, complementarization, and embedding all conventionally expressed.

Here are some further examples of didactic questions:

9.   35 to 30 years depending how old you are – and then what?

10.   Save some money, what with the building society or what?

11.   See we're talking about single people, now you see, men or women . . . and what about married people?

Basically, none of these poses a specific question. Even though the sentences are grammatical (except possibly 10, but "or what" is a conventional question-marker), it is not apparent what form an appropriate answer would take. One might speculate that these are deviant attempts to ask more specific questions. However, the tape provides several instances of well-formed direct questions:

12.   What are you earning nowadays, I think 3,000, isn't it, the average?

13.   Oh you mean to say he had, he has had two wives?

This contrast supports our analysis of example 8; the questions in examples 6, 7, and 9–11 serve as rhetorical markers that topicalize details previously mentioned.

We conclude that the variations in the social worker's speech reflect shifts in her communicative intention, i.e., that *she speaks the way she does in order to be understood and to elicit appropriate responses*. We have further evidence of this; she apparently gets the response she seeks. If the class members were experiencing difficulties of the sort we have described for ourselves in following her longer descriptions and questions, we would expect these to be followed by pauses. None occur; the students respond promptly. Furthermore, the social worker's and the students' speech exchange is rhythmically coordinated. While she is speaking, their supporting comments ("yes," repetitions of her words) are in synchrony (Erickson and Schultz 1982); when they answer her questions or enter the conversation with comments or questions of their own the transitions occur smoothly, without any breaks in rhythm. In other words, all the participants are successful in processing the ongoing talk; they are speakers of English who share a code. All the speakers in the class have used English for most of their lives: not only do they all 'know English,' they all know and use a systematic set of discourse principles; they are mutually attested as competent producers of meaningful and intelligible discourse.

It is conceivable, from the examples given so far, that the oddities we perceive merely reflect a grammar which differs from standard English; that is, that these are matters of purely syntactic interference from their native languages. When we examine equivalent styles of these languages, however, we find that the grammatical provision for the expression of anaphora, subordination, relativization, conjunction, and similar cohesive features bears a one-to-one relationship to those of the speakers' English. In other words, whatever oddities there are, are not the result of lack of syntactic knowledge. They simply reflect native language discourse strategies. It would be possible to construct perfectly grammatical translations of English sentences in which the cohesive relations we find missing were syntactically and lexically expressed. These would not be idiomatic translations, however; they could not retain the same relative formality or colloquial connotation of the originals. For example, in a sequence like, "I saw him yesterday. Today I did not see him," the second "him" would not ordinarily be included by Indian speakers except for special emphasis. Use of anaphoric pronouns signals, in addition to reference, further connotations of contrastiveness or expressive emphasis. So the 'interference' we must consider is not simply previous knowledge of a grammatical system as such, but of previous experience with the various constituents of a 'system' of *style*.

Indian speakers of English frequently, and apparently systematically, differ from native speakers of English, in the devices they use to signal 'communicative intent' through lexicalization, syntax, and prosody. When we speak of style we mean the verbal realization of differences in communicative intent through shifts in the balance of the signalling load carried by these channels. The *interdependent* functioning of these surface features of communicative acts accomplishes the requisites of discourse cohesion: topicalization, relativization, establishment of perspective, indication of illocutionary force, contrastiveness, etc. When we examine Indian discourse from the perspective of native English-speaking expectations we are confronting two systems within which these functions are accomplished differently.

In what sense are topicalization, relativization, etc. 'requisites of discourse cohesion'? That is, what must participants in a conversation *do* that these devices enable them to accomplish? These devices describe relations among textual elements, the establishment of which signals aspects of an utterance's meaningfulness in its context. What are these aspects which are signalled? A listing is necessarily partial and composed of overlapping or, more accurately, largely coextensive categories. Nevertheless, for discourse to be cohesive, speakers must signal and hearers interpret (1) what is the main part of a message and what is subsidiary or qualifying information, (2) what knowledge or attitudes are assumed to be shared, (3) what information is old and what is new, and (4) what is the speaker's point of view and his/her relationship to or degree of involvement in what is being said. In other words, an utterance to be understood must be contextualized – this sort of information must be signalled in such a way as to fit into the goals and expectations of participants.

We are talking about what linguists call discourse functions, and we are suggesting that these functions do not inhere in the text, i.e., are not 'given' in the text; they are expressed through prosody and the syntactic and lexical choices such as are illustrated in this volume. In addition, signalling at the level of discourse functions has direct consequences for interpreting what linguists refer to as indirectness, i.e., the implied, or to use Grice's term, the 'implicated', meaning of utterances. It is true of all conversation that participants must read between the lines, and interpret information signalled through multiple modalities. To explain any indirect communication we must understand where and to what extent speakers rely on obligatory convention and where and to what extent they have expressive flexibility. To some extent, languages, as modern research in linguistic typology reveals (see also Chapter 11) are arbitrary with respect to the disposition of such possibilities. Where groups of speakers of the same language differ in their interactive experience, in their background as members of social systems with differing schemes of rights, obligations, and norms, they will differ in the systematic balance of verbal convention and flexibility and in the functioning of particular behavioral and linguistic devices to signal meaning.

We have said that Indian discourse sounds odd to Western ears, which is to say that it is hard to follow; that 'followable' discourse is discourse which is cohesive; that cohesion in discourse is accomplished by the interplay of several aspects of verbal and paraverbal behavior to establish the relationships among textual elements which embody the intended significance of the message; and that speakers with different experience and conventions of conversation will differ precisely in how they signal cohesive relations. We must recall the crucial fact that conversation is *processed as it occurs* to appreciate how critically we depend on conventional systems for signalling cohesion, on our ability to read between the lines. Speakers, finite and temporal creatures, must rely on strategic expectations as to the balance of the contributions of various kinds of behavior to conversational meaning in order to render interpretable the constant stream of speech. What this means, furthermore, is that to be able to follow also requires that we be able to anticipate. Relationships that are established do not merely shed their light retrospectively; they also enable *necessary predictions* as to where the discourse is going. We recognize, for example, that something is a culminating statement of opinion, or a punch line, or, as in examples 6 and 7, a rhetorical question, in part only because we have known that something of the sort was coming.

Conversation is always a multichannelled activity. Syntactic and pragmatic considerations have received the most attention from linguists concerned with cohesion and communicative intent. Prosody, as we have pointed out (Gumperz 1982), has generally been examined only to see how it reflects linguistic options. Yet we can never say anything without intoning it, and changing the intonation of an utterance entails changing some aspect of its meaning. Any one way of saying something is understood as a choice – it can only be explicated by contrast with other possibilities. To take a relatively simple case, starting an utterance with the word "but" frequently signals that what follows will involve a contradiction. Then what it is that is being contradicted will be signalled by stress. In other words, *but*, which plays a syntactic role in conjoining the utterance to what has preceded it, also entails that stress will have a particular role to play in the signalling of information which further explicates that conjunction.

So when we speak of the multichannelled nature of conversation we *are speaking of 'channels' that are not clearly independent, nor are they completely mutually determined and therefore merely redundant*. The relationship of the several available modes of signalling and the concomitant inferences drawn from their co-occurrence vary with context and with the communicative experience and conventions of the speakers. Thus when we investigate the occurrence, sources, and consequences of such variation, and particularly when we examine the speech of speakers with widely differing social and linguistic backgrounds, we cannot extricate one element and seek its isolated role in accounting for observed differences in behavior. The differences we find will ultimately be differences in the texture of what must for each individual speaker be a unified and comprehensive system of expression. So we are seeking to characterize such systems, to the extent that they are shared among a group of speakers, in terms of how interactive exchanges function jointly to create a texture.

Our terms 'Indian English' and 'Western English' refer to two such expressive systems. These are not systems in the same sense as a grammar is a system – here, achieving adequacy is not the same for all speakers. We cannot articulate for all speakers of a variety what will be starred or unstarred, appropriate or inappropriate sequences. To say that individuals speak Indian or Western conversational English, despite their extensive individual and dialectal variation, that each is a system, means that each has a logical and motivational consistency, a texture, which shapes the universe of features and which we can endeavor to clarify although we do not expect to account for all specific choices. To state the point more succinctly, while not all Indian speakers will do all or precisely the things of which we give examples, the manner in which stylistic determinants covary in their speech will be the same.

So, resuming our search for sources in the previous linguistic background of Indian speakers of their English stylistic conventions, what we are concerned with are differences in the linguistic devices for signalling semantic relationships among the various bits of information that are conveyed within a stretch of discourse. In any conversation, speakers must signal what is to be chunked together and what is to be kept separate, whether some stretch of talk is complete in itself or whether it is a subpart of a larger utterance. There must furthermore be ways of signalling the relative weight or importance assigned to component units, of distinguishing main clauses from qualifying phrases or of signalling the distinction between old (or given) and new information. In spoken discourse this type of relational information, often referred to in the literature as 'discourse function,' is signalled as a result of the interaction of three channels: prosody, syntax, and lexical choice. What we want to show is that the way these channels interact in Indian English is different from Western English.

Features of prosody relevant to our discussion are treated in Gumperz (1982). In what follows, we will employ the strategy of first pointing out syntactic differences between Western English and the colloquial styles of many North Indian languages, and then showing how, in interaction with prosody, these differences tend to affect the speakers' Indian English.

Word order

English is basically an SVO (subject, verb, object) language in both its spoken and written forms. In many Indian languages the written and formal spoken order is SOV (subject, object, verb) but in colloquial speech styles, word order is highly flexible and signals topicalization and emphasis. (Our examples are from a particular language, Hindi, but the features we will be discussing are common to most of the languages spoken in what we may call the North Indian linguistic area group of languages – Hindi, Urdu, Punjabi, Gujerati, and Marathi.) Consider the English sentence:

14a. The book is lying on the table.

Translated into Hindi with unmarked word order, 14a is:

14b. kɪtab mez par pəʀi hæ

      book table on lying is

or with marked word order is:

14c. *mez pər pəʀi hæ* kɪtab
  d. *pəʀi hæ* kɪtab mez pər
  e. *kɪtab pəʀi hæ mez pər*
  f. *pəʀi hæ mez pər* kɪtab
  g. *mez pər* kɪtab pəʀi hæ

The italic portions here are emphasized by virtue of sentence position. First, consider some immediate problems of direct translation. Keeping the same order of the three basic elements 'book,' 'table,' and 'lying,' we can make grammatical translations of 14b–g as follows:

14b'. The book on the table is lying
  c'. On the table is lying a book
  d'. It is lying, the book, on the table
  e'. The book is lying on the table
  f'. Lying on the table is a book
  g'. On the table a book is lying

What have we had to do just to make grammatical constructions? In all of these translations the two-part verb "is lying" and the prepositional phrase "on the table" had to be inverted from the

Hindi. In d' it was also necessary to add "it" as nominal subject and to create a separate structure, i.e., an appositive, serving as a modifying aside. In all of them, furthermore, it was necessary to select and insert the appropriate article – is the topic "a book" or "the book" which has been the subject of previous conversation? All the sentences 14b'–g' would have been equally grammatical, though in some cases pragmatically odd, if the article modifying "book" were different. However, even though in the original Hindi sentences there were no articles, there was no ambiguity – in fact, the choices we made in constructing b'–g' were those *strictly implied* in the original sentences. In other words Hindi word order alone serves to signal features of meaning that in English require optional syntactic devices like choice of modifiers, dummy pronouns, and dependent clause constructions.

These features have to do with the discourse notions of topicalization and perspective. Such discourse choices on the part of the speaker do not merely make speech grammatical but make it effective as discourse. And much more signalling of topicalization and perspective is accomplished in the Hindi alternatives than is represented by grammatical translation. b'–g' are translations *but they are not equivalents*; if we consider each set, the shades of meaning and appropriateness that differentiate b–g from each other are not mirrored in the range of implication of b'–g'. We said of the originals that the italicized portions are 'emphasized' – that is, merely by occurring at the beginning of the sentence these elements are topicalized. We have attempted to capture one feature of such topicalization in the Indian languages in our translations by our choice of articles; i.e., is the current topic something which has already been talked about? In addition, b–g convey more precisely than b'–g' a main topic-modifying statement relation. One consequence is that, for example, sentences e' and f' do not capture the subtle change in the significance of the verb which is implied by e and f, where f is actually talking about the physical position of the book whereas in e "paʀi hæ" could more accurately be said to mean something more like "can be found."

The important point however is not the problem of adequate direct translation, but of determining where speakers have expressive flexibility. The most crucial contrast between b–g and b'–g' is that the Hindi examples convey information through a range of alternatives that are meaningful options for colloquial, informal talk in a way that the English examples are not. For similar expressiveness, considering for the moment only lexical and syntactic options, we might say things like

14h. You'll find the book on the table.
  i. The table's got a book on it.
  j. There's a book over there on the table.

which differ from each other in something of the same way as do the Hindi e, f, and g, and are similarly colloquial.

So in these Indian languages sentence elements, nouns, verbs, and prepositional phrases (and qualifying expressions in general) can be treated independently and simply juxtaposed to meaningful effect. Does it appear that Indian speakers avail themselves of similar freedom in speaking English? That is, do we find examples in Indian English of (1) odd word orders and (2) juxtapositions of phrases where native English speakers would minimally provide syntactic ties, if not say the whole thing differently? The answer is yes:

15.   And weekend you can spend with your brother.
      (vs. And you can spend *the* weekend with your brother.)

16.   And I realize my mistake that I couldn't bring it early.
      (vs. And I realise *that it is* my mistake etc.)

17.   Twenty-five years after yours house.
      (vs. Twenty-five years after (later) *the* house *is* yours.)

Example 18 strikes us as particularly odd since a transitive verb is separated from its direct object:

18.   But I deposited the other day over $300 in my account.
      (vs. But I deposited over $300 in my account just the other day.)

How does prosody fit into this discussion of syntactic differences? A simple declarative sentence like 14a will be spoken by a native speaker of English as a single tone group, with a nuclear stressed syllable. Such sentences have a conventional, unmarked declarative intonational contour, in our case:

    The 'book is lying on the table //

If we change the assignment or shape of the nuclear stress, we create an implicit contrast:

The 'book is lying on the tàble // (not somewhere else)

The nuclear tune has changed, but the sentence is still a single tone group; the intonations of the parts of the sentence are mutually codetermined. If there are any pauses or breaks in saying such a sentence, these will be interpreted as rhetorical pauses signalling, for example, a desire to pause, or reflect for a moment, or the desire to make one's hearer think for a moment.

In contrast, in Indian languages, sentence elements can be treated independently in prosody. A phrase or phrases, e.g. those italicized in examples 14c–g, acquire emphasis automatically by occurring at the beginning of the sentence, but any aspect of the sentence can be further highlighted prosodically. This is done by isolating that portion through both rhythm and pitch: the stressed phrase will be set off in a higher or lower pitch register (notice, phrase, not syllable) and if it is not the initial sentence constituent it will also be preceded by a tone group boundary. Contrastiveness is only one possible consequence of emphasis in such cases. This flexibility in the chunking is immediately apparent in Indian English data:

19.   Can we go back / again on it please //

20.   Put that chair / over there in the corner //

Clearly, with more complex sentences and more complex communicative acts, matters become more complex. Making colloquial equivalents of complex Indic constructions is not simply paraphrasing as we did in examples 14' and 15–18, but additionally involves signalling prosodic ties. When we consider relativizing, subordination, attributing differential emphasis, complex question construction, etc., the Indian English signalling system involves other aspects of the Indian languages interacting with word order, and this interaction becomes quite intricate. While there is no space for details, we hope to have demonstrated that the balance of expressive options differs between Western and Indian English, and that the flexible word order of Indian languages is one of several determinants. We can outline broadly three ways this balance of options appears to enter into the Indian English signalling system:

(1)   Speakers can map word-order freedom directly onto English, reordering words and phrases to signal emphasis primarily through juxtaposition, rather than through either periphrastic construction or prosody.

(2) Speakers may use the standard English word order and treat the utterance prosodically as that word order could be treated in an Indian language, by juxtaposing prosodically independent chunks. Something like this is involved in the example from the mortgage discussion, example 6, where one part of the "if" consideration in an *if, then* construction is not tied prosodically to the rest.

(3) Speakers may use a prosodic pattern which would go with a word order which is not available in English.

The verb system

Another important feature of Indian languages is that the system of verb inflection is very specific in signalling the speaker's perspective on the action or event referred to and the degree of involvement of individuals. In Western English when we say,

⌐You left / the door open //

using a high tone of voice on "you left" we imply that the person indicated by "you" is at fault. If the stress pattern remains the same, but "you left" is spoken at low pitch, there is no longer the same implication of personal involvement. In any of the Indian languages this difference would have to be signalled through choice of verb or through verb inflection. In particular, these languages rely on their system of verb auxiliaries to express perspective on and attitudes toward actions. Here we have another set of examples of how some languages and conversational conventions use grammar to signal certain types of information while others use stress and tone of voice. The following example from Punjabi demonstrates how verb inflections can signal four degrees of causation:

o ṭhik dɪkhda ai
(he appears to be OK)

o ṭhik dekhda ai
(he sees OK)

o ṭhik dɪkhanda ai
(he shows it (to someone) OK)

o ṭhik dɪkhənda ai
(he makes (someone else) show it (to someone) OK)

This specificity signalled by verb inflection complements the freedom in word order; the relation of subject and predicate is always signalled through the verb – there will be no ambiguity of case relations, i.e., who the actor or agent is. One consequence of the effect of the Indic verb system on Indian English is that such relations may be, for Westerners, ambiguously expressed. The following example is an illuminating case of self-correction by a student in the mortgage discussion:

21.   And the block they call their flat . . if there're many flats they call it a block.

Here the speaker has had to reorder the sentence and make paraphrastic verbal constructions to specify her meaning. A direct translation of the first English version in an Indian language could, by verb inflection, convey exactly the same meaning as does the second English version.

One possible strategy used by Indian English speakers seeking to highlight causative, temporal, or volitional aspects of verb phrases is to employ intonation, stressing that element which literally carries the modification closest to the intended meaning. Consider the following example:

22.   D: You you s . . you will say/that uh may have spoken for me on Friday or ( ) //

Here, by stressing both "will" and "say," D intends something like "you will agree" with what he then goes on to say. To a Westerner, both the word choice and intonation carry a conventional attributive connotation, something like, "Well, you would say that." In another example,

23.   B: In the ⌐third school / in which I had been ˌtransferred //

a likely reading is to interpret the stress on "had" as contrastive: despite what you may have thought, I had been transferred. In fact, B is highlighting the passive construction "had been," emphasizing that his being transferred was none of his doing, that others were responsible.

Our interpretations here are by no means unassailable. They simply follow from the lines of reasoning we have adopted. Yet the form in which we put them yields questions which informants familiar with the relevant style can readily answer. Examples 22 and 23 derive from our analysis of the counselling interview, another aspect of which is analyzed by Mishra in Chapter 3. When relevant sections of the tape were played to Indian English speakers, our interpretations were confirmed, and, as Mishra points out, when such interpretations are taken into account, the entire speech event becomes interpretable.

As we have returned to the consideration of problems arising in conversations where participants are using different signalling systems, we will round out this discussion of the effect of the Indic verb system on Indian English with two more examples. In these, the Indian speaker, D, seriously misconstrues the actions and attributions signalled by C (perhaps as a result of the kind of interference we have been examining) in C's interpretation of D's speech.

24. C: I don't understand / why you are so insùlted with me //
     D: mm I.. I am not 'in'sul'ting y̧ou /

25. C: Mr. D 'stop tèlling me / what I'm doing /
         what I'm "not doing / I knòw what I am ᵈoing //
     D: No / I'm not telling "you / what you "do /
         or what you 'not to 'do / but I I "know the fact /
         what you 'are / and what you what ( ) your opinion will be //

In 25, C accuses D of telling her what she is doing, meaning what her job entails. The charge D refutes is the different one of telling her what she should do; that is, he argues that he has not attempted to tell her what specific action she should take. D then says, "I know . . . what you are," i.e., what power C has – exactly what C objected to in the first place.

Emphatic particles

North Indian languages have a special set of particles that affix to words, whose function is, very abstractly, to indicate emphasis. Such particles also exist in European languages and have been discussed in some detail for German. Our preliminary data, however, suggest that their role in the signalling of discourse functions differs from that in the North Indian and some other Asian languages. In the North Indian languages, there are extensive syntactic and contextual constraints on the occurrence of these particles, determining which one will be used in which sort of sentence, etc. Description and analysis of the behavior of emphatic particles have provided material for several manuscripts; we will not go into any such detail. We will demonstrate some generalized features of their functioning, and how the shifts in meaning they signal may be accomplished by Indian speakers in English, where they are not available.

In a context-free description we would say that the emphatic particles of Indian languages can occur after any word in a sentence. They have implications which have to do with such matters as the definiteness or indefiniteness or the inclusive or exclusive attributions of modifiers and qualifiers. They may intensify the meaning of a particular word, or affect the sense of entire noun or verb phrases. In general, if they occur in the topic nominal phrase, they underline the topic; if in subsidiary or predicating phrases, they effect some form of relation of that phrase to the stated topic. Thus, they may carry some of the burden of clarifying deixis, of conjoining, and of subordinating sentence parts. Something of this range in the contribution of emphatic particles is demonstrated in the following example. The basic sentence and most of the variants and their paraphrases come from a footnote to explain "Indian English" in Varma (1971). We have added a few variants to round out the set and reveal some further contrasts. The emphatic particle is italicized in each instance.

26. ye   tin   ləɾke mɪthai kha rəhe   hæ̃
    these three boys sweets   eat present particle are

(i.e., these three boys are eating sweets)

With a particle in the noun phrase:

26a. ye *hi* tin ləɾke . . .
    (these particular three boys . . .)
  b. ye tin *hi* ləɾke . . .
    (only three of these boys . . .)
  c. ye tin ləɾke *hi* . . .
    (only these three boys, and no one else . . .)

Or with a different particle in the noun phrase:

26d. ye tin ləɾke *to* . . .
    (at least these three boys . . .)

With the particle in the predicate phrase:
With *hi*:

26e. ye tin ləɾke mɪthai *hi* kha rəhe hæ̃
    (these three boys – what they are eating is sweets, nothing else)

f. ye tin ləɹke mɪṭhai kha *hi* rəhe hǽ
    (these three boys are eating sweets right now)

With *to*:

26g. ye tin ləɹke mɪṭhai *to* kha rəhe hǽ

(This would be said when it is unexpected that the boys would be
eating anything, pointing out that in fact they are eating sweets.)

26h. ye tin ləɹke mɪṭhai kha *to* rəhe hǽ

(This would be said when it is unexpected that the boys would eat
sweets, pointing out that in fact they are doing so.)
With both *hi* and *to*:

26i. ye tin ləɹke mɪṭhai kha *to* rəhe *hi* hǽ

(This does not make sense by itself, but implies or requires a
reference to some other aspects of the situation concerning which it
is relevant to note that the boys are at this moment eating sweets.)

The emphatic particle *hi* can also combine with the negative *na*,
and can differentially negate part of a sentence without further
syntactic modification. In our example there are two places where
nahi could be inserted in accordance with colloquial usage:

26j. ye tin ləɹke mɪṭhai *nahi* kha rəhe hǽ
      (it isn't sweets that these three boys are eating)
    k. ye tin ləɹke mɪṭhai kha *nahi* rəhe hǽ
      (these three boys aren't eating sweets [i.e., they're doing something
      else with them])

If a pause and an additional particle are added, *nahi* can also
modify the subject noun phrase:

26l. ye tin ləɹke *to nahi*/mɪṭhai kha rəhe hǽ
      (it is not these three boys who are eating sweets)
Negative placement can further combine with word order changes
to achieve the following connotation:

26m. mɪṭhai ye tin ləɹke *to nahi* kha rəhe hǽ
      (sweets is not what these three boys are eating)

Here as elsewhere in Indian English either a single noun phrase,
or a combination of phrases, can have sententiality, i.e., it can serve
as an independent unit of discourse. In any stretch of speech
therefore each noun or verb phrase can receive separate stress or

emphasis by addition of a particle. In Western English a sentential unit must consist of a noun phrase plus a verb phrase, i.e., a sentence, and negation or emphasis will apply to the sentence as a whole. To single out a sentence constituent we must add a topicalizing phrase, as we have done in translating the previous examples, e.g., "it is not these . . ." (ex. l), or "X is not what . . ." (ex. m).

In more complex contexts, emphatic particles additionally convey judgmental or evaluative meanings, bringing in elements of the situation and contextualizing the utterance. They may signal the relative importance of parts of a message, how convinced the speaker is of what he or she is saying, whether the speaker is irritated with a previous speaker, etc.

Emphatic particles also occur in what has been called performative function: they are involved in formulaic idiomatic locutions which are adverbial performatives, expressions which indicate the relation of a contribution to the prevailing topic or effect a shift in topic, locutions which function like English expressions, such as "My opinion is . . ." or, "Not only that, but . . ."

Since there are no emphatic particles in English, Indian English speakers make use of several options. One is simply to translate what can be translated of the Indian expressions which contain particles. The results then signal adverbial or performative information in ways which are pragmatically odd by Western conventions, as in examples 27–9 (the phrases which would contain an emphatic particle are italicized).

27.   A: Which one would be the cheapest?
      B: *I think so*, Miss . . . this terrace house . . .

28.   Certain councils in the country, they allow you to buy the house that you do live in, but not every council. *I don't think so* Ealing does.

29.   *I can tell you*, I bought it in good faith, and, *I can tell you*, and actually, I didn't wear it, for a single moment.

Another possibility is to translate the particle itself replacing it with a word or phrase which embodies the additional connotation supplied by the particle. Again, by Western conventions, the results do not have the same signalling effect and are pragmatically odd.

4.   (from p. 23) Building societies and the council have got no objection, *doesn't mean* if a council house, council mortgage, you can still sell it.

30.   *It's all the time* one person selling it to the other.

31.   Block of flats, yes, and *even* houses are as we said three types.

32.   First of all there are two types of property *again.*

Other possibilities involve the use of stress. Stressing a word through intonation and highlighting it with an emphatic particle are similar, and it appears that the general observation that Indian English speakers use stress more frequently than Western speakers is in part the result of stress acquiring the signalling function of these particles. In simple cases we see odd or isolated word stress where there would have been a particle, instead of a reformulation: (the stressed word is italicized)

33.   My record I have to explain *my* self, *my* position.

This sentence is ambiguous, with both readings oddly expressed. On the one hand, one does not explain oneself in the same sense in which one explains one's position. On the other hand, if the speaker means to say that he himself must explain his record, then we would expect first of all that the chief stress be on "self," and also that "my position" be topicalized along with "my record." Similarly with example 5 from the mortgage discussion above:

5.   . . . if they want to buy a house / they go to / a building society // not even bànk //

The heavy stress on "bank" occurs here in the place of an emphatic particle: "bank *hi* nahi." The particle here emphasizes the topical role of "bank," i.e., a bank is not where they would go. The result in English is first of all that the central contrast, that they *would* go to a building society and therefore they *would not* go to a bank, is not prosodically signalled, as it would be if "not" rather than "bank" were stressed. With "bank" stressed, one possible interpretation for a Western English speaker would be that it is quite extraordinary for someone not to go to a bank. A related, converse, phenomenon occurs in the following example (the speaker has just been given a deposit form by a bank teller):

34.   No no / nòt this one /

In Hindi, "not this one" would be "ye to nahi." So in English the element which most directly conveys the role of the particle *nahi*, "not," receives stress (rather than, as we would expect, "this"). Here the most likely Western reading involves attribution: the speaker seems to imply that the addressee is at fault in giving him the wrong form.

In these examples, in mapping their native contextualization strategies onto English, Indian speakers correctly assume that the role of emphatic particles corresponds to the role of marked stress in English. They then locate the stress at the available location closest to that of a particle; that is, they do not take into account that Western English has other pragmatic and syntactic rules and conventions governing stress placement.

Question particles

The Indian languages each also contain an additional particle that serves as a question marker, either making a direct question of the entire proposition expressed or differentially questioning a particular aspect, without any inversion or further syntactic modification. Taking our Hindi sentence, the entire proposition can be questioned by placing *kya* at the start or at the end of the sentence:

14n. (*kya*) ye tin ləʀke mɪṭhai kha rəhe hæ̃ (*kya*)

Basically, this asks, "Is it true that these three boys are eating sweets?" There are two options for making a differential or contrastive question of this sentence. The first is to place the particle at either the start or the end and then stress a word. With *kya* at the beginning one can stress any of *tin, ləʀke, mɪṭhai,* or *kha.* With *kya* at the end one cannot stress the noun phrase, but one can stress either *mɪṭhai* or *kha.* The second option is to insert the question particle within the sentence, preceding the item which is its focus; this has the same effect as stressing. Thus:

26o. ye *kya* tin ləʀke mɪṭhai kha rəhe hæ̃
    (these three boys – is it they who are eating sweets?)
  p. ye tin ləʀke *kya* mɪṭhai kha rəhe hæ̃
    (these three boys – is it sweets they are eating?)
  q. ye tin ləʀke mɪṭhai *kya* kha rəhe hæ̃
    (are these three boys eating the sweets? e.g., as opposed to doing
    something else such as wrapping them)
  r. ye tin ləʀke mɪṭhai kha *kya* rəhe hæ̃

This last version implies some question of whether "eating" really accurately describes what they are doing. That is, it does not question the truth of the proposition, but rather something of how the proposition describes the situation.

The key point is again that in the Indian languages one can signal through independent elements intentions which in Western English must be further embodied in syntactic transformations, paraphrastic or relativized constructions, and/or prosody. Most generally, this difference is reflected in the sort of questions we presented earlier as examples of the social worker's didactic questions in the mortgage discussion, where the specific intention of the question is not clear:

6. Mortgages. If you are to buy a house. Who can get and who cannot get. What assumptions we made, what? If you work. If you don't work, can you get a mortgage?

10. Save some money, what with the building society or what?

Informally we could describe these questions as noun phrases or sentences with an affixed question marker. Colloquial Western equivalents might use tag questions, something like:

6'. . . . We made some assumptions, didn't we?
. . . It matters whether you're working, doesn't it?

10'. The building society is one place to save money, isn't it?

Another sort of interference in Indian English question formation involves the combined effects of question particles and verb morphology. Indian English speakers frequently phrase two-part questions with modal verbs in ways which are not just odd, but strictly speaking ungrammatical. In English there are three forms for such questions. Using "can" as an example we have either:

Can you or can you not . . .?

or

Can you . . ., or can you not?

or, inverting only the second phrase:

You can . . ., or can you not?

Choice among these possibilities has to do with variation in expectations, such as what the speaker thinks is the most likely response. In literal translations into Indian languages such considerations would not have to be expressed syntactically, but would probably be signalled through prosody. The syntactic distinctions operating in English would not apply because (1) pronouns would not necessarily be used, since who was the actor, patient, or experiencer referred to would be signalled in the verbs, and (2) a question particle would cover equally both propositions expressed. Thus in Indian English, grammatical deviations such as the following are quite common:

35.   Once you have established that this is the house you want . . . you do or do you not have some savings, some money?

36.   What about miss, if we see somebody's house and we want to buy, so we can't go to building society or we can?

Conjunctions
The use of conjunctions is governed in Indian conversation by conventions that differ substantially from those obtaining in Western English. Most important for our discussion of the signalling of discourse continuity are the three following observations: in Indian languages, conjunctions never receive stress; they are relatively dispensable syntactically compared to English. Consequently, the occurrence of an optional conjunction carries signalling value.

Turning directly to Indian English, these observations account for typical instances where Westerners encounter comprehension difficulties. One such instance is our example 5:

5.   So therefore / normally / most of the young people / who are / getting married / newly / they have got no families / meaning no children / or single people / professional people / if they want to buy a house /they go to / a building society //

We have already remarked that when "or" is used to mean "or alternatively," this would be signalled prosodically by a Western speaker.

In the following example the speaker shifts his focus in the course of extended speech; the shift is marked only by the unstressed use of "and," with no further prosodic cues:

37.   B: So so what was the outcome Mr. A?
         A: Outcome was that they they had recommended that he has class discipline problem / language problem / so much problem / and but his lesson was well prepared / and he had told us he needs more help . . .

Here A uses a listing prosodic pattern, i.e., a level tune is employed and the stress is placed on the last noun phrase in each clause. But he does nothing to signal the distinction between the list of criticisms in the first three clauses and the contrasting commendation in the last. This last clause is marked off only by being conjoined with "and."

An additional difference between Indian English and Western English in the use of conjunctions appears in how these words are used as 'butting-in' devices to take turns in conversations. In Indian English "and" and "but," and also "yes" and "no" can be used simply to signal "I've got something to say" without necessarily connoting how one's comment ties to preceding speech.

Deixis and referencing

For both English and Indian languages, most of the work on deixis and referencing has treated formal or literary language; it has been essentially grammatical work. Little has been said about the interaction of prosody with grammar that is useful for the descriptive analysis we are doing. In this section our focus shifts away from native Indian languages. We will be comparing in fairly broad outline the Indian English and Western English conventions of anaphoric reference, and proposing a generalized explanatory logic for the Indian English system, without being able to say how this logic is embodied in a rule-governed system in either the Indian languages or in Indian English.

In Western English pronouns, ostensives (this, these, etc.), and temporal and spatial locatives (then, there, etc.) must be anchored in the text of the discourse if they do not refer to places, persons, or objects in the presence (sight, hearing, etc.) of the speakers. When referring words do have textual referents, there is a complex set of conventions governing disambiguation. For example, unless otherwise marked, a personal pronoun will refer to the last-mentioned person of appropriate sex. There are also conventions concerning how much and what sort of material can intervene between a referring word and its referent. Indian English differs substantially on these points. In some cases explicit textual referents need not be present at all; where they are present and particularly where there are multiple possible referents, speakers use pragmatic rules very different from those of Western English. The general nature of the contrast is that Indian English users rely to a greater extent on shared assumptions about speakers' knowledge of the situation being talked about, rather than on structural features of the explicit textual context.

The following are some easily interpretable examples where back referents are unspecified. Example 38 is an excerpt from a monologue describing an incident at the speaker's workplace: (the oddly used referring words are italicized)

38. Johal noticed that thing they are looking us surprisedly, you know, when we are having our dinner. I told her, "Don't care about this, we are having our dinner, finish our dinner and go *back*. Don't think about these little things." Anyway, when we finish our dinner we went *there*, but *that* we think that never mind you told something but you feel it in your heart. Never mind. We went afterwards *there*.

Both "back" and "there" here mean "back to work," but this full phrase never occurs. In the next two examples it is not quite correct to say that the referents do not occur, but the referring words are used in a much looser sense than Western conventions allow.

39. I had a phone call and I had to go *there*.

Rather than indicating a particular location, "there" means "to answer the phone"; the spatial connotation of "there" is invoked only very metaphorically. Its function, perhaps, and this will require further investigation, is to intensify the intentional component of "so," rather than to carry locative meaning.

Example 40 comes from later in the same narrative as 38. The speaker has just been asked, "Were they eating as well?"; her answer is:

40. They had *that*.

"That," rather than indicating a particular thing, implies something like "that which you speak of."

In cases where textual referents are present, disambiguation can be highly problematic for Western speakers. Returning once more to example 5, we have noted that "they" must be interpreted by virtue of content to mean all the subjects mentioned – young newlyweds, single people, and professional people – although the utterance flouts Western English conventions in two ways. First of all, the structure and quantity of material in the utterance is such that "they" is a very fragile link, not sufficient to effect such a cumulative tying together. One reason is that there has been an intervening clause which also has "they" as subject, but with an exclusive reference. Secondly, "they" is stressed, which by Western conventions makes it marked and thereby contrastive, i.e., signals that what follows applies to those indicated by "they" and not to others. Here, the only two sets of referents which could be contrasted in this way are young marrieds on the one hand and single professional people on the other. In fact the stress on "they" is most likely intended to signal exactly the opposite of this contrastiveness, namely coordination of all referents. The stress is emphatic rather than contrastive; what is emphasized is in effect the act of referring itself. The stress is probably the result of the sort of interference we have described where stress replaces emphatic particles. An emphatic particle following a pronoun could convey exactly this intention of extent and inclusiveness of reference.

In the next example, a contrast between two referents *is* intended:

41. But you can't ⌐'know / and ⌐'can't ''tell a 'per'son /
     'just to come into 'this 'course /
     if suppose I 'came to 'this 'course from uh / had you taken this
     impression /
     that I am not ''suitable because ⌐'I took this còurse //

The first two occurrences of "this course" refer to a course the speaker wants to get into, and the last to a course he is currently enrolled in. All three occurrences are similarly marked by stress on both "this" and "course." Again the strategy seems to be connected with the use of emphatic particles which could be used in a manner which would disambiguate, not by specifying or contrasting, but by signalling a shift of focus. In Indian English, stress alone cannot signal this shift; so the speaker is also using prosody. He marks the contrast by raising his pitch register on the last occurrence of "this course." We can describe the speaker's strategy metaphorically. The two different courses are both assumed to be present as topics under consideration; it is as though the speaker is holding an object up in each hand and saying, "Look at this one. Now look at this one." The use of pitch register shift to signal contrastiveness in Indian English is discussed further in chapter 2 of Gumperz (1982).

An extended example of the very real intelligibility problems that arise in such cases is given by Mishra in Chapter 3.

Repetition

Repetition and reduplication of words and larger utterance elements can be observed at several levels in Indian English discourse. In the next section we consider repetition by one speaker of parts of another's speech as a discourse strategy. Here we discuss some uses of repetition within the speech of a single speaker.

A direct influence from Indian languages appears in the reduplication of single words to effect a slight change in meaning. So far we have only observed this in the case of adverbs. Some examples of reduplications in Hindi:

42. dhire dhire (slowly slowly, i.e., gradually)
    kərib kərib (close close, i.e., almost)

And an example from Indian English:

43. I just make sure to eat slowly and slowly.

Indian English speakers may also repeat longer phrases or whole stretches of discourse with subtle alterations to convey additional meanings, where Western speakers are more likely to make a more thorough reformulation, as in this example:

44. 1 I said /
     2 it's nothing to do with us why somebody put in the bin /
     3 or why / because it's the Hayer food //
     4 but I'm taking objection with Shirley //
     5 why she pick up from the bin / and offer us //
     6 if she pick up from the bin / if she want to offer us /
     7 to tell us / to look we take this from the bin /
     8 and you want to eat / you can eat //

First of all, the facts of the event being described are that someone unknown threw the food belonging to Hayer into a dustbin. The woman Shirley then picked up the food and offered it to the speaker and another woman, who ate it, which they would not have done had they known it had come from the dustbin. Thus in lines 5–8, the speaker is saying what she thinks Shirley should have done, namely tell them the food had come from the bin. This shift from talking of what actually happened to description of a hypothetical

9213

721

87213

action is signalled through repetition with alternation of the conjunction "if" and the addition of the verb "want." These lead up to the high stress on "tell." The stress in this context thus signals that what is being talked about is a hypothetical, volitional, and desirable act. The use of "if" here is not strictly logical. "If" can signal entailment two ways. It can signify "if such and such which really is the case" then something logically follows, or "if such and such, other than what is the case, *were* the case" then something follows. Neither of these is quite what this speaker is saying, which is something more like, "this is the case, but if the case were what it should have been . . ." S *did* pick up the food from the bin, and she *did* offer it, but she did not *want* to offer it in the way she should have, and she did not tell anybody anything.

In extended Indian English discourse, repetition of key words and phrases is commonly used to establish thematic continuity. This is not to say that Western speakers never repeat themselves. What we are saying is that the difference lies in how repetition is used as a strategic choice. In Western discourse it tends to be used to rhetorical or persuasive effect in connection with the unfolding of a logical argument. In Indian discourse the function of repetition seems rather to be connected to the establishment of a cumulative and holistic picture. In the following example we have italicized the repeated elements.

45.　　1　A: The following day a then a th . . . there was
　　　　2　　　nothing no problem nothing of the past just
　　　　3　　　I know how to handle the class and a what
　　　　4　　　is the ⌈condition
　　　　5　B:　　　⌊hu
　　　　6　A: and how
　　　　7　B: hu　hu
　　　　8　A: I have to do through that *condition*
　　　　9　B: hu
　　　10　A: am a because I felt I cannot
　　　11　　　exist anym . . . anymore without *criticize*
　　　12　　*criticizing* his own ⌈lesson
　　　13　B:　　　　　　⌊that's right
　　　14　A: so that he feels ⌈(　) and
　　　15　B:　　　　　⌊yes　yes
　　　16　A: he is not pushing me hard on
　　　17　　　his own *criticism*
　　　18　B: yes yes　　　yes

```
19 A: I had started criticizing ⌈and he was
20 B:                          ⌊yes
21 A: puzz . . . puzz . . . a puzzled
22 B: very puzzled . . puzzled hu
23 A: because he had discipline ⌈problem by himself
24 B:                           ⌊hu hu h hu
25 A: he had been putting in cl . . . class discipline
26    which I didn't
27 B: yes
28 A: even he was putting some . . . some of the
29    children in detention and I didn't ⌈put
30 B:                                     ⌊hu
31 A: even a single child in ⌈detention
32 B:                        ⌊hu   hu
33 A: you could feel my position, I could have
34    done some of the things in the class
35    with the children difficult children
36    but I didn't put even a single child
37    in detention because I thought if I am
38    going to put it it's coming on the record
39 B: Right
40 A: that I've I've ⌈got some discipline problem
41 B:               ⌊yes I see yes
42    yes yes yes
43 A: so I did ⌈what I could do best in the class
44 B:         ⌊yes hu
45    without putting
46 A: without without putting (  ) evidence
47    that I have got some problem but
48    because other teacher by himself
49    was not out of any problem
50 B: hu
51 A: he had some problem
52 B: he had problems
53 A: he had some problem, so I when
54    I critic . . . ⌈criticized ⌈he take it very ill ⌈but
55 B:               ⌊hu yes    ⌊yes  yes   yes   ⌊yes
56 A: he couldn't do anything a a that was
57    the only way I could make him to ⌈shake
58 B:                                   ⌊I see
59 A: not to criticize so badly
60 B: yes that's right
```

There are three main interconnected themes here: (a) the overall conditions A had to work under (lines 4, 8, 33), (b) the deputy head's problems with his own class (lines 23, 25, 29, 48, 49, 53), and (c) A's solution to the deputy head's unfairness (10–18, 53–9). He moves quite freely back and forth among these three main themes, emphasizing through repetition their relatedness and importance. In similar presentations a Western speaker would be likely to state the three themes (a), (b), and (c) sequentially and be quite explicit about the connection between them, making verbal ties, such as, "this was the case," "so what I did was," "the result was," etc.

There is a serious irony here in that this use of repetition by Indian English speakers to establish important points of thematic progression is likely to lead to impatience on the part of Western English speakers whose own conventions of how an argument will be presented are so different. The very information which an Indian speaker is trying to make important is likely to be judged as irrelevant and redundant material.

So far we have focused on conventions that create textual cohesion within the speech of individual speakers. These have been *conversational* conventions in two senses: first, these conventions account for usages we find colloquially, i.e., in conversations, and secondly, we have assumed a listener in that we must consider that ties are made in order that someone be able to follow what is being said. But conversation does not simply depend on each speaker's making his or her own speech internally cohesive, nor even on all participants' making textual connections between their own speech and that of the other speakers. Understandable discourse is interactively appropriate discourse; speakers employ conventions at the further level of how an utterance is integrated into the social commitment which is a conversation, which could be called conventions of discourse management.

Elsewhere in this volume we examine how such discourse conventions are sensitive to participants' understandings of the goals of a particular interaction, and how a lack of shared conventions can prevent people from arriving at a mutual understanding of the situation in which they find themselves. Here we focus on two aspects of the different conventions of discourse management of Indian and Western English: the use of repetition of the previous speaker as a polite strategy in Indian English, and a comparison of the Indian and Western English use of metatalk, or talk about the conversation itself.

Repetition of other speakers

In this section we turn to some features more commonly considered under the rubric of rhetorical strategies. Such features and their consequences for stereotyping are treated in Young's discussion of Chinese/English discourse in Chapter 4. In Indian English discourse it is polite, that is, a sign that one is intending to be cooperative, to open one's remarks with some repetition of the previous speaker's words or ideas. We will illustrate this convention with some examples from interethnic conversations, which will at the same time indicate how this strategy can cause problems in combination with all the diverse differences in signalling conventions between Western and Indian English. In the following example an Indian worker, A, is talking to his British supervisor, B:

46.   A: Dave //
      B: Yeah //
      A: I've got something 'wrong with the pàyslip //
      B: O yéah 'Jaswinder /'what's your problem thìs week //
      A: 'Well uh /'I think I'm paid shòrt //
      B: 'No I don't thiňk so /I think that's your nòrmal
         amount /isn̩'t it //
      A: Well /it's ''not normal am̃ount /'you / 'you remember
         I worked the 'extra 'time last ẁeek //

This example ties in with our discussion of emphatic particles; the heavy stress on "not" here is by Western conventions straightforwardly contrastive, i.e., the payslip is not for the normal amount. What A is clearly saying, however, is that the payslip is for the normal amount, but it shouldn't be. In other words, the entire situation, the payslip being for the normal amount, is being called into question by the negation. A's strategy is to do this by using B's own words and modifying them. The consequences here are not terribly serious; A is likely to appear to have lost some of his command of language in his excitement. In the next example the Indian speaker appears to be rude where his intention is in fact to be polite, since he misinterprets the other speaker and thus in repeating her words appears in fact to have not really heard them. The example is an excerpt from an interview. W, the British interviewer, has asked M, who is Indian, to describe his work. He says his job involves "costing of the expenses," and proceeds to give a quite detailed account of what this entails. Our excerpt comes in the middle of this account:

47. M: Now if this is not a special type of furniture, general furniture, used by all the departments in routine with the ( ) desks and the chairs like that . . .
   W: Yes
   M: then it goes into general folio. Now, end of the year . .
   W: That's something special is it?
   M: That's right, something special work, costing is special work. Now at the end of the year you see I take the total of the furniture, money spent by the department . . .

M misinterprets W's deictic use of "that" which is intended to refer to what happens at the end of the year. He takes her to mean the general topic, costing. That is, her interjection is off the current point, but he acknowledges her politely by repeating her words and confirming them, and then returns to where he left off, which is of course what she was referring to in the first place. The impression, given W's intention, is that M is either stupid or not paying attention, and his repetition patronizingly passes over her comment.

   Another form of repetition frequent in Indian English discourse is to paraphrase what has been said by other speakers before going on to add a new point. The following example is of an instance where Western speakers do not recognize that such repetition is merely preparatory. Instead, the comment by the Indian speaker, G, appears to be redundant. It is not apparent that he has anything new to add on the subject, he is interrupted, and he loses the opportunity to make his point.

48. C: no / when you get busy you take things that you need // you don't pick out what they need /you don't need the whole box
   G: ya . . ba . . ba but both forms are justified . .
   C: right
   G: anthropologists have their own emphasis // linguists have their own emphasis // and / but uh / there is no connection // what we need is really a bridge uh . .
   A: ya uhu ⌈m
   K: ⌊may be the problem is / there is no faculty person that really has that oversight // (I mean) . . .

One significant general contrast between Indian and Western English is that Western speakers make much greater use of meta-talk, or talk of which the topic is the interactive situation itself.

Such talk can be used as what might be called therapeutic strategies. For example, in the case of turn taking, if one Western speaker happens to interrupt another, there are formulaic expressions like "excuse me," "go on," which may be used to maintain the cooperative nature of the conversation. If one Indian speaker interrupts another Indian speaker either the former will successfully gain the floor, or he won't, but they will not talk about it, nor will they necessarily be annoyed.

The following example demonstrates the sort of talk we mean and the contrast. The example consists of two versions of a role-play situation in which a worker makes a request of a supervisor:

49.   *i. Both speakers are British*
      E: Good morning. Uh, well, I got a request to make actually.
      F: Yes?
      E: Um, it's very important to me. I wonder if you could possibly give me next week off.
      (later)
      E: I can see the problem, but you see it's very important to me. My brother is coming from India, I haven't seen him for eight years, and he is only spending a week in England. So I really must have the week off.

      ii. Both speakers are Indian
      G: Hello H. Good morning.
      H: Hello, good morning. I want to one week off, please. I my brother is coming to the, India.
      G: (   )
      H: And . . . want one week off.

Elsewhere, this example is discussed in terms of how conversational conventions governing the use of metatalk, and talk about one's intentions in general, are concomitants of social conceptions and expectations. Western expectations are that polite conduct in certain situations entails making explicit one's communicative actions, such as stating that one has a request to make before one actually does so; Indian norms of politeness are different.

This difference in what communicative behavior is polite in given situations is an aspect of a comprehensive difference in what speakers expect to be lexicalized. It is not only in order to be polite that Western speakers use metatalk; we do so also as a part of how we signal thematic relations. Expressions such as "What I'm trying to say is . . .," "the point is . . ." are used in Western English to signal how parts of an argument are connected, to highlight information, and to direct the hearer's attention. The following examples are utterances by a British speaker in a counselling interview.

> But it isn't a followup. That's the point.
>
> But Mr. D. it's . . have I said anything about your English?
>
> But Mr. D look, I mean be fair, if . . .
>
> I don't know what to say to you.
>
> Well, I'll tell you what I'm doing.

Obviously this category is not a clear-cut one, and we must do further work on explicating what kinds of behavior constitute metatalk and in what communicative function they occur. But there is certainly an essential difference here between Western and Indian English. Defining our category as simply "comments whose focus is the interaction at the moment," i.e., comments on one's own or the other speaker's verbal behavior, we counted the instances of such talk by each participant in the above-mentioned counselling interview. For the British woman, there were 36, for the Indian man, 14.

These considerations are connected to what we said about example 44, where we said a Western speaker would have reorganized his thematic material and used lexical tying devices to highlight and to mark shifts in topic, where the Indian speaker instead uses repetition for cumulative effect. Indian English speakers are apparently able to move far more freely among topics than Western speakers; not that Western speakers do not switch topic, but the tendency would be to tell the listener *about* the shift by saying things like, "We'll come back to this later."

There is an underlying difference here in *what kind* of thematic progression speakers expect discourse to have, as well as in the devices they use to signal progression and effect cohesion and to identify discourse tasks. Indian English discourse is frequently judged by Western speakers to be loose, illogical, and slow, i.e., lacking in adequate structural clarity. However, this is not to say that there is no thematic structure to Indian English discourse, only that it is of a different sort.

3

Discovering connections
ARPITA MISHRA

In order to show how prosody (including rhythm and register shifts) and paralinguistic cues signal interpretive meaning, and how this affects evaluation of an individual's performance, I have analyzed part of a counselling interview between Das, a school-teacher, born in South Asia and Beth, a British born staff member in an adult education center specializing in industrial language and communication problems. Das is typical of numerous Asian professionals working in the urban West, whose written English is good, and who have no difficulty on their day-to-day affairs in English, but who experience what to them seem unexplainable difficulties in oral exchanges. After completing his professional training he had received several probationary appointments. Probationary teachers are regularly evaluated, but normally such evaluations are routine. The vast majority of probationary appointments are eventually regularized. Das, however, had been released from three positions and seemed unable to obtain regular employment. He reports that in his last post the principal had at first assured him that he was doing well, but when he was then once more released, he was informed that this was because he lacked communication skills and that he needed more training to improve his language before he could be appointed to another post.

He thus turned to the center for advice on how to proceed. In the following extract from a 90-minute interview, Das attempts to explain the circumstances that led to his dismissal. The interviewer, Beth, is a center staff member in charge of curriculum planning, not a regular member of the teaching staff.

The example demonstrates the difficulties a Western English speaker can experience when trying to follow an Indian English

narrative which relates a temporal sequence involving several
different actors and distinct events.

1.   D: In the ⌐thīrd school / in which I hàd been ˌtransferred //

2.   B: yes //

3.   D: I hăd ˌbeen / . . . I contācted / duȑing the ˌhalf / . . . and ˌduring
     the / . . 'during the teˌrm //

4.   B: yẹs //

5.   D: when / ˌI had completed the . . . traìning / ˌten 'day traịning /
     ˌat the ⌐langụage school //

6.   B: Lat the language school //

7.   D: ⌐ ˌand yōu know that . . . whát happẹned there . . .

8.   B: Lyes what happẹned there //

9.   D: and there was anōther / . . . wèek / for thē / . . . vacaṭion //

10. B: yẹs //

11. D: and duȑing that ˌvacation I /

12. B: you ⌐'contacted

13. D: L ⌐contacted ˌthe unìon / 'and un̄ion person ˌcontacted the
     (1) hìs / represẹntative / àt the school and /
     (2) "that reprešentative / contacted the headm̌aster /
     (3) and heādmaster / had contạcted the auˌthority //
     (4) ⌐but before 'that instạnce / ⌐in the mòrning /
     (5) ⌐first day / òf the term / 'I 'had mèt him /
     (6) ˌand toḷd ˌhim that / ⌐I'm wōrried /

14. B: yẹs //

15. D: and / I ˌdon't know ⌐whēre I stand / . . .

16. B: hum //

17. D: ⌐he told that / ˌit's alrịght / ˌyou are okày / ˌI'm happy /
     ˌyou're hạppy /

18. B: th . . th . . the ⌐head'master ˌsaid this //

19. D: Lh . . . headmaster yēs //

20. B: befòre he contacted the authòrity //

21. D: before hē contācted the authōrity / ⌐and ¹before ¹he leàrnt /
    ⌊that I have sèen/anóther ₁union person //

22. B: frọm / you mean from a^{acc}¹different ⌐uñion //

23. D: ⌊different ₁union ₁person //

24. B: ¹which ¹union wạs it //

25. D: ⌐it was uhm . . it was ¹not NAS / it ¹was uhm . . .

26. B: NŬT

27. D: ⌊^{acc}NỤT

28. B: NỤT // and ¹you were a mèmber / of ⌐. . . of the NẠS / yes /

29. D: ⌊no I ¹I was NĄS member /
    uhm so uh . . uh /

30. B: so yọu ¹contacted the NỤT //

31. D: and so / . . ⌐dùring this ₁time/

32. B: yẹs //

33. D: becāuse the / heádmaster ₁didn't know /
    ⌊that ₁I have seen the óther union /

34. B: hm

35. D: and uhm / hè didn't had cont / ⌐. . hè hadn't ₁contacted the /
    educạtion office / so hè had the impression that / ⌊¹everything is
    okạy //

36. B: before he ¹contacted the office //

37. D: yẹs // whèn / the uñion person / tóld him that / hè has /
    he ⌊^{acc}has con¹tacted oùr union representative

38. B: yẽs //

39. D: and ₁he has / askẹd / ¹for hìs help and /

40. B: yẽs

41. D: ⌊^{acc}I want to see whạt is / ⌐so ¹he contacted thè advisor / ⌐told
    ¹th . . thè advisor / ¹that . . ¹this is the situation / ⌊he has
    contạcted/

42. B: yes

43. D: anòther union member / (1) so ⌐hē was annoyed //

44.   B: who //
45.   D: ⌐advisor ˏmath math advisor //
46.   B: the math advisor / yes /

Das here is reporting on a set of events to explain why the
mathematics advisor (the officer responsible for evaluating his
professional performance) became, as he puts it, "annoyed."
Apparently, Das received his present job after attending the language school. When he realized that things were not going well, he
had contacted his union, who then referred the matter to the union
representative at the school. The principal had at first told Das that
everything was alright, but when the principal learned that the
matter had been referred to the union, he contacted the mathematics advisor: this was the source of the problem.

Most English readers attempting to follow Das's account will
share the comprehension difficulties revealed in Beth's frequent
queries and interjections. She clearly seems to have difficulty in
following Das's use of deictic expressions and anaphoric pronouns
and in deciding what is being referred to at what time. His
utterances, moreover, seem to lack connecting links and it is not
easy to see how they fit together, so that in the end (turn 43), when
Das makes his main point, she responds by asking "who?"

Turning now to a more detailed examination of the characteristic
prosodic features used by Das in this passage to signal thematic
continuity, the first question we ask is "what kind of prosodic cues
is Das using to tie his arguments?" I assume, of course, that what
Das is saying makes sense to him. Since there are no compelling
criteria to accept or reject his account as incoherent, we begin by
accepting it as having some kind of semantic relevance which seems
to bypass the British speaker's understanding but which would be
understood by someone who shares his background.

I have analyzed the conversation from Das's and Beth's view-
points on the basis of (a) some of the possible explanations of each
of the utterances, (b) the supporting evidence we may get from the
conversation itself, (c) personal interviews with the participants,
and (d) research with other speakers of the same background, thus
reaching the most likely explanation of each of the utterances. We

are able then to get to the intended meaning at each step of the conversation, and are able to discover when and why the intended meaning was misunderstood and resulted in miscommunication (see Table 1).

In Table 1 we will deal with turns 1–21 to illustrate the different interpretations that can arise during conversation.

There are two main reasons why a British English speaker encounters special problems in understanding: (a) "he" is used a number of times with no special clarification of its referents; (b) the relationship between sentences and parts of sentences is not clear.

Just what does "he" refer to in each occurrence? Among other things, prosody serves to highlight particular actors, to establish a sort of hierarchy of who is being spoken of. In turn 13 "headmaster" is stressed both times it occurs. The focus is thus on the headmaster and it is he who is referred to by "him" in turn 13.5 and "he" in 17. Notice how Das stresses "he" quite emphatically, in turn 21, when he is trying to make it clear to Beth who he is talking about. The headmaster remains in focus until turn 37, when Das begins to describe what the union person did and said, and the action being talked about is no longer the headmaster's contacting the authorities, but the union's having been contacted by Das. Thus the stressed "his" in turn 39 refers to the union representative. All the pronouns referring to the headmaster (turn 37) and Das himself (turns 37, 39 and 41) are destressed, since neither are the highlighted actors in the events in focus. In turn 41 the final figure enters the story. The stress on "the" advisor seems at first gratuitous, but in fact it signals that the advisor is now the central figure in the narrative, and the "he" of turn 43 refers to him. It seems that stress rather than syntax or lexicon serves as the primary signal of anaphoric coreference. What and where are the connections? One additional reason why the passage seems incoherent to Beth is because she has problems connecting the arguments and is unable to figure out what the central issue is. The British speaker looks for syntactic cues in the passage to determine the relationship between two parts of the message, but such cues are absent in this conversation. With analysis we find that semantic functions referring back to given information, linking of effects, subgrouping one or more facts as part of a major argument, etc., are instead indicated through intonation and prosody. In the absence of

Table 1. *Alternative views of the conversation*

Turn	Das's view	Beth's view	Comments
1	"In the ... third ... transferred//" 'In the third school, to which against my wishes I had been transferred.'	Ambiguous. A possible explanation: 'in the third school, in spite of what you may have thought, I had really been transferred.'	Das is stressing the auxiliary "had." By over-stressing the passive form and de-accenting the agent, Das is showing his helplessness in the action thus taken.
3–5	3. "I had been/ ... term//" 5. "when/ ... training//" 3 is a complete sentence by itself. 5 refers to a new, i.e. different, event.	5 seems to qualify 3 contributing to the act "contacted" in 3.	Tone group boundary after "when" in 5 seems to suggest to Beth that the sentence following it is somehow related to the preceding sentence.
11–13.1	11. "and ... contacted" 13.1 "contacted ... and" 'union person contacted the representative who was a representative at school.'	'union person contacted his representative not when he was at home or anywhere else but when he was at school.'	Ambiguity not clarified by syntactic markers.

13.4–13.6	13.4 & 13.5 "but … met him." Das took initiative and went to see him personally.	Peculiar stress. Sounds strangely expressive.	Extra stress on "met."
	13.6 "and … worried//" Das is quoting.	Peculiar intonation. Same as above.	Das's use of high pitch vs. normal pitch to distinguish a quotation from a statement respectively. Das constantly uses high pitch in 13.4 and 13.5 and flat tone on "worried" (in 13.6). Flat nucleus sounds odd to Beth. Similarly in 17, Das is quoting 4 short sentences, all on low pitch as against the pitch and high head of the previous sentence.
21	"before … person": 'person from a different union.'	Ambiguous. Two meanings: (i) 'person from different union'; (ii) 'another union person from the same union'	In IE, one way of contrasting information is not by contrasting single words (as in BE) but by contrasting a whole phrase as one unit with another phrase as the other unit through use of prosodic features like high pitch and stress. In such cases we find that the stress begins from the linguistic unit just before the content words.

syntactic markers to indicate semantic relationships between arguments, how does Das (1) signal old and new information, (2)
arrange events in a temporal sequence, (3) indicate distinctions
between personal opinion and a general fact, and (4) signal a
change in the focus of the argument?

We can begin to answer some of these questions by looking first
at how Das relates different arguments. The first step includes
dividing the entire conversation into several 'blocks'; by 'block' we
mean a stretch of speech which, on the basis of initial reading of
content, contains one major new piece of information. Our procedure, then, is to use these blocks as the starting point in our search
for the basic conversational units by which speakers mark the
development of thematic continuity. For instance, turns 1 and 3
pertain to one major piece of information, namely "in the third
school to which Das has been transferred, Das contacted (somebody)." Therefore, 1 and 3 can be grouped into one block. Further,
turns 5 and 6 jointly furnish another major piece of information,
namely "Das completed the ten day training at the school." Since
the information given in turns 5 and 6 is crucial to Das's narrative
is different from the information given in 1 and 3, and is one
separate piece of information, 5 and 6 can therefore be grouped
into another block. In this manner, the entire passage is divided into
ten blocks (see table 2). I have mentioned only those sentences
which are crucial to the chain of events mentioned in the discourse.

Now that the different pieces of information supplied by Das are
clearly recognizable, the next question can be posed; namely, how
are these different blocks arranged by Das to make one cohesive
piece of argument? Since the account relates several incidents that
took place at different times, the problem is not in understanding
the literal meaning of the individual sentences, but in comprehend-
ing the right temporal sequence. The listener is unable to link these
different pieces of information supplied by these sentences either
logically on the basis of the literal meaning they imply or sequentially on a real time scale. Thus we ask ourselves, why is it that the
account makes sense to Das but seems to be so confusing to Beth?

Looking at the account for the chronological order of information and from the point of view of the story schema, we find that
Das switches to and fro in time frame very frequently. He presents,
in what looks like the same time frame, events that really happened

Table 2. *Blocks of information*

Block	Turn	Utterances (Bracketed items indicate the analyst's clarifications)
A	1,3	In the third school in which I had been transferred; during the term I contacted [somebody].
B	5,6	I had completed the ten day training.
C	9,11,13	There was another week for the vacation and during that vacation, I contacted the union.
D	13.1	And union person contacted his representative at the school.
E	13.2	That representative contacted the headmaster.
F	13.4, 13.5, 13.6 15, 17	But before that instance, in the morning, first day of the term, I had met him [headmaster] and told him that "I don't know where I stand." He said that "it's alright. You are okay. I'm happy; you're happy."
G	21, 23, 25, 27, 29, 31, 33, 35	Before he [headmaster] contacted the authority and before he [headmaster] learnt that I have seen another union person. During this time because the headmaster didn't know that I have seen the other union and he [headmaster] hadn't contacted the education office, so he [headmaster] had the impression that everything is okay.
H	37, 39	When the union person told him [headmaster] that he [Das] has contacted our union representative and he [Das] has asked for his [representative's] help.
I	41, 43	[Note that this is a repetition of 13.3: "headmaster contacted the authority"] he [headmaster] contacted the advisor. Told the advisor that this is the situation. He [Das] has contacted another union member.
J	43.1	So he [advisor] was annoyed.

much earlier and much later, thus creating an unclear picture of the actual sequence. If we represent the time scale of events on the horizontal dimension and the major steps in the development of the story on the vertical scale, we can summarize the basic discourse structure of Das's account of the events in the form of a diagram (see Fig. 1).

Observations
Below is what we can observe about the story based on (a) a knowledge of Indian English discourse conventions and (b) participants' comments.

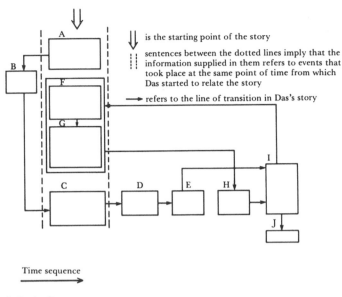

Figure 1. Basic discourse structure

(1) *Going back and forth:* If we mark the direction of the arrows joining two blocks, we find that Das not only goes backward in time, but also constantly refers to events that took place much later in the real time sequence, shifting from one event to the other. For instance, he goes from block A to block B, which in a real time scale is going backward in time and then from B to C, thus returning to the original point of time, then moving on further ahead in time, to D to E, then to I and then suddenly going back in time to F and G and so on and so forth.

(2) *Mentioning events in disjoined order:* The events mentioned in A, C, F, G all occur at the same point of time but they are arranged out of sequence as is evident from their alphabetical order. In other words, instead of giving one complete picture of the events at one time, Das relates parts of them on several different occasions.

Referring back and forth to several events when telling a story is not uncommon surely, but in that circumstance the speaker must clearly spell out the shifts so that the hearer can easily follow the connections and can relate the different events together.

The important question is: Does Das relate these different blocks together and if he does, how does he connect and differentiate them? That is, is he clear in his own mind about what he is saying? We find a surprising lack of syntactic constructions to indicate relationships between successive sentences. If the relationships between sentences are not lexicalized, then how exactly are the relationships indicated?

On carefully scanning through each of the sentences of the passage spoken by Das, we are surprised to find that as the story progresses Das is using some very definite and regular prosodic devices, not only to mark these different blocks but also to indicate the relationships between them whenever an explicit mention of the connection would be necessary. Prosodic markings of a definite nature are also used to indicate the 'sudden shifts' in the line of argument, or of perspective, which occur when there is a change in the focus of the discourse. In these instances, prosody serves as a marker for these shifts and thus serves as a signalling mechanism for the building and the cohesion of the discourse. Figure 2 displays the specific prosodic characteristics of each of the sentences semantically crucial to the block they are part of.

After specifying prosodic markings for all of the crucial sentences, some very interesting observations can be made:

(1) *Sentences having one major argument in common share the same prosodic characteristics.* For instance, in block B, turns 5 and 6 are both in low voice and in accelerated speech. In block F, turns 13.4, 13.5, 13.6 and 15 together make one complete statement of fact. They also share prosodic markings; *viz.* they are mostly spoken in very high pitch, and the first set of syllables of minor tone groups is set off from the following ones.

(2) *Shifts in the focus are marked prosodically.* Given that each of the blocks constitutes one complete statement of fact or one argument, the blocks that appear next to each other which do not follow each other logically, are marked prosodically to indicate the shifts in the focus of the argument. Each block is set off from the previous block either by a different intonational pattern or by a different rhythmic pattern. For instance, block A is differentiated from block B by a change in the voice level and in the speech rhythm.

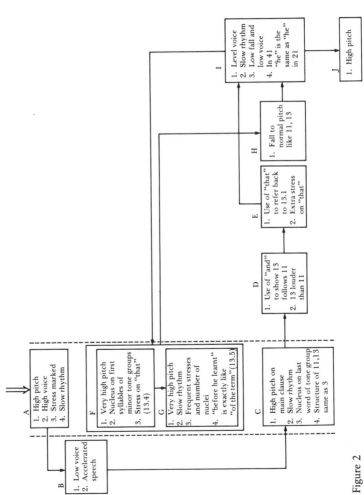

Figure 2

Corollary
Blocks that do follow sequentially on the time scale do not receive any characteristic prosodic markings. We can see that block E directly follows after D; i.e., they are connected by an arrow with no interim block en route. We see that the two blocks are not marked prosodically in any significant way either. The stress is on the main content word, namely, "that" of 13.2, a way of indicating that Das is referring back to the "representative" mentioned just before in 13.1.

(3)   *Repetition of prosodic pattern: a way of relating information.* The prosodic structure of 3 (high pitch on main clause, slow rhythm, definite stress markings) is repeated in 13, and that of 13.4, 13.5 (high pitch and staccato) is repeated in 21. Figure 2 shows that blocks consisting of these sentences have the same time reference (between the dotted lines). It is interesting to note that the main clauses of the sentences of all these blocks receive high pitch. The use of high pitch appears to be a way of suggesting transitions in the development of the story that refer to events occurring at the same point in time. Hence repetition of the prosodic characteristics appears to relate two or more sentences that occur at different points in the discourse but that refer to events occurring at the same point in time.

Corollary
A shift in the prosodic pattern indicates the speaker's intention to convey that the current information is not immediately related to the previous information. (Note: this is similar to the observation indicated in (2) above.)

   At times Das uses an utterance consisting of several pieces of information, with several minor tone group boundaries and with only one major tone group boundary at the end. In such cases, a British speaker is likely to interpret these several pieces of information as part of *one* whole argument; or at the least, he may see them as being closely related semantically and temporally, lacking any syntactic information to the contrary. For example, the utterance represented by 13, 13.1, 13.2, and 13.3 has 7 minor tone groups, with a major tone group boundary after the word "authority."

Turns 13, 13.1, 13.2, and 13.3, although falling within the same major tone group, refer to two separate incidents that occurred at two different times. 13.2 starts with high pitch register to "that" and also receives extra stress and high tone on the last word; 13.3, on the other hand, starts with a *flat* nucleus and has no heads at all. By treating these segments differentially on the prosodic level, Das indicates the difference in the time of the occurrence of two events. Similarly, there is a shift in the pitch register of 13.3 and 13.4 and we see from Figures 1 and 2 that the two incidents occurred at two different times.

To summarize, after we consider the prosodic features that Das used to mark semantic functions of discourse, we see that Das not only distinguishes between two semantically different arguments but also uses definite prosodic cues to tie in several different messages in whole or in part. Without specifying the main point, he gets into several minor details so that by the time he comes to the main point, the staff member is thoroughly confused. Moreover, his way of indicating main and subsidiary information is so different from the Britisher's linguistic system that communication breaks down.

A real time rearrangement
Having resolved the basic question regarding Das's method of signalling communication intent, we are tempted to ask another question: would Das have made himself clear to a BE speaker if he had followed his line of narration according to the real time sequence, as depicted in Figures 1 and 2?

Now, if we were to substitute for each block the topic sentences of each, keeping the temporal sequence of the blocks as is (i.e., B→A→F→G→C→D→E→H→I→J), we get the passage given in Table 3.

If we read through the column "after minor modification," we get a cohesive narrative and the account makes sense. The chain of events seems to follow in a logical order, the cause and effect relationships are explicit, and the hearer gets a complete picture of the line of argument as presented by Das. Note that I have not made changes in the grammatical structure of Das's constructions.

This points out that in spite of the fact that Das gave all the

Table 3

Turn	Verbatim	After minor modification
5	when I had completed the . . . training/ten day training at the language school	when I had completed the ten day training
1	in the third school in which I had been transferred	I had been transferred to the third school
13.5	I had met him	at the language school, I met the headmaster
11	during that vacation, I contacted the union	later, during a vacation, I contacted the union
13.1	and union person contacted his representative at the school	and the union person contacted his representative at the school
13.2	that representative contacted the headmaster	that representative contacted the headmaster
37	when the union person told him that he had contacted our union representative	when the headmaster came to know that I had contacted the union
41	so he contacted the advisor, told the advisor . . he has contacted another union member	the headmaster told the advisor that I contacted the union
43	so he was annoyed	so the advisor was annoyed

relevant information, Beth could not process it because of the way Das framed and marked it.

Das's strategies have many similarities to those discussed in Chapter 2. There is good reason to believe that he represents a significant group of English-speaking South Asian professionals. Minority speakers who use this style may feel that their opinions and views are not taken seriously and see themselves as subjects of racial discrimination. The Britishers, on the other hand, think of minorities as inefficient workers who make excuses and speak incorrect English. Much of the problem lies not in knowledge of grammar, of syntactic constructions, or of accent for that matter, but in the way linguistic and paralinguistic cues signal syntactic and semantic functions of day-to-day discourse.

4

Inscrutability revisited

LINDA WAI LING YOUNG

> For decades, Westerners referred to 'oriental inscrutability', which was only a way of saying that their own cultural inheritance had not prepared them to 'read the signals' of interpersonal relations in Chinese society.
>
> Richard Solomon, *Mao's Revolution and the Chinese Political Culture*

Introduction

Considerable work has been done on the factors that promote or mitigate understanding of contact across different cultures, both within nations as well as between nations. The theoretical apparatus has been drawn from various disciplines. For example, recent writings by anthropologists of ethnic process explain the persistence of ethnicity as an aspect of socioeconomic considerations and power relations and as a major factor in generating misunderstanding in ethnically mixed industrial societies. Previous work by social psychologists on the problems in cross-cultural interaction attributes cultural differences to variation in values and attitudes.

Philosophers and historians, for more than three centuries, have grappled with characterizing Chinese ethos, values, and perceptual framework. Many of them seek to define the differences in logical processes between the Asian mind and the Western mind. Moreover, they attempt to delineate the differences in social processes between Asian cultures and Western cultures. Their emphases have been reliance on either historically or religiously based explanations, or the search for the nexus between language and culture. Unfortunately, their excursions into the role of language in specifying modes of thinking have been mired in the study of vocabulary and isolated grammatical paradigms. Conversely, their comments on the overarching framework of social values have not been linked to linguistic evidence.

This chapter argues that some Western claims concerning the peculiarities of the Chinese mind and the Chinese preference towards harmonious social relationships can be traced to culture-specific notions of acceptable discourse strategies. The data to be analyzed here are derived from a variety of formal speech encounters, including an academic conference and a number of business meetings involving Chinese speakers of English as active participants. This study will be guided by the assumptions that these speakers will have transferred some of the mechanisms of their native speech patterns and discourse expectations into English.

Background information

When a Westerner listens to a foreigner whose English sounds odd, he often attributes it to grammatical inadequacies or to phonological characteristics, i.e., 'accent.' When he encounters someone with an unusual discourse style, he may misjudge that person's intention or ability, leading to severe social consequences. Likewise, some Chinese users of English are convinced that an improvement in the communication process with English speakers resides in a modification of accent and an increase in vocabulary. What both groups fail to realize is that there are substantial differences in basic sentence type as well as in certain discourse strategies.

Chinese, as well as many other mainland South-East Asian languages, has utterances that show a topic–comment grammatical relationship, as in the sentence (from Li and Thompson 1976: 479):

(1) *Huang se* *de* *tu-di dafen* *zui* *heshi*
     yellow color rel. soil manure most suitable
                   clause
                   marker
     THE YELLOW SOIL (topic), manure is most suitable.

Y. R. Chao has suggested that 50% of the utterances in Chinese are topic–comment types. He has also claimed that the topic–comment utterance is "the favorite sentence type only in deliberate connected discourse" (Chao 1968: 83).

The topic–comment grammatical relationship is in sharp contrast to the preferred subject–predicate format of many European languages, English as well. However, the topic–comment structure itself is not unknown in English. It functions least like:

(2)   As for the President's men, they're all a bunch of liars.

where a contrastive relationship is presumed. It is more in tune with the following:

(3)   You know the blue surfboard, a giant squid ate it.

The Chinese version of the topic–comment utterance would eliminate the "you know" and "the" portion. The sentence would read, then:

(4)   Blue surfboard, giant squid ate.

Li and Thompson (1976) argue that the topic–comment structure is a basic sentence type and point out some of the differences between subject-prominent and topic-prominent languages: the topic is definite, selectionally independent of the verb, sets the framework for the predication and occurs in sentence-initial position. Other writings on topic–comment in Chinese have acknowledged that the topic bears a loose relationship with its comment. Chafe (1976) suggests that the topic sets the spatial, temporal or personal framework for the following assertion. Chao (1968) has stated that the topic carries the old information whereas the new or significant information is found in the comment.

To put it all succinctly then, the Chinese topic–comment utterance eliminates the necessity of the lexicalized "you know," "a," "it," and "the" parts of a sentence like (3) since it is understood from the context, and their appearance would consequently be redundant.

Chinese also has subordinate clauses that set the evaluative framework for the main clause. The appearance of these subordinate clauses is in the order prescribed for the topic of the topic–comment utterance. In other words, they must precede the main clause (Chao 1968). Both the subordinate and the main clauses have pairs of specific lexical markers that occur in clause-initial position. The markers can be optionally dropped in either clause.

These subordinate clauses can be divided into three types:

the causal
   because . . ., therefore . . .
   since . . ., so . . .
the conditional
   if . . ., then . . .
the concessive
   although . . ., yet . . .
      but

Guided by the insights of these scholars, I will extend their analyses of the functions of the topic–comment utterance to reflect beyond the sentence boundary. I will suggest that in such discourse tasks as explaining, justifying, and persuading, the organization of the discourse mirrors the order presented in the topic–comment utterance. The relationship of the main point to the rest of the discourse is in the order of the semantic relationship of topic to comment.

Analysis
In general, the total configuration of the Chinese responses in the following conversational exchanges reveals a distinctive tendency in the production and management of discourse. In most cases, the Chinese discourse patterns seem to be the inverse of English discourse conventions (see Kaplan 1966) in that definitive summary statements of main arguments are delayed till the end. Thus, as we shall see, "because" and "so" are used, respectively, in Chinese discourse to initiate the discussion and mark the transition to the definitive summary statement.

The first example comes from a recorded discussion by a group of Chinese businessmen who manage the various divisions of a large Hong Kong business corporation. They are discussing the qualities desired in a good salesman. The discussion is capitalized, summary statements are italicized.

(5)   Irving: Oscar, anything else to add? Your line of business is, again, quite different from what PK and Tony have. And, in your line of business, I presume market information will be quite important.

Oscar: Yes. What have been mentioned previously by the three gentlemen, I think they are quite sufficient to cover all the basic requirement of a salesman.
My business is textile. The salesman is . . . The quality of the salesman, need something different. BECAUSE THE VOLUME OF MAKING A SALES IN TEXTILES IS ABOUT, AT LEAST, TO OVER TEN THOUSAND US DOLLARS, SOMETIMES. SO THAT IS THE PROBLEM. THAT IS, WHENEVER ANYBODY WHO MAKES A DECISION TO BUY SUCH . . . WILLING TO PAY SUCH AMOUNT, WE'LL MAKE SURE THEIR FINANCIAL AID IS STRONG. AND, THEN, SUCH . . . SOMETIMES THE MARKET MAY SUDDENLY DROP IN TEXTILE. MAYBE WE'RE WILLING TO BUY ONE MONTH AGO, BUT MAY NOT BE BUYING . . . WANT TO BUY NOW. THINGS LIKE THAT. *So, the so, for a salesman, also have to understand about the financial situation and things like that.*

The next .example comes from a tape recording of a budget meeting.

(6)   Chairman: So by purchasing this new machine, do you think we need to recruit additional workers or our existing workforce will cope with our requirement?

Alpha: I THINK THAT WITH THIS NEW MACHINE, THE PRODUCTION TIME WILL BE SHORTENED OR WILL BECOME MORE EFFICIENT. AND THE NUMBER OF STAFF REQUIRED, I THINK WE CAN UTILIZE THE EXISTING STAFF FOR THE TIME BEING. AND NO MORE NEW STAFF IS NECESSARY. *So that we can solve the problem in recruiting the new staff.*

Another example was collected by the author during a discussion period, following a talk given by a visiting professor of nutrition from Peking, China.

(7)   American: How does the Nutritional Institute decide what topics to study? How do you decide what topic to do research on?

Chinese: BECAUSE, NOW, PERIOD GET CHANGE. IT'S DIFFERENT FROM PAST TIME. IN PAST TIME, WE EMPHASIZE HOW TO SOLVE PRACTICAL PROBLEMS. NUTRITION MUST KNOW HOW TO SOLVE SOME DEFICIENCY DISEASES. IN OUR COUNTRY, WE HAVE SOME NUTRITIONAL DISEASES, SUCH AS X, Y, Z. BUT, NOW IT IS IMPORTANT THAT WE MUST DO SOME BASIC RESEARCH. *So, we must take into account fundamental problems. We must concentrate our research to study some fundamental research.*

Although illustrations can be multiplied from other taped inter-changes involving native Chinese speakers, these examples give credence to the fact that a systematic pattern in the organization and presentation of information exists. That is, there is a Chinese preference for the steady unravelling and build-up of information before arriving at the important message.

These remarks may serve to set the scene for the following, more detailed analysis of data derived from a simulated budget meeting conducted by Chinese businessmen in English. There were five participants, one of whom chaired the meeting. He began the meeting by asking the participants, who were members of various departments, what should be done with an excess sum of £180,000 in the budget. Several of the participants, for various reasons, requested a portion of the funds.

There is a remarkable coincidence in the presentation of requests. Like the topic of a topic–comment utterance, the reasons or justifications for the request appear initially, represent old informa-tion and establish the situational framework for the request. In more prosaic terms, the listener is given a build-up before the punchline is delivered. The following example comes from the tape:

(8)   Theta: One thing I would like to ask. BECAUSE MOST OF OUR RAW
MATERIALS ARE COMING FROM JAPAN AND ( ) THIS YEAR
IS GOING UP AND UP AND UH IT'S NOT REALLY I THINK AN
INCREASE IN PRICE BUT UH WE LOSE A LOT IN EXCHANGE
RATE AND SECONDLY I UNDERSTAND WE'VE SPENT A LOT OF
MONEY IN TV AD LAST YEAR. *So, in that case I would like to*
suggest here: chop half of the budget in TV ads and spend a
little money on Mad magazine.

Note again that the subordinate marker "because" initiates the listing of reasons while the conjunction "so" signifies the shift from the reasons to the request. Between the two markers are several independent clauses, connected by the conjunction "and," which itemize the reasons. The example shows a series of conjoined sentences that not only repeat old or assumed information but also provide the hypothetical context with which to evaluate the significant information to follow. The same structure is revealed in the next two examples. Note that the topic–comment structure can be juxtaposed to another topic–comment-like structure:

(9) Chairman: . . . I would like to have your opinion on how we should
                 utilize the extra amount of one hundred eighty
                 thousand pounds to improve . . . (Beta's answer follows
                 another presentation).

     Beta: AS YOU KNOW, I HAVE SPENT FIVE HUNDRED AND
                 SEVENTY THOUSAND POUNDS LAST YEAR TO ON THE
                 MACHINERY AND COMPONENTS AND AH IF AH IF MR.
                 AH LINCOLN WOULD LIKE TO INCREASE THE AH
                 PRODUCTION IN AH THROUGH THE COMING YEAR, I
                 THINK WE HAVE TO MAKE OUR BUDGET TEN PERCENT ON
                 TOP OF THE AMOUNT FIVE HUNDRED AND FIVE
                 HUNDRED AND SEVENTY THOUSAND POUNDS BECAUSE
                 THERE WILL BE A TEN PERCENT ON UH INCREASE IN PRICE
                 ON AVERAGE. AND, UH, *in other words, I need another
                 sixty thousand pounds to buy the same material and
                 quality.*
                 AND AS YOU KNOW WHENEVER THERE'S A SHORTAGE
                 OF COMPONENTS ON THE (   ) AMOUNT OF TIME AND AH
                 ALTHOUGH WE HAVE ARRANGED DELIVERY OF NORMAL
                 SUPPLIES FOR FOR FOR AT LEAST SIX MONTHS. BUT WE
                 STILL NEED AH AN EXTRA MONEY TO BUY AH THE
                 REPLACEMENT WHICH COST US FIVE HUNDRED MORE.
                 *So, in other words, I need at least six hundred thousand
                 sorry six hundred thousand pounds for an extra, uh,
                 extra money for the for the*

(10) Chairman: Uh, Mr. Lincoln do you think the new machinery that
                 you just mentioned that will cost us sixty thousand
                 pounds will cater for the the (   ) the new model, that is,
                 the portable TV set that was just mentioned by Mr.
                 Jeffrey?

     Alpha: I think this new machine will certainly reduce the
                 production cost. And, uh, AS WE HAVE AN EXTRA
                 BUDGET OF ABOUT ONE HUNDRED EIGHTY THOUSAND
                 POUNDS STERLING AND WE JUST SPENT ABOUT ONE
                 THIRD OF THE TOTAL AMOUNT BUYING THIS NEW
                 MACHINE AND AS THE SALES OF IT INCREASING THE
                 PRODUCTION OF HOURS, *therefore I think it is very
                 worthwhile at minimal to invest in this new machine by
                 buying a sixty thousand pounds sterling new machine.*
                 I have also one thing to say. BECAUSE THE PERSONNEL
                 MANAGER, HE MENTIONED A FEW DAYS AGO THAT UH
                 THERE ARE SOME DIFFICULTIES IN THE EQUIPPING
                 MORE NEW WORKERS AND ASK THE EXISTING WORKERS
                 TO WORK OVERTIME BY PAYING THEM SOME EXTRA
                 MONEY, AND *therefore I think that we have no
                 alternative but to buy a new machine or otherwise incur
                 a lot of cost by using the existing one.*

What is striking about the data is the similarity in the majority of the presentations, the smoothness of the interactions, and the evident ease of comprehension among the participants. This demonstrates that the topic–comment effect cannot be limited to a single person's idiolect and reduces the possibility that these patterns may simply be chance occurrences.

Nonetheless, native English speakers who listened to the tapes experienced many difficulties with the discourse. The main point was initially lost on them because it lay buried in a mass of information. Adding to their confusion was a lack of understanding of how the important information was highlighted. In fact, their appreciation of the significance of any one feature proved elusive.

Moreover, sentence connectives, which play an essential role in guiding the listener's journey through the discourse, had been invested with meanings which are somewhat different from their usual associations in English. For example, the English speakers were not fully cognizant of the fact that, in the Chinese discourse, single word items such as "because," "as," and "so" had replaced whole clause connectives commonly used in English, such as "in view of the fact that," "to begin with," or "in conclusion."

The English speakers' attempts to sift through the information were complicated by another problem. The opening lines of the Chinese discourse did not provide a thesis or preview statement which would have oriented the listener to the overall direction of the discourse; the presence of a clear and concise statement of what was to be discussed would have made the discourse more precise, more dramatic, and more eloquent. As it was, in their view, the clarity and the forcefulness of the main points were absent. Worst of all, the lack of precision and the failure to address the point directly led to suspicions that the Chinese speakers were beating around the bush.

Thus, the implication would seem to be that the presumed shortcomings mentioned above were influenced by the lack of the English speakers' familiarity with the contextualization cues of the topic–comment format. It becomes easy to see how a basic unawareness of alternative linguistic structures and discourse conventions can shade into doubts concerning the reasoning abilities of the Chinese mind.

A closer examination of the linguistic data provoked another interpretation that might shed light on the view that Chinese tend to minimize confrontation in formal social relationships. The native English speakers called attention to the indirectness of the discourse style. When asked to appraise the effectiveness of the presentations, they commented that the Chinese arguments lacked sufficient aggressive and persuasive power. In line with these sentiments were remarks concerning the construction of the discourse. The absence of a preview statement and the mere item-by-item listing of justifications, blocked the development of a positive tone in the Chinese arguments. As a matter of fact, the listeners sensed a reluctance on the part of the Chinese to have to make a request, that they had to slide inevitably into it as a result of a convergence of forces. Likewise, it was pointed out that, instead of stating their proposition somewhere in the beginning and then proceeding to build their case, the Chinese first established a shared context with which to judge their requests. Only after carefully prefacing the request with an avalanche of relevant details, as if to nullify any opposition, did they present the requests.

In view of the fact that there are correspondences between linguistic behavior and social evaluation (Giles and Powesland 1975), the Chinese examples led some Westerners to the interpretation that the Chinese were employing a deference tactic so as not to press their claim too forcefully upon the other person. The framework provided by Brown and Levinson (1978) would lead one to conclude, then, that the user of such a discourse strategy was minimizing his particular imposition by operating on the basis of "negative politeness."

The aforementioned interpretation is compatible with Western writings on Chinese ethos. As a matter of fact, it obliquely lends support to Western impressions that the Chinese prize harmony in social relationships. Whether it is a genuine demonstration of deference or simply the consequence of a particular discourse style needs further investigation.

While such an examination lies beyond the scope of this chapter, curiosity led me to make a few inquiries of several native Chinese speakers. I asked each of them to enact a similar budget meeting. The result was that they all began by providing the rationale behind their requests. The overall consensus was that one must always state one's request or one's main point last, after first articulating the reasons for it. They provided some illuminating comments when pressed further as to the reasons for this and as to the kinds of consequences that can develop when the opening line of the discourse indicates their position. One person flatly stated that he would not listen beyond the first sentence as he already would have heard what was wanted. Two other individuals claimed that it would be rude. It would sound as though the person was demanding something. Moreover, it made the person seem immodest, pushy, and inconsiderate for wanting things. Another person elaborated: in giving the impression that you were demanding something, you would lose face for acting aggressively. He added that the use of such a discourse strategy might suggest that you are not considering the other members of the group. Thus you'd be hurting people by claiming something for yourself. And, finally, he said that if you started out with a statement that strongly hinted at a request for something, despite your eventual elaboration of the rationale behind it, and furthermore, if the chairman didn't grant it, you'd lose the respect of the others. One other person stated that it would be a foolhardy approach to hint about or mention your desires at the outset, because you're not aware of what the chairman is prepared to give you and what the others are planning to ask. In such a situation, it's considered a smart strategy if you carefully delineate the justifications that will naturally lead to your request.

Generalizing from their responses, then, there is an attempt to refrain from making prestige-damaging statements when there might be an open recognition by others that the request may not be granted. Also, there is an effort to resist any appearance of presumptuousness and overeagerness. In addition, in clarifying the circumstances behind the individual's request, such a discourse strategy avoided disagreements as to the justness of the request and the rigidity of the individual's stance. More fundamentally, their comments and the data suggest that there are significantly divergent assumptions about the appropriate linguistic behavior for a given communicative task. The different ways of structuring information receive different valuation in English-speaking and Chinese-speaking cultures. Viewed callously, the Chinese discourse appears imprecise, unwieldy, and downright inept. Cast more charitably, it is seen to emphasize cooperation, prudence, and clear-headed caution.

Additional remarks
The validity of these findings on the preferred style of Chinese discourse is strengthened by the following observations on Oriental rhetorical form. By "Oriental" the author is referring to Chinese and Korean (see Kaplan 1966, footnote). Although he focuses on written discourse, his comments are directly pertinent to the examples provided earlier in this paper.

Some Oriental writing on the other hand, is marked by what may be called an approach by indirection. In this kind of writing, the development of the paragraph may be said to be 'turning and turning in a widening gyre'. The circles or gyres turn around the subject and show it from a variety of tangential views, but the subject is never looked at directly . . . Again, such a development in a modern English paragraph would strike the English reader as awkward and unnecessarily indirect.

He goes on to scrutinize a composition written by an Oriental.

The concluding paragraph-sentence presents, in the guise of a summary logically derived from previously posited ideas, a conclusion which is in fact partially a topic sentence . . . The paper arrives at where it should have started . . . (Kaplan 1966: 10–11)

In order to gain further perspective on the validity of Kaplan's analysis, I interviewed a number of Chinese speakers. They have all had to take English writing classes while enrolled as foreign students in various American universities. It is an index of their difficulties when faced with an unfamiliar sociolinguistic tradition that all of them immediately disclosed their confusion and consternation with the task of mastering English rhetorical form. Among other things, they were unable or unwilling to come to terms with the common English tendency to begin with a topic statement. Most significantly, the more fluent bilinguals went on to contrast, from a Chinese viewpoint, the critical social implications that lie behind Chinese and English styles of rhetoric. One individual neatly summarizes their sentiments with the following statement.

I don't find the American style, where the topic sentence appears first, to be effective. It's not necessarily more persuasive nor convincing than the

Chinese style, where the speaker, at the same time as he is speaking, is reasoning with the listener to allow the listener to see whether what he says makes sense or not. This Chinese speech style is more open-minded, less biased, not constrictive as the American style, where it immediately sets you up to a particular frame of mind. You see, with the American style, you can react immediately to what the speaker says without listening to the rest of his explanation.

While this statement merits further investigation, nonetheless, it sheds considerable light on the divergent premises underlying Chinese and English discourse construction. Put in capsule form, the difference between Chinese and English expectations of discourse norms boils down to the distinction between 'where the argument is going' and 'where the argument is coming from,' respectively. Moreover, the statement lends clarity to the social considerations implicit in the construction and structure of Chinese discourse. That is, there is a genuine concern that the ability to retain the listener's attention not be jeopardized. Such a task is accomplished in Chinese discourse, then, by a deliberate maneuvering in the direction of a less aggressive and more consensual appearance, with the intent to create and maintain a receptive environment for one's remarks. Simultaneously, respect for the listener is insinuated by the 'laying out' of information – revealing the manner of one's thinking, so to say – to elicit the listener's judgment. The speaker and listener become bonded in a cooperative endeavor. In view of this, the high Chinese premium placed on the avoidance of an immediate stance becomes transparent.

Conclusion

Although people have been able to coexist in intercultural contact, there remains an undercurrent of tension. This tension is not only just a product of resource competition and power relations; it can also stem from failures in the communicative process. The fact that different sociocultural assumptions underlie message construction on the discourse level is not easily recognized. Speakers from different cultural or subcultural backgrounds, in attempting to formulate a sensible interpretation when faced by an unfamiliar or unexpected discourse style, fall back on their knowledge of the evaluative frameworks conventionalized by their own culture. Unfortunately, in cross-cultural interactions, what are generally explained as problems in grammaticality at the sentence level often become interpreted as behavioral differences of motivation, attitude, and personality on the level of discourse. It is no exaggeration to say that continuous misperception, misinterpretation and misunderstanding in face-to-face linguistic encounters can develop into stereotypes that are reinforced over time.

5

Negotiating interpretations in interethnic settings

MARK HANSELL AND CHERYL SEABROOK AJIROTUTU

The notion of a "speech community" has long been recognized as problematic since competent language users who are geographical neighbors may be linguistic distant cousins at best. They assume they share a common code, but their ability to enter into fruitful exchanges may at times be limited. Our data derive from an ethnographic group interview recorded in 1969 involving a university professor and a group of inner-city teenagers enrolled in an urban alternative high school. The meeting took place in the home of a young black social worker less than a mile away from the professor's residence located in a medium-sized California city. The researcher had asked the social worker to arrange the group discussion to give him an opportunity to tape informal Black English conversation. Communication problems at the meeting provide striking evidence of the interpretive difficulties that can arise even among long-term residents of the same urban environment.

Although linguists concerned with Black English have concentrated on phonological and grammatical differences, the problem here is rather one of conversational conventions embodied in prosody and formulaic speech which draw upon knowledge specific to the Afro-American cultural traditions in the United States.

In attempting to isolate the relevant conversational conventions, we begin by focusing on empirical evidence of conversational breakdown occurring in the course of the discussion. Our purpose is to identify culturally specific contextualization cues that have signalling values for individuals familiar with the Afro-American tradition but that are not noticed or interpreted by the middle-class white interviewers.

Conversational conventions are those organizational filters that
the listener uses when making the connection between speaker's
intent and meaning. They act as sifters in processing conversational
information. As such they tell us what the intended agenda is and
how the speakers expect to present their point of view. This agenda
is always negotiated among speakers and listeners, and the ability
to reach agreement is crucial to the achievement of conversational
cooperation. The strategies employed to maintain and to control
the flow of conversation allow for nonverbal and prosodic, as well
as verbal, signs. And many of these conventions are specific to
individuals regularly interacting in particular social networks. We
have found that often in shared familiar surroundings such as the
home, with family and friends, conversational conventions are not
problematic. However, once conversation moves to broader
spheres, use of conventions easily understood in the home may lead
to serious misreading of intent.

Our analysis identifies two types of contextualization conventions, reflected in prosodic cues and formulaic speech. In context,
these cues may seem idiosyncratic and to rely heavily on style for
effect. But we have found that the listener who shares the relevant
cultural knowledge is able to give the expected response. That is,
we are dealing with systematic differences at the subcultural level,
not individual peculiarities.

Prosodic features in Black English include rhythmical stress
placement and marked intonation patterns. Our data substantiate
three distinct kinds of prosodic cues. The first is a shift of pitch
register. The second type is a change of voice quality, the 'quotational style.' In this type, the speaker assumes the role of some
character, imitating the prosody associated with the character or
role. The third type of prosodic cue includes such features as voice
tensing and the use of falsetto, characteristics often discussed under
the heading of paralinguistic features. Prosodic cues can also be
signalled through a marked use of vowel lengthening.

Formulaic speech on the other hand is metaphoric in nature and
occurs in context-bound instances. Its meaning draws upon specific
cultural knowledge that requires reference information as to place
and to time. Often it is marked by a 'quotational style' in which the
speaker's voice quality further signals speaker's intent.

The cues under investigation are related to conventionalized discourse strategies – ways of planning and negotiating the discourse structure (conversational agenda) over long stretches of conversation. Our examples are therefore whole or partial episodes within a conversation, each episode consisting of a stretch of conversation involving the same participants, the same setting, and the same subject matter. Only by tracing the progression of the discourse from the use of the cue in question through its ultimate outcome in the episode can we provide empirical, internal evidence for the discourse-directing nature of these cues. In cases where a misunderstanding occurs, the discourse is heading in different directions in the minds of the participants (without either's knowledge) until the discrepancy is so great that the miscommunication becomes obvious to all, in which case it can be negotiated and resolved. Sometimes the discrepancy never becomes great enough to be obvious; the miscommunicating participants interpret the others' conversational contributions in a way consistent with their own idea. Each comes away with a different sense of what happened. A third type of miscommunicative episode is the conscious manipulation of culture-specific conversational conventions by one group of participants to gain conversational control over another group – 'putting them on' or 'running a game on them.' A precondition for this type of episode is that those on the same 'team' share conversational conventions and, therefore, coordinate their strategies through prosodic and paralinguistic cues invisible to the other 'team.'

Our first example is one where both the white and black participants are aware of this third possibility, and where the black speakers maintain conversational control because of the doubt in the minds of the white participants.

Active participants in the interview are the researcher (G), his research assistant (M) and two black teenagers (W) and (B). Several other black teenagers are listening. "What do we talk about?" marks the beginning of the interview proper.

Transcript 1

1.   G: What do we talk about? //
2.   W: Oh you guys pick a subject / any old subject you know //
3.   G: Any old subject //
4.   B: Any old thang .. /
5.   W: Are you opposed to .. / to the draft? //

6. M: Yeah //
7. W: Are you? (laughter) . . . opposed to the draft? //
8. G: Yeah / Well I can be I can afford to be opposed //
9. W: Tell me about your war life / Was it interestin' // I mean you
        military // service // life // Was it interestin' //
10. G: Oh, it wasn't very interestin' / no //
11. W: Tell me / what part of the service you go into the army //
12. G: I was in the army //
13. W: Well / what war was you in //
14. G: Second World War //
15. W: Second . . did you . . how you . . you where did you go //
16. G: I was in Europe //
17. W: That's the only place //
18. G: That's the only place //
19. W: um hum
20. G: England / France / and Germany //
21. W: O-h / well . . .
22. G: In those days / well . . .
23. W: I mean was you really in action //
24. G: Oh / once or twice //
25. W: Did you kill anybody //
26. G: I don't know / I shot a couple of times //
27. W: You busy shootin' huh //
28. G: I don't know / I never saw anybody I killed / . . I saw some dead
        people //
29. W: Yeah / ah . . Have you ever got shot? //
30. G: No . . I got hurt one day (I 'member) // We were out . . out in the
        morning and I got hurt / they put on KP / they made me get up at
        four o'clock and peel potatoes / choppin' potatoes and I
        chopped off this part of my finger // (laughter)
31. W: ( )
32. G: That's my 'War Wound' //
33. M: It's a french fry //
34. B: That was the first time you tried smokin' that weed huh? //
35. W: Hes trippin' . . you peelin' potatoes //

W's and B's speech in these examples reveals many of the
linguistic variables characteristic of Black English. Note the vowel
[æ] in "thing" (line 4), the loss of "r" in "your" (line 9), the lack of
agreement in "was you" (line 23). As is common with speakers of
Black English these variables alternate with more 'standard' variables, such as the (i) in "thing" (line 13, Transcript 2) and the [ŋ] in
"interesting" (line 9). But use of these Black variables is more than
simply a marker of ethnic identity. It serves clear communicative

ends and the researchers' failure to perceive this significantly affects the success of the interview.

The researcher's goal was to initiate a relatively informal discussion, a free exchange of personal opinions about a subject of sufficient interest to induce participants to display their persuasive skills. To that end he was willing to allow the group to choose a topic of their own. The actual interview, however, takes a quite different form. From the very start, W and B are 'running a game' on G and M in a way obvious only to themselves. In line 4, B's pronunciation of "thing" as [θæŋ] is in his case an exaggeration of Black English pronunciation – and in fact is a pronunciation he never uses again, his segmental phonology being much closer to White than to Black English throughout the rest of the tape. This use of the exaggerated Black English form can be seen as a metaphoric switch, indicating to the others his willingness and ability to lead the researchers astray (as in "If they want to hear Black English, I can give them all they want and more"). W then completely takes over the role of interviewer – switching the interviewer–informant roles around. In line 9 he uses a conventionalized Black prosodic marker on the words "military service life" – tense voice quality, with a repeated marked intonation pattern and tone-group boundaries after each word – to express dissociation of himself from his actual words, as if marking them 'foreign vocabulary' or 'things that other people would say.' If one were forced to give a verbal paraphrase of this prosodic marker, perhaps the best one would be 'so-called.' Its use is analogous to the use of quotation marks in academic papers – e.g., if a linguist uses the word *meaning* he can be justifiably asked for a definition of it, but if he writes 'meaning' instead, he can avoid responsibility for defining it, and can in fact even express doubt that such a definition exists.

Then follows a long question and answer session in which W tries to elicit a war story from G. Rhythmically, synchrony starts to break down in this section. W tends to accelerate at the end of his questions, but G's answers lag behind in speech rate. W seems to be insistent on getting a story, while G is reluctant. G later reported that he hesitated to say anything because he had no idea what was going on, whether the questions were serious or if he was being made fun of. W also is indicating prosodically what the most important element of the story should be, using high-level pitch and stress on the salient items in each sentence: "action" in 23; "kill" in 25; "shootin'" in 27; and "shot" in 29; that is, a lively, entertaining war story is in order. G finally resolves his dilemma by taking control of the context – telling a story that is humorous, and through which he gently pokes fun at himself – thereby ending the ambiguity of serious vs. joke and eliciting confirmation of its joke status in the form of a humorous contribution from each participant (lines 32–5).

This episode is an example of what we mean by the negotiation of interpretive frame. In line 9, W establishes control of the conversation and maintains it in 17. In 23 he even interrupts G to keep G on his subject. W's use of question after question, and his use of prosodic markers to show where his main areas of interest lie, suggest an interview style, where he asks all the questions and G gives all the responses. The interpretive frame is ambiguous, however, since there is an element of joking in the conversation as perceived by G, and as visible in W's mock surprise in line 21, and as cued in "military service" in line 9. This conversational strategy of maintaining ambiguity between the joking and serious interpretive frames allows W to maintain conversational control, until G, by his choice of a story, insists on the joking interpretation, relieving the ambiguity. The joking comments by everyone at the end of the story show that the renegotiation into a joking frame has been accepted by all. Lack of acceptance here – that is, continued insistence on a blood-and-guts war story – would have strained the conversation to the limit, because it would have constituted total inflexibility in negotiation. Conversational cooperation in natural conversation depends on this willingness and the ability to negotiate, rather than to dictate, changes in interpretive frame.

The second sample episode takes place a few minutes after the first, with the same participants:

Transcript 2

1. W: Did you agree with elections? //
    (laughter)
2. W: Did you agree with the elections? // You first //
3. M: Me first // No / next question //
4. W: Why do you not agree? //
5. M: Why do I like what? //

6. W: Why do .. Why don't you agree with the elections? //
7. M: Oh
             (laughter)
8. M: thought it was a joke //
9. G: huh
10. M: thought it was a joke / joke / a joke / you know //
11. W: Oh / it was a joke //
12. M: yeah //
13. W: Oh Oh the whole thing was a joke to you? //
14. M: right //
15. W: I hear you //
16. G: Who'd you vote for? //
17. W: I oh well / if I just had to //
18. G: Yeah if you just had to //
19. M: Next time you have to //
20. W: Oh //
21. G: Next time around you have to vote //
22. W: Well like ah / I ain't had to register from the git go //
23. G: um //
24. W: I ain't had to register to vote from the beginning //
25. G: You didn't? //
26. W: I mean – I mean don't don't I have that choice? //
27. G: That's right //
28. W: Well then –
29. G: So you not gonna vote / ⌈huh? //
30. W: ⌊No, for what? //
31. G: ( )
32. W: For what now either one of 'em git up, there / you know what
        they gonna do //
33. B: right on
34. W: The dogs gonna git the in / you know they gon just
35. W: put us lower in the ghetto / and throw a little black man on
36. W: TV and / make you thank [think] they doin' somethin' for you //
             (laughter)
37. W: Now you know I'm right about it / you know I'm right about it //
38. M: You think (Nixon) is worse than Humphrey? //
39. W: ah ain't one ain't no better than the other one //
40. M: I think Nixon is worse //
41. ?: ( )
42. W: one ain't man they all terrible //
43. W: Now they make it look like Wallace is a dog / and Nixon is the
        next dog / and Humphrey is / well . . (laughter) you know / a
        little bit higher than the other two dogs . . (laughter) but he's still
        a dog //

The episode begins with W again taking the role of 'interviewer,' a role made explicit by M's formulaic reply in line 3 "next question." M's use of an interviewee formula foregrounds the interview frame, and W responds by using a grammatically more formal style ("do you not" rather than "don't you"). By the quotation style prosodic marker (tense voice quality), exaggerated pitch contours and rhythmic stress placement in his next question, W acknowledges M's recognition of the 'interview' frame with his use of an 'other' voice; i.e., he takes on an interviewer's voice as well as his role. For M, however, this prosodic shift is so unexpected and uninterpretable that he is unable to understand the sentence at all, so that W has to translate it into colloquial speech with unmarked prosody (line 6). In lines 11–15, as in the previous episode, W plays on the ambiguity of inference – using joking forms, making fun of M (his mock surprise in lines 11 and 13), then suddenly agreeing in line 15.

In lines 16–29, starting with G's question at 16, G and M are asking the questions and W is answering. The tone is now unequivocally joking, as shown by M and G giving false information (in lines 19 and 21) without intending to be believed. The banter continues until line 30, where a sudden shift occurs. W breaks the previously established rhythmic pattern by starting in line 30 before 29 is finished; furthermore, 30 is much louder than preceding utterances, and he makes an upward pitch register shift. In line 32 W has completed the shift from conversational give-and-take to a more formal 'public address' style similar to that used by black preachers and politicians. He signals his change of speech activity with a sharp upward pitch register shift (on the word "now").

That this style shift is a significant use of a black-specific discourse strategy whose meaning is lost on the whites is clear from the different reactions to W's 'sermon.' B, who has not spoken previously in this episode, utters the formulaic back channel response "right on" in line 33, exactly in keeping with black audience call-response conventions, and his response is timed perfectly to come during W's pause. The formulaic nature of B's interjection, the appropriateness of its timing, and the fact that he chooses this point to enter the conversation all indicate that a shift has occurred to a ritualized speaking style which W and B drawing on shared cultural knowledge cooperatively produce.

M, not sharing their communicative conventions, does not realize that W has recontextualized his speech – that W has indicated that his statements in lines 32–6 are a proclamation of his convictions and not just a position taken for the sake of argument. In line 37 W indicates that it is his last word on the subject – yet in 38 and again in 40, M questions and then challenges W's beliefs – because M has missed the shift of context and is still operating in a debate-like framework. W (in lines 39 and 42) refuses to enter a discussion (in 42 he uses the upward pitch register shift as a prosodic marker just as in 32, perhaps as a kind of reference back to the frame established earlier), until in 43 he re-explains the content of 32–6 in less eloquent, more relaxed conversational style.

This again is a case of breakdown in the negotiation of interpretive frame because of lack of shared conversational conventions. W's shift in line 32 is ratified by B in line 33, but M hasn't perceived the shift, and hasn't reacted one way or the other to it. When M finally speaks in 38 he and W are operating under different sets of assumptions as to what is appropriate talk. As in the previous episode, successful negotiation of a resolution finally occurs when one of the participants (in this case W) arrives at a summation that is appropriate in both frames of interpretation – in M's interpretation as an explanation and justification of W's previous statements (appropriate in debate-like give-and-take speech activity), and in W's interpretation as simply a restatement of what he said earlier (for those who didn't understand the first time).

This brief illustration of conversational conventions shows that mutual intelligibility is not solely contingent upon a shared language base but also upon shared discourse features.

Conversational control and cooperation are signalled through contextualization cues. These cues signal the preferred interpretation of a speaker's utterance through the process of conversational inference. Since the discourse structure of a conversation is being constantly negotiated by means of the participants' shared conversational conventions, someone not sharing the conventions cannot participate in the negotiation and has no control over the direction the conversation takes. The inability to determine through conversational inference whether a conversation is being presented as a serious or humorous matter is problematic.

We have found prosodic cues and formulaic speech in black rhetorical style that, when occurring together in context, convey significant conversational meaning through inference. Black conventions include much greater use of rhythmic stress placement, vowel elongation, pitch register shifts, and different voice qualities than white conventions. Speakers unfamiliar with the black conventions interpret them as stylistic and not significant. They are forced to rely solely on the grammatical and semantic information in the speaker's utterance for meaning, missing the wealth of information in prosodic and paralinguistic features that can disambiguate the speaker's intent.

6

Strategies and counterstrategies in the use of yes–no questions in discourse

ADRIAN BENNETT

Native speakers of English overhearing the following two-speaker exchange would have little trouble getting a general idea of what is going on, even though they might not be able to contextualize some of the referential content of the exchange:

(1) A: Do you do you think that you have a right to stop
         me from walking into the Fairmont hotel to listen to
         Dean Rusk? ⌈ / Do you? /
     B: ⌊ / I have never / I have never stopped you
         from walking into / the hotel /
     A: / But this is what those / people wanted to do that night //

I want to suggest that, despite the apparent ordinariness of this exchange, it can be made to appear upon analysis to consist of a number of peculiarities and that if we can make ourselves aware of these peculiarities we can gain some insight not only into what the participants are doing but also into how they manage to accomplish it.

This sort of interactional analysis might be seen as a way of making the ordinary seem strange so that we can understand how it is put together (Fred Erickson, personal communication). There are several ways we might go about doing this. For example, we might look at the exchange in (1) from a syntactic point of view, following the lead of the very valuable work of Sacks, Schegloff, and their associates on sequencing in conversation, or of work by Labov on the taxonomic analyses of recognizable discourse types such as ritual insults or narrative. If we took this approach we might notice that in (1) we have ABA exchange in which A asks a question, B replies, and A takes the floor again to make an assertion. We could

see this as three separate but related events and note that, especially
with the first two events, we have a kind of constructional unit in
which given event A, it is a safe bet that event B will follow. Sacks,
Schegloff and Jefferson (1974) have characterized a large class of
such discourse units under the rubric of "adjacency pairs," and they
have given this unit a specific and perhaps too restrictive definition,
noting that adjacency pairs have these three features: "(1) two
utterance length, (2) adjacent positioning of component utterances,
(3) different speakers producing each utterance." Without quib-
bling over the details of this definition, it should be noted that one
of the important consequences for speakers of organizational units
like adjacency pairs is that, given the performance of a 'first pair
part' by one speaker, the failure of a second speaker to produce a
'second pair part' is a noticeable absence in a conversation, and
being noticeable can have consequences. Labov (1972) has expressed this notion of consequence in discourse very succinctly with
regard to the pair question–answer: "If we consider the compelling
character of all questions . . . it is clear that all requests, even the
most mitigated, are to be heard against an unrealized possibility of
negative consequences if they are not answered."

While we will need to call repeatedly on the insights of these
workers in our analysis, we will not want to follow their approach
exactly, because we want to know more than the empirically
observable recurrent patterns of discourse; we want to know how
they get there in the first place and how they are made use of by
conversationalists. The model of the actor implicit in the work of
these scholars inclines toward a mechanistic view of speakers and
hearers as relatively inflexible beings, more rigidly constrained by
algorithmic rule-systems than perhaps real people actually are.
They have not been able to present a fully convincing characterization of the decision making processes actors use to construct
meaningful exchanges nor of the relatively high degree of flexibility
involved in these processes in everyday conversation.

Another source of insight is the work in the ethnography of
communication. Research in this field has not concentrated much
on everyday conversation, but has focused primarily on relatively
formal exchanges in exotic cultures or subcultures. In an attempt to
formulate the cultural knowledge required of participants in particular kinds of communicational events, such as the Japanese

Rakugo performance (Sanches 1975), entering a Yakan house (Frake 1975), or the obtaining the use of drugs by heroin addicts (Agar 1973), this work shows that the most ordinary conversational exchanges could not take place at all without the establishment and use of a wealth of cultural background knowledge. Given a characterization of this knowledge, however, we still need to know how conversationalists make use of it to put a discourse together into a meaningful whole. For our purposes here we do not need an exhaustive characterization of the shared cultural understandings of the two speakers in (1), but will need to know only the following. This exchange is taken from a larger piece of talk which was a panel discussion conducted on public television in a major American city between several representatives of opposing political groups. The discussion is about race relations and the exchange is a small part of an informal controversy between the participants, A and B. Both A and B were well-known public figures at the time and their respective positions on race relations would have been part of informed public knowledge. The immediately preceding discussion focused on demonstrators (i.e., "those people") who threw bags of blood at people going into a hotel to listen to a speech by Dean Rusk. Prior to the exchange in (1) speaker B criticized the police for beating up and arresting some of these demonstrators.

The analysis of (1) can be seen as an exercise in the reconstruction of what Schutz (1970) called the "in-order-to" motives of actors, meaning by this "state of affairs, the end, which the action has been undertaken to bring about." That is, instead of looking at discourse either as constructed of repeated surface patterns such as adjacency pairs, or as exchange events taking place against a formal set of culturally specific rules, I want to make the assumption that discourse is composed of more or less reasonable and reasoned acts which actors perform on their way toward achieving particular goals. I use the term 'reasonable' here not as any kind of claim for a rationalist epistemology but merely to characterize what I take to be a fundamental working assumption of conversationalists; that is, that people say and do things in order to accomplish various communicational goals. Actors then go on to make inferences about what others are trying to accomplish. This process is a kind of circular, self-contained system such that we can often say either "A performed act X because he wanted to accomplish goal Y" or

"A has accomplished goal Y which explains why he did act X."
These inferences are based both on what speakers say and on how
they say it. Where choices are considered to be available for saying
the same thing in terms of both propositional content and primary
speech act (Searle 1975), at least sometimes particular choices
senders make signify something about their intentions or in-order-
to motives. As speakers, we project plans across slices of discourse
and as hearers we try to infer ahead of time what those plans are.
Furthermore, in some cases these plans are designed to be transparent to hearers, while in other cases at least parts of them are
designed to be opaque. In exchange (1) we will find both opaque
and transparent plans working together simultaneously, and also
some possibly universal principles of discourse carrying out these
plans.

To begin with I will attempt to reconstruct what speakers A and
B are trying to do in (1) and then go on to test this reconstruction
against what we can actually observe there.

A is trying to construct a successful argument against B. Part of
A's strategy is to avoid making this intention explicit. B tries to
countermove against that argument, not by presenting either an
answer to it or a counterargument against it, but by attempting to
prevent that argument from being brought to completion in the first
place. Furthermore, B's attempt to countermove involves treating
that argument as a nonargument. Then, following B's countermove, A comes back with an effort to complete his argument
anyway, and not by moving against B's countermove in any direct
way, but by in turn treating it as if it were not a countermove at all.
That is, A treats B's countermove neither as a failed attempt nor as
irrelevant, but as if it were in fact a 'bad' move that causes B to fall
into the trap A had set.

Accepting for the purposes of our (tentative) analysis that this
characterization is more or less correct, let us go through exchange
(1) and look at the ways language is being used and see if these can
be made consistent with our reconstruction of the underlying
action.

First note that A begins with a yes–no question that asks B to give
an opinion. B gives a reply but notice that it is not exactly a reply to
the question asked. Instead, by virtue of the fact that answers to
yes–no questions – at least in the prototypical case – either affirm

or deny the propositional content of the question, and by virtue of the operation of the Gricean maxim of relevance, B's answer pragmatically presupposes that a different question has been asked that might go something like,

(2) A: Have you ever stopped me from walking into the hotel?

Finally, notice that A does not take exception to this answer by calling attention to its irrelevance but treats it instead as a "no" answer. We can tell this at least partly by his use of the connective "but" and by his use of "this" as a discourse deictic. The word "this" in A's comeback, if his utterance is assumed to be relevant, necessarily refers to the proposition "x PREVENT y from ENTERing HOTEL z." The use of "but" makes sense here if we assume that A takes B's answer to be a negation of the proposition. If B's answer were taken to be a yes, the use of "but" here would be distinctly odd, as we can see in the following exchange:

(3) X: Do you think you have the right to block my driveway?
     Y: Yes, I do.
     X: But you're blocking my driveway!

The important thing to notice in (1) is that, despite the literal irrelevance of B's reply, A takes no remedial action, such as rephrasing his question or pointing out that B's answer is not to the point. This fact alone might lead us to suspect that as far as A is concerned B's answer is good enough for the purposes of the moment.

Given these few observations about the language use in (1), can we connect them meaningfully to our reconstruction of the actions going on in (1)? This will involve asking questions like the following: If A wants to make an argument why doesn't he just assert his beliefs and give his reasons for believing them? Why does he go to the trouble of asking B a question? Furthermore, why does he ask him a question that, given that A knows B's political position, A can probably predict the answer to? We can also ask why B doesn't answer the question directly but instead answers a different question. And finally we can ask why A in his comeback to B's reply doesn't do some kind of repair work.

We can begin to answer some of these questions by looking first at the question A asks. If A is in a position of wanting to make a certain kind of argument, his use of a yes–no question can be seen to have certain advantages. First, as we noted above in our quote from Labov, the asking of a question creates the expectation of a reply such that not replying may be seen to have consequences. Secondly a yes–no question puts fairly strong constraints on the acceptability of the answer. In general an appropriate answer to a yes–no question either explicitly affirms or denies the propositional content of the question. This fact, plus the Gricean maxim of relevance places fairly strong limitations on what constitutes relevant propositional content in the reply. That is, the answerer cannot disregard the question and he cannot just talk about anything either. The answerer is thus constrained to commit himself. Compare this to a WH-question of similar propositional content:

(4)   A: What is your opinion about your right to prevent me from going
             into a hotel to listen to Dean Rusk?

This type of question does not put the answerer into quite such a tight corner. He need not commit himself to the question of whether he has a right or not. In contrast, a yes or no answer to a yes–no question commits the answerer to a belief in the truth or falsity of the propositional content of the question by virtue of the sincerity condition in the type of speech act Searle (1975) calls "representatives." This condition is that the speaker of an assertion commits himself to a belief in the truth of that assertion.

A third advantage of using a yes–no question in this context is that questions not only can be used to select a next speaker but have the further property that upon completion of a reply the rights to take the floor again can legitimately go back to the asker of the question and are even likely to do so. Thus, A can expect that if B gives a straight answer to his question, he, A, will get a turn to speak upon completion of the reply. If A wants to make a further point this has an obvious advantage (see Sacks, Schegloff, and Jefferson 1974).

Thus from the point of view of making an argument, especially one in which you wish to defeat an opponent, the use of yes–no questions is particularly valuable because they can put pressure on your opponent to commit himself to a position. Given this commitment you can then easily make use of it as the antecedent to a conclusion which you can then draw. Since the answerer has already affirmed his belief in the truth of this antecedent, he cannot very easily deny the consequent, assuming you have obeyed the rules of logical inference.

I believe that this use of yes–no questions is simply one particular application of the general property of such questions that they can be used – and ordinarily are used – to get a hearer to commit himself to the truth of some assertion. There are thus a number of related uses for them in discourse which can be seen from the following examples:

(5) a. *Focusing the hearer's attention; helps speaker to determine how to parcel information into given and new, topic and comment, etc.:*
Do you remember that woman we were talking about last night?

b. *Preliminary to a request; helps speaker to make sure his request will get him what he wants:*
X: Did you get paid yet?
Y: Yeah.
X: Then how about paying me back the money you owe me?

c. *As a polite request; the speaker can avoid imposing on the hearer by presupposing he is willing to do X:*
Do you have the time?

d. *Preliminary to a suggestion; helps speaker to determine whether the suggestion will be in order:*
X: Do you like Truffaut's movies?
Y: Yeah.
X: Then let's go see *Adele H.*

e. *Preliminary to an offer:*
Do you need any help?

There are of course cases of this type, but the main point is that yes–no questions get hearers to make a commitment which then gives the speaker something concrete to go on in carrying a plan to a successful conclusion.

We can now turn to B's reply and again ask why he gives the kind of answer he does. As regards this there are at least three assumptions we might make. First we might assume there is a misunderstanding: either B thinks he is answering the question presupposed by his answer, or he knows he didn't quite catch the question but just wants to give some sort of answer, etc. Second we could assume that B intends his answer to be construed as an implicit negative answer to the question asked by way of implicatures based on

Gricean maxims of relevance. In this case we would say that he
intends to convey this meaning by getting A to recognize this intent.
There are reasons in the rest of the conversation from which (1) is
excerpted for not supposing either of these alternatives, but I will
not take space to go into them here. Instead I suggest a third
possibility, and that is that B has recognized A's unavowed attempt
to lay a trap for him and seeks to prevent this. In order to make this
assumption, B has further to assume that A is (1) not just asking for
information, and (2) not trying to convey an implicature by getting
B to recognize certain intentions of A to do so. B will have to
assume instead that (3) A is using language strategically. This
assumption is I believe based on a rhetorical principle of language
in discourse which I will return to in a moment.

   If B's reply is a counterstrategy to A's strategy then we can see it
has certain advantages. B is in a position of obligation; he must say
something. A failure to reply in this debate situation may give the
audience the impression he is inept or is hiding something. By
giving an answer that presupposes a different but related question
has been asked, he manages to do two things: (1) he avoids giving a
yes or no reply to the actual question asked, (2) he gives an answer
which is at least topically relevant and wards off the charge of
evading the issue.

   There are other strategies that B might have used to serve these
purposes, some of which have been investigated by Weiser (1975).
For example he might have said one of the following:

(6)   a. Why do you ask?
       b. I won't answer that, you're just trying to trap me.
       c. Oh ge–, I left my keys in the car.
       d. Wait a minute, I think the moderator is trying to tell us
          something.

B could also give a false answer, such as saying yes when he really
believed no. This could be taken either as a joke or as serious. If a
joke then B could be charged with being unserious about serious
issues. If serious he could be accused of being against democratic
principles of free speech. The replies in (6) also have serious
drawbacks in this context of informal debate. (6a) would allow A
to say "I'm just trying to get your views clear" and then to repeat
the question. (6b) leaves B open to the challenge that he is afraid to
engage in open discussion. If B uses (6c) he will seem particularly

inept as a political leader. (6d) might get him off the hook more gracefully but it has three disadvantages: one being that the moderator will say "No, go ahead"; a second being that the moderator will talk and then reselect A, giving him a chance to pursue his question; a third being that the moderator will talk and then select some other panel member, neither A nor B, thus not giving B a chance to make any further points of his own.

There is another strategy B might use which happens to be fairly common and that is to hedge his answer in some way and use this as a wedge to make a point which has the effect of disarming A's conclusion before it is made:

(7)   B: No, but it's not a question of whether I have the right or not; the question is whether people like Dean Rusk should be in power at all.

This last strategy might have been effective because it might have turned the argument around to B's advantage. It has the disadvantage of giving A the opportunity to parry it by saying something like, "No, we're talking about rights of free speech, not whether Dean Rusk is or is not a good leader." (This in fact does happen earlier in the conversation before the exchange in (1) occurs.)

None of these strategies is airtight, and that includes the strategy B actually does use. This leads us to the final utterance in (1), A's comeback to B's reply, which, as we have seen, treats B's reply as if it were a negative answer to the question A had originally asked. Why doesn't A take explicit notice of the skewed quality of B's reply and come back with something like, "No I'm asking about what you think your rights are, not about what you have or have not done in the past"? I suggest that A doesn't do this because he is less concerned with the clear and efficient exchange of information than with drawing the conclusion of his argument. That his comeback overlaps B's reply might lead us to suspect this in fact.

In order to treat B's reply as constituting a negative answer, A must treat it as the second of the three alternative ways we mentioned earlier of treating this reply, i.e., as being meant to convey an implicature by virtue of getting A to recognize this intention. This involves the further assumption that B's reply actually does accord with the Gricean principles of cooperation and relevance. The point here is not whether B's reply was meant to be taken this way but that A goes on to act as if this were the case, and

he does this in order to serve his own purpose, which is to defeat B
in a debate. Thus A's argument can be roughly sketched along these
lines:

(a)   You have said that you do not think you have the right to prevent me
       from doing X,
(b)   therefore you will think it wrong for others to do this (given certain
       assumptions that civil rights are equally true for all members),
(c)   but you have implied earlier that you support 'those people' who
       attempted to do just that;
(d)   (b) and (c) cannot both be true in the same world at the same time,
(e)   therefore you contradict yourself;
(f)   if you contradict yourself you are wrong, etc.

Notice that in his comeback to B's reply A does not make this
argument explicit. He especially does not directly accuse B of being
self-contradictory. This has the advantage in the context of this
kind of informal political debate of letting the audience draw this
conclusion for themselves. Furthermore, if A had made such an
explicit accusation he would leave himself open to the charge that
he was less interested in discussing issues than in discrediting B.

We can now return to a question raised earlier, which was: given
that B sees A as setting a trap when he asks his question, what
enables him to make this recognition? We can note in passing that a
variety of factors go into such recognitions and that they range
across all channels of communication as well as involving making
use of any other information that might seem relevant at the time,
derived either from general cultural knowledge or from the rest of
the discourse. I want to pass over these however to suggest an
operating principle that may have universal or at least widespread
application in the processing of language in discourse. I will refer to
this principle as the Principle of Expressivity. I mean this to be not
so much a rule of conversation that should be added to Grice's
maxims, but as a rhetorical principle which can be derived from
one of the four 'charges' that Slobin (1975) places on any natural
language, namely that a natural language should be clear, processa-
ble, simple and expressive. The last of these he divides into two
categories, semantic and rhetorical, and it is the charge to be
"rhetorically expressive" that is particularly relevant here. However, instead of seeing this charge as a requirement for a complete
natural language, I want to present it as an assumption that

speakers can make use of in both the construction and the interpretation of discourse. I will give it a tentative and informal characterization as

> *The Principle of Expressivity:* Assume that language with its accompanying paralinguistic and nonverbal channels of communication has the capacity to enable speakers to perform any communicational act they may want to perform.

I call this a rhetorical principle for two reasons. First, it has a Speaker Corollary that, like the much-maligned mythical beast, the High School English Teacher, tells language users what to do:

> *Speaker Corollary:* Be as effective in your use of communicational channels as you need to be or want to be.

Second, the Principle of Expressivity does not seem to operate in quite the same way as the Gricean rules of conversation. In fact it is more akin to those metarules in board games like chess that tell players they are supposed to be as effective as they can be. But there is something like a Hearer Corollary that nevertheless can enter into the decision-making process that hearers are involved in when making inferences about what speakers are trying to do:

> *Hearer Corollary:* Assume that speakers are being as effective as they need to be or can be.

Turning now to B's reply in (1), I would argue that the Hearer Corollary enables B to understand A's question as being 'more than it seems'; conversely for B to assume that A's question is not more than it seems would require B to 'set aside' the Hearer Corollary as not relevant for this exchange and to assume that A is not being as effective a language user as he could be. If he made this latter assumption, B might then conclude that A was just asking for information and would expect B – if he understood the question – to give a relatively straight answer, which he of course does not do. Furthermore, the Gricean maxims won't necessarily lead B to make the assumption that A has something up his sleeve because A is not trying to get B to recognize this intention but is in fact masking it.

This argument has been theoretical in two ways. First, I do not want to claim that the particular imputations about A's and B's in-order-to motives are facts which I have 'proven.' I have merely tried to demonstrate a method of analysis whereby, trying to make the ordinary seem strange, we make a reasoned attempt to reconstruct the motives of actors, 'reasoned' insofar as hypotheses are tested against observable communicational phenomena in a systematic way. There is no ultimate method that will without fail tell us in any absolute sense what actors are 'doing' in any given exchange. Once an analysis has been done it should be tested against judgments of what actors themselves see each other as doing. Ways of doing this have been suggested in Gumperz (1975) and Erickson (1975). Secondly, this discussion has been theoretical in that it tries to show what assumptions people operate on when they try to make a skilled use of language to accomplish certain goals. Some of these assumptions might be candidates for universal principles operating in language use, such as certain aspects of Searle's speech act theory, particularly the sincerity condition on speech acts, Grice's rules of conversation, especially the maxim of relevance and the rules for implicature, certain principles of sequencing and turn taking, such as those suggested by Sacks, Schegloff, et al., and perhaps some rhetorical principles like the Principle of Expressivity.

Finally, I want to emphasize that, as Weiser (1975) has usefully pointed out, we can look at communication as being accomplished in two ways, one involving what she calls 'communicative devices' whereby speakers intend utterances to accomplish purposes by means of getting the hearer to recognize this intention, and the other which she calls 'conversational stratagems' whereby speakers intend utterances to accomplish purposes by some other means than by getting the hearer to recognize this intention. We can make two extensions of this distinction. First, we can extend the accomplishing of purposes beyond the utterance level to include all channels of communication including the nonverbal. A rich understanding of what goes on in communication can only be accomplished by looking at both verbal and nonverbal levels together. Second, the two ways of accomplishing purposes Weiser has delineated should not be seen as mutually exclusive alternatives for doing the same things, but as two melodic lines that run through communicational exchanges simultaneously working in counterpoint to each other. That is, the two means of accomplishing ends function reflexively in the sense that communicative devices make possible the use of conversational strategems, and conversational strategems constrain the interpretation or decisions speakers and hearers make about what communicational devices are in effect. There has been an understandable emphasis in linguistics on the study of communicational devices, but I would suggest that in so doing we are not only missing half of what is going on in the use of language in its practical applications, but that without understanding both we cannot fully understand either one.

7

Negotiations of language choice in Montreal
MONICA S. HELLER

Something strange is going on in Montreal. Every encounter between strangers, however casually, especially in public places but by no means exclusively, has become a political act. Buying a pair of socks has become problematic, as witnessed by the following article from *The Montreal Star* of January 26, 1978, reporting one person's frustration:

> The other day I walked into a department store and had a conversation which made me feel foolish. It was also frustrating . . . It's the kind of conversation I have an awful lot nowadays . . . The conversation always goes something like this:
> I walk up to the counter, intent on buying some socks. "Bonjour," says the woman behind the counter, smiling. 'Est-ce que je peux vous aider?" "Oui," I smile back. "Je voudrais acheter des bas comme ça." I point to some socks on display in the showcase. "En beige, s'il vous plaît." "Yes, of course, Madame," she responds in English. "What size?" "Er . . ." I pause, "nine and a half, please."
> Our transaction continues smoothly and I thank her and leave the store. But inwardly, the whole time this pleasant bilingual woman is fishing my socks out of the showcase and putting them in a bag and taking the money, I am cursing. Dammit, I want to say. Dammit, lady, why do you always switch to English? . . . [Does] my French sound so terrible that you'd rather not converse in it with me? . . . [Do you] recognize an anglophone . . . and presume I'd prefer to use my own language? . . . Could it even be that . . . you're telling me . . . that you're a federalist? . . . (This happened once, in such a conversation. I stopped in a garage . . . and struggled to explain . . . that my windshield wipers were congelé and I wanted to make them fonctionner. He listened in mild amusement and then said: "You don't have to speak French to me, madame. I'm not a separatist.") . . .

Language choice in Montreal used to be a fairly clear-cut issue, but sociopolitical change over the past 18 years or so has led to the dissolution of old norms. And, as that change continues, new and widely accepted norms have not replaced them. In the place of unconscious, or semi-conscious, use of language in everyday life is an extreme awareness of language, a new way of holding conversations that involves the negotiation of language choice in every interaction. That awareness of language comes from the symbolic role it has in political life, and from the social value it has acquired as an obvious characteristic of the social groups involved in sifting relationships. Negotiation in conversation is a playing out of a negotiation for position in the community at large. It is made up of implicit and explicit strategies for seeking the kind of information that seems necessary in order for the participants to be able to hold a conversation, and that information is information not only about what a person's mother tongue is, but also what his or her ethnicity is. The fact that conversation often halts, and that negotiations have often to be made in explicit terms, is evidence, I think, of the necessity of shared social knowledge and norms of language use in order for conversation to take place.

Background
Originally, Quebec was a French colony. The British acquired it in 1763 as a result of having won the Seven Years' War. The upper classes of New France left and went back to France, leaving behind an agricultural society made up largely of peasants, their seigneurs, and the Catholic Church. The British made little attempt to assimilate them; the result was a French rural laboring class and a British urban Protestant ruling class, engaged, respectively, in agriculture and business. The French, then, maintained their separate identity through physical isolation, the strength of the Church, and sheer numbers: they perpetrated what has come to be called 'la revanche du berceau' (the revenge of the cradle). At the time of the Industrial Revolution the countryside could no longer support its burgeoning population, and many Canadians moved to urban areas and formed an urban proletariat, a position they have maintained to this day, although since about 1960 they have begun to rise socially and to threaten the economic hegemony of the English.

The geographic isolation was maintained in the cities; in Montreal, for example, the east end is French, the west, English, divided down the middle by a buffer zone of immigrant areas dating from at least the turn of the century, and by the downtown financial and commercial area. The geographic isolation is reinforced by a total reduplication of cultural institutions: school commissions are divided into Catholic and Protestant, and within those there are French and English schools (although in fact, of course, the great majority of Catholics are francophone, and the great majority of Protestants are anglophone); there are French and English hospitals, French and English department stores. It was, until recently, rare, in short, for the groups to come into contact. Those who did were usually the francophones who sought work in English enterprises, and as most business was, and still to a large degree is, English-owned, most Québecois had to learn English. It should be noted as well that the position of English was strengthened by two factors: the presence of the English-speaking majority in the rest of Canada and the United States, and the tendency of immigrant groups to assimilate to the English population. This assimilation can be explained by the greater economic opportunities offered to immigrants in the English sector, and by the greater ease of entering the group: French social life tends to be based on the ascribed characteristics of the group members, whereas that of the English is based on achieved ones.

Since about 1960, francophones have become increasingly aware of their unenviable social position, and increasingly able to do something about it. Their strength, however, lies in their solidarity as a group, and it is this very solidarity that, ironically, is being threatened by the very same economic and demographic forces that have enabled them to change their lot, namely, the rise in productivity and hence in standard of living, rise in level of education, the decline in influence of the Catholic Church, and the corresponding tendency to have smaller families. Rather than assimilate to the English population, they would like to replace it; but in order to do that they have to maintain their integrity as a separate group. One of the ways that they are attempting to do this is through political action, most particularly through legislation about language use. Specifically, they are trying to legislate the use of French into existence, where it did not exist before, and to assure its continued use in areas where it seems to be losing ground to English. They are also concerned with the form of the language; that is, it has to be purified from the effects of past onslaught from within, and protected from any future damage other languages may do. Much of this legislation is directed towards allophone immigrants (that is, immigrants whose mother tongue is neither French nor English), as they are in a position to control the population balance; the French are reeling from the counter-revenge: 'la revanche du bateau' (the revenge of the boat). It is felt, at any rate, that it is morally more acceptable to make demands of people who have chosen to live in Quebec than of those who were merely born there. As the present provincial government is committed to a policy of nationalism and separatism such legislation is coming thick and fast, and a process which started slowly in the early 1960s is quickening its pace to the point where things are changing daily. The population, too, is changing, as many people are leaving and few are coming in. Moreover, as everyone's lives are directly affected, everyone has feelings about the situation, and interpersonal relations are perforce drawn into question. The overwhelming feeling is that you just can't take anything for granted anymore.

The current situation
A few examples of interaction show how these events affect everyday life. I did my field work (from June to September 1977) in an English-speaking hospital, but the majority of the patients in the Out-Patient Department are francophone or non-anglophone. The majority of the doctors are anglophone; the clerks however, in order to be hired, must be functionally bilingual in English and French. The questions then arise: What language do hospital employees use with each other and with patients? How might we interpret these choices? How do they make them, and what happens when they do? Does the choice ever appear to be problematic?

Prior to these questions of use is the question of *norms*. The norms involving how and what to speak to patients appear to be as follows:

(1)   The hospital is an English one; thus the staff should expect to speak English among themselves, and with the patients.

(2)   Hospital staff have an obligation to give the best medical care possible, and this means facilitating communication. Politics should not be involved; communication difficulties should be resolved on a one-to-one basis.

(3)   The languages of work in Quebec are French and English, and
      all staff, especially clerical staff, should be bilingual. Doctors
      are usually exempt from this norm, especially if they are
      older. (In fact, the language of work is now French, but
      English still has a special status.)
(4)   The language of the majority of the province is French, and
      thus all communication should be in French, unless it has
      been established that the interlocutors are anglophone and
      choose to talk in English. It is possible for one person to hold
      norms 1, 2, and 3 at the same time.

It is difficult to tell a priori, however, what norms one's
interlocutor holds. Furthermore, it is impossible for a clerk to tell
what norms, if any, are held by any patient s/he may speak to; and
if this is true, the likelihood is slim that the patients are fully aware
of the norms held by the clerks. What prevents anyone, then, from
just imposing one's own? At times, of course, this is all one can do,
to begin with. But, as I have said, it is not unusual for one person to
hold conflicting norms. Also, it is rare that in such a situation
people will choose to initiate conflict. A patient who has come
seeking medical care is not in a position to impose conditions on
how s/he receives it, unless s/he is willing to do without. Hospital
staff are not in a position to refuse their services, unless they are
willing to lose their jobs. How then do they go about the business of
talking?

Here is an example in which the only cues interlocutors have
about each other are verbal ones: the telephone conversation.
Clerks at the Appointments desk sometimes answer the phone in
both French and English ("Central Appointments, Bureau de
rendez-vous"), but this is felt to be somewhat abrupt and time-
consuming, and more often is replaced by the more polite, if
monolingual, "Central Booking, may I help you?"

> Clerk: Central Booking, may I help you?
> Patient: Oui, allô?
> Clerk: Bureau de rendez-vous, est-ce que je peux vous aider?*
> Patient: [French]

* The French here appears to be a calque from the English formula, as it is a
word-for-word translation, rather than the normal French order. French Cana-
dian formulae often reflect equivalent English word order, as is the case in contact
situations of this type.

```
Clerk:   [French]
Patient: [English]
Clerk:   [English]
Patient: [French]
Clerk:   [French]
Patient: Êtes-vous française ou anglaise? (are you French or
         English?)
Clerk:   N'importe, j'suis ni l'une, ni l'autre . . . (it doesn't matter,
         I'm neither one nor the other . . .)
Patient: Mais . . . (But . . .)
Clerk:   Ça ne fait rien (It doesn't matter).
Patient: [French] [Conversation continues in French]
```

What we have to explain here are the code switching and the explicit question about the clerk's ethnic identity, and then we must ask what role these play in determining what language will be used.

At all points in the conversation both participants theoretically have the option of using French or English, as they show here that they master both. In the first place, the initial turn need not determine what language will be used. In this case, the obvious conventionalization of the clerk's response may indicate nothing to the patient as to his/her linguistic preference, as the 'Englishness' of the institution may determine the telephone-answering behavior of its staff. Patients often, then, act as though they haven't really heard. By forcing a repetition they may then find out what the clerk really prefers (i.e., does s/he repeat the salutation in English or French?) By saying "Oui, allô?" the patient is doing something analogous to what she would be doing if she said "Hello?" but she is also introducing another factor into the conversational turn taking: she is saying, "We can't have this conversation until we decide whether to speak English or French."

Alternatively, the patient may ask "Parlez-vous français?" In this case, the clerk may switch, call a bilingual clerk (theoretical bilingualism not being the same as functional bilingualism), or say "Oui, un peu" (Yes, a little bit), expecting, in this last case, that the patient will either switch to English or make an effort to speak simple French, slowly and clearly. This last option, however, often leads to frustration and misunderstanding when the clerk's expectations are not fulfilled. The clerk feels that she is doing her best, and they both, or maybe only the patient, may feel that her best is just not good enough. (It might be noted that some doctors feel that having to deal with such communication difficulties is 'dirty work' that is not part of the job they have taken on, although this is probably more true with non-anglophone patients.) Clerks whose French is passable but not perfect tend to feel that speaking French is, on the one hand, part of their duty to be as helpful and as pleasant as possible, and, on the other, a favor which the patient should appreciate. They are more likely to speak French with a patient who is polite, calm, and presents no problems. If the situation is complicated, if the patient is hostile, senile, or disturbed, or merely insistent about speaking French (which is often interpreted as hostility), or if the clerk is tired and feels the net emotional losses of the interaction are bound to outweigh the net gains, she will try to get someone else to handle it. Thus one clerk once said to me: "Monica, please take [line] 1902. She's French. I understand her, but I'm just too tired." The clerk did, however, want to make it clear to me that she was competent (as she was expected to be). Admitting that you are not perfectly bilingual (for an anglophone) entails loss of face; but speaking French constitutes a favor. However, for a Québecois to accept that 'favor' lets the anglophone keep his position of power in the conversation (indicative of his position of power in the community).

The fact that this conversation then continues in French may be explained if we assume that the clerk feels her French is good enough, that the patient has made an implicit request that the conversation be held in French, and the clerk feels it is incumbent upon her to comply with that request. Why, then, does the patient switch to English? Because the clerk's accent was not typically Québecois (it should be noted that the speaker may be a fluent, even native speaker of French, but if his accent is not typically Québecois, that will engender a switch to English as fast as, if not faster than, an English accent will), or her use of some non-Québecois lexical item (such as 'rendez-vous' instead of 'appointment') led the patient to believe that the clerk may not be Québecoise. And her switch may mean "She speaks English really, and I want to make sure she understands me, so I'd better speak English." It may also, or alternatively mean, "We can't have this conversation until I find out whether you are French or English." The clerk may then feel, "Doesn't she think my French is good enough?" If the clerk had persisted in speaking French, which also happens, the motivation would probably have been, "Nice of her to try to make it easier for me, but this will be easier and clearer if we do it in French." (The clerk may feel it was genuinely nice, or she may feel it was snide.) The fact that switching keeps occurring probably means that the patient is not getting the information she needs, and so finally has to ask explicitly. She still gets no direct answer. How do we interpret the fact that the conversation continues in French? If we take the question to mean "What language do you speak?" we have to explain it as an attempt to speak the language of the clerk. The hesitation afterwards would come from not wanting to have to make a decision, as would the switching, possibly in an attempt to take back the initial French used, as having been an unconscious slip. If we take the question to mean "What *are* you?" we have to assume that language choice is directly related to ethnicity for this speaker. And we have no way of choosing between the two. The clerk, however, makes a choice as to what the language of the interaction is to be. By doing so she has done two things: (1) she has refused to identify her social group; and (2) she has taken the position of determiner of language away from the patient. The fact that she has done (1) enables her to do (2).

The patient in this last case, unconsciously or not, has identified herself first. Other patients do not. In those cases the clerk is met with silence, and is likely to begin the conversation all over again. Or, if the clerk decides that there is something in the way the patient talks that leads her to believe that he is a speaker of the other language then the tables are turned, but the problems are the same. But all missed turns or infelicitous turns are interpreted as linguistic difficulty; the problem lies in figuring out whether or not it is politically motivated. Thus:

Clerk: Lombard, Anne-Marie? [in French]
Patient: (Silence. Glare.)
Clerk: C'est bien ça votre nom? (That's correct isn't it? That's your name?)
Patient: (Silence. Glare.)
Clerk: (pointing to card with name on it): Is this your name?
Patient: Yes.

The conversation continued in English. But the issue can get extremely confused, for example:

```
Clerk:   May I help you?
Patient: (Silence.)
Clerk:   Est-ce que je peux vous aider?
Patient: (Confused look.)
Clerk:   Anglais ou français?
Patient: WHAT?
Clerk:   MAY I HELP YOU?
Patient: Oh, yes, yes, I'm sorry, I'm just a little deaf.
```

Or simply, when one hasn't quite caught what the other person said. A record store employee once asked me something. I didn't hear him and said "Hmmm?" He repeated himself in French. If I were monolingual the conversation might have been rocky. As it was it was just ironic that two anglophones, who might just as well have been speaking English, held an entire conversation in French. (It used to be, and still to a certain extent is, the case that bilingual francophones will speak English to each other. The fact that the opposite is occurring simultaneously is more evidence of the extreme state of change in social relations and group identification.)

But to return to the explicitly phrased question: there are situations where the one who calls the language of interaction into question does not necessarily want to be the one who determines the language of interaction. For example, three people were in a downtown delicatessen late one night, speaking English among themselves. Two were fluently bilingual, one had only a working knowledge of French.

```
Waiter:       Anglais ou français, English or French?
2 Bilinguals: Bien, les deux ... (well, both ...)
Waiter:       No, mais, anglais ou français? (No, but, English or
              French?)
2 Bilinguals: It doesn't matter, c'est comme vous voulez (Whatever
              you want).
Waiter:       (sigh) OK, OK, I'll be back in a minute.
```

He was trying to do them a favor, and they wouldn't let him. Instead he had to make a choice, and speak French, and identify and assert himself, or speak English, and risk offending his customers in case they didn't want to be identified as anglophones (which they probably didn't, or else they might have given him some kind of answer, however indirectly they may have put it).

The importance of the negotiation is such that when subtler tactics, involving norms of conversational turn taking, facial gestures, and code switching, fail to elicit the required information, the question has to be made explicit. Whether it is made in English, French, or both is not necessarily relevant, except that it may be harder to find people with perfect accents in their second language than without. The question has become a conventionalized part of interaction among strangers, and often initiates the interaction. To do so it need not be phrased explicitly: "Bonjour, hello" is a good substitute, unless the other person responds with a smile, in which case, you have to ask "Anglais ou etc."

> Patient: Bonjour, English or French, anglais ou français?
> Clerk: Czechoslovak (or tchecoslovaque, depending on your point of view)
> Patient: Bon, est-ce qu'il y a un endroit où je peux acheter un journal?
> Clerk: (Silence.)
> Patient: Can I buy a newspaper somewhere?
> Clerk: Un journal?
> Patient: Oui.
> Clerk: At the tuck shop, au bout du couloir.

The point about this conversation is that the choice of language did not have to be resolved one way or the other. With experience you learn that it's very hard to tell, when someone asks you if you are English or French, whether or not you are seriously expected to answer the question one way or another. On top of which the way in which it is raised forces one to take sides, something that not everyone is willing to do. All of this only makes conversational inferences harder to make, whereas, one would assume, the explicit question is an attempt to make it easier by bringing it out into the open. Thus the fact that some people promote bilingualism and others oppose it (one PQ member of the National Assembly has said: "They could all be bilingual tomorrow, this wouldn't change the fact that they live and think in English") has led to a curious dance, in which the very same explicit question, and the very same strategies, especially code switching, might have two or more possible interpretations. Selecting the wrong one can have disastrous effects, viz.: I carried on a conversation at work over the phone with a patient in English. I went to find his Emergency slip, read his name, and went back to the phone.

Me: St-Pierre, Robert? [in French]
Patient: St. Pierre. Robert. [in English, and he sounded angry]

Thus the negotiation of language has to do with judgments of personal treatment, that is, how one expects to be treated in such a situation. But such judgments are dependent upon social knowledge, knowledge about group relations and boundaries and ways of signalling them, and knowledge about other social differences, e.g. status differences. For example, a young anglophone doctor interviewed an illiterate male French-Canadian patient who was about 50 years old, and the patient's female companion in French, although his accent and difficulty with the language were noticeable. When the doctor asked a question that the woman felt was important she would often repeat herself in English. Her interaction with the clerks was entirely in French. There are things about situations and their relative importance that determine such language choices, but there are also things that one expects of clerks that one would not expect of doctors.

This negotiation itself serves to redefine the situations in the light of ongoing social and political change. In the absence of norms, we work at creating new ones. The conventionalization of the negotiating strategies appears to be a way of normalizing relationships, of encoding social information necessary to know how to speak to someone (and which language to speak is but one aspect of this). Macro level events, then, have had a direct effect upon people's communicative strategies. But by the same token those events are affected by how people work out their relationships to each other, for on the basis of how they are treated in the community people reformulate their feelings about their role in the community, and hence the political role they choose to play. In this way we can see how it is that language can come to have social values attached to it, and equally how those social values affect language use, and hence the very system itself as its use alters through recourse to aspects of the system. The way in which English and French are spoken in Quebec, and the rate at which they change, will be directly affected by these aspects of their use.

8

Performance and ethnic style in job interviews
F. NIYI AKINNASO AND
CHERYL SEABROOK AJIROTUTU

1. Introduction
This chapter provides a theoretical framework for analyzing
conversational data derived from job interviews and reports a
case study using such a framework. Our data derive from simulated interviews given to 12 Afro-American students of a CETA
(Comprehensive Employment and Training Act) job training
program in Oakland, California in the summer of 1978. Our
goal is to highlight those communicative conditions that can lead
to negative evaluation in stressful speech encounters like job
interviews.

We describe (1) the structural and communicative characteristics
of the job interview, (2) the nature and inferential implications of
interview questions, and (3) the nature of communicative tasks,
showing how interview conversation differs from ordinary conversation. We then go on to compare the responses of two
candidates to a similar set of interview questions, using three major
parameters of communicative effectiveness in interview conversation: stylistic expectations, content, and underlying patterns. The
comparison shows how the accretion of ethnic discourse features
that diverge from established conventions of interview talks leads
to a negative evaluation of one of the candidates.

2. The job interview
The interview as a kind of conversation is probably as old as
language itself. In its simplest form, it is prototypically manifested
as an interrogative encounter between someone who has the right
or privilege to know and another in a less powerful position who is

obliged to respond, rather defensively, to justify his/her action, to explain his/her problems, to give up him/herself for evaluation. (God's interview of Adam after the latter had eaten the forbidden fruit provides an archetype. That the origin of human problems is traceable to God's decision during this interview is symbolic of the role of interviews in modern society.) Such an encounter frequently occurs between interlocutors whose statuses reflect a power differential which occurs for reasons external to the encounter itself: parent–child, adult–youth, teacher–pupil, diviner (doctor)–patient, arbitrator–offender. While the interviewer is often more powerful than the interviewee, there are some exceptional cases where the power asymmetry may be reversed, as in the case of a journalist interviewing a successful politician, or a field worker interviewing an informant. In both situations, the interviewee is certainly more powerful; s/he can decline to answer questions with impunity, and the outcome of such interviews often has no direct impact on the interviewee's life chances. This paper will not be concerned with this kind of interview.

With the growth of complex social and political institutions, the division of labor, and the development of the bureaucracy, the interview has become the major medium for determining people's access to political, social, and economic rewards. Perhaps the most pervasive kind of interview today is the job interview; it is by far the most formalized and perhaps the most crucial face-to-face encounter in ethnically mixed industrial societies.

In bureaucratic settings where personnel selection procedures must be standardized, the job interview has become a major gate-keeping situation where several potential candidates compete for limited economic rewards through intense, face-to-face, verbal interaction usually with unknown persons. Today, it has grown into a key situation where social inequality is ritually dramatized, where basic differences in class, ethnicity, access to power and knowledge, and culturally specific discourse conventions mediate the interaction between participants.

The job interview differs from ordinary conversational interaction in several ways. In general, there are structural, linguistic, and paralinguistic differences. Structurally, the job interview is a formal speech event that normally arises out of a scheduled appointment. Though the outcome of the encounter is not normally known beforehand, the scheduled nature of the encounter presupposes that the purpose of the interaction is known to the participants and that the results of the encounter will be used "to settle future decisions about an issue known prior to the commencement of talk" (Silverman 1973:39). Thus, unlike ordinary conversations, which are not normally prearranged, the purpose of the job interview is to settle certain practical outcomes. The interviewee wants the job; the interviewer wishes to select the most suitable candidate(s). Neither party is interested in the interview as conversation; rather, the aim is to achieve a successful outcome.

Several other structural features further distinguish the job interview from an ordinary conversation. One is the use of some agenda or some form of program in directing the course of the interaction. Another feature is the deliberate recording of the proceedings of the interview. These features facilitate future accountability: the proceedings of the interview may be reported to superior authorities (e.g. Board of Directors) and used as the basis for future decisions. However, neither an agenda nor a formal record can be introduced into an ordinary conversational encounter without seriously disrupting the interaction.

But perhaps the most pervasive structural feature of the job interview is its fixed organizational structure and the strict allocation of rights and duties. Basically, the interviewer has power over the interviewee. S/he controls both the organizational structure of the interview and the mechanics of the interaction. S/he has the privilege of starting it, of introducing new topics or changing topic lines (see Covelli and Murray 1980), and of terminating the conversation. Perhaps the interviewer's greatest weapon is the legitimate responsibility for asking questions designed to elicit responses by which the interviewee will be evaluated.

The interviewee is more or less powerless vis-à-vis the interviewer, with a role mostly confined to responding to the interviewer's questions, giving information about his/her background and experiences for purposes of evaluation. Unless explicitly permitted to do so, the interviewee has no right to ask questions, except for clarification. The interviewer is not, even then, obliged to answer questions: the interviewer may plead lack of expertise or shift the responsibility for answering a question, as in the following example (I = interviewer, C = candidate):

I: OK, ah do you have any other questions?
C: Yes . . . I'm interested in furthering my education, and I was
     interested in if the university has any kind of program that I can
     get involved in as far as furthering my education, not so much
     during my office hours or working hours, but maybe even after
     in the evenings or in between my . . .
I: OK. Yes, we do. There are several possibilities. And the girl in
     the outside office has some brochures with all the information.

In this exchange, the power asymmetry between interviewer and
interviewee is evident in the allocation of turns and the pattern of
linguistic choice. The interviewee had to wait for explicit permission to ask a question. She acknowledges this special privilege by
asking her question pragmatically through the illocutionary force
of her statement rather than through interrogative syntax. The
interviewer further asserts power by doing two things which could
be damning if done by an interviewee: (1) interrupting the speaker;
and (2) shifting the responsibility for answering a question to
another party. Besides, he uses "we," the pronoun of power, as
opposed to the interviewee's "I." All this and more lie within the
interviewer's prerogative. It is the interviewer who alone may
decide to relax the level of formality of the interaction. Thus the use
of formal address terms in reference to the interviewer is obligatory
throughout the interaction whereas the interviewer may use the
interviewee's first name. This power asymmetry is enhanced by the
role differential between the interviewer and the interviewee, by
the differences in the kinds of information they give, and by the
differential treatment given to such information. Notice, for example, that while the interviewee is expected to provide information
about background and experience for purposes of evaluation, the
interviewer has no such obligation. Indeed, information about the
interviewer's background and experiences are irrelevant to the
encounter whereas the interviewee's major role is to provide such
information.

As a matter of fact, both participants often come to the interview
with differential knowledge of each other. While the interviewer
usually has prior knowledge of the interviewee through the latter's
résumé or dossier, the interviewer is often completely anonymous
to the interviewee. Such prior knowledge available to the interviewer provides a powerful tool which may be used during the interview

to manipulate the interviewee, thus perpetuating the power asymmetry between them (cf. Kress and Fowler 1979).

This inequality is further enhanced by the anchorage of the established conventions of interview interaction on the linguistic and cultural norms of the dominant group in mixed populations. This is, of course, part of the historical and sociopolitical processes of the development of the bureaucracy, the standardization of language, and the control of the educational system by the dominant group in ethnically mixed populations. To the extent that deviations from such standardized norms often receive negative evaluation, minority candidates often bring with them into situated interviews a major disadvantage based on pre-existing factors outside the interview interaction itself. Conversely, candidates from mainstream middle-class culture who, in the course of their upbringing, normally acquire linguistic and cultural conventions similar to those of the interview genre enter the interview situation with that advantage. In other words, the patterning of interview conventions and systems of learning according to the cultural conventions of one group will surely disadvantage others whose systems of social and cultural reproduction are entirely different (cf. Bourdieu 1973; Ogbu 1978). Such disadvantage increases exponentially with the degree of differences in discourse conventions between interviewer and interviewee.

In most social interactions, the skewed distribution of social and cultural resources among interactants is best expressed in the pattern of linguistic and paralinguistic choices. The pattern of communicative choice is much more crucial in an interview than in ordinary conversation not simply because the stakes are greater in the former situation but also because the burden of the interaction is placed on the candidate's communicative effectiveness which is often evaluated by culturally specific and unstated criteria other than those in which it is portrayed. We shall be concerned with the three major parameters which determine the communicative effectiveness of interview candidates and, thus, underlie evaluations.

1. *Stylistic expectations:* which conventionalized surface signs are used to signal what intention?
2. *Content:* what is the general meaning of what is said as signalled by linguistic and paralinguistic cues?

3.   *Underlying patterns:* what body of knowledge of social structures is needed to infer what an interview utterance 'really' means or signifies?

A distinction between stylistic expectations and content has been described by Halliday (1967) and Halliday and Hasan (1976) as one between the relational and the ideational features of an utterance. Both features seem to merge in what Gumperz (1977:199) describes as contextualization cue: "any aspect of the surface form of utterances which, when mapped onto message content, can be shown to be functional in the signalling of interpretative frames." A number of case studies in this volume show how miscommunication can arise where such cues are not shared by interactants. In the job interview where the focus is more on the outcome of the encounter, miscommunication and negative evaluation often arise when participants do not share the same cultural and linguistic background, and therefore use different strategies to signal "interpretative frames."

But perhaps more crucial from the point of view of the interview is the problem of discovering underlying patterns. Even when background is shared, miscommunication or noncommunication can occur if one party, especially the interviewee, lacks the ability to 'go beyond' surface meaning. The interviewee must go beyond the surface semantics of interview questions to infer the questioner's intent and select the necessary information about his/her background and qualifications in order to produce effective responses.

Consider the following extract from our data (taken from the interview of C_2):

I: What about the library interests you most?
C_2: What about the library in terms of the books? or the whole building?
I: Any point that you'd like to . . .
C_2: Oh, the children's books, because I have a child, and the children . . you know there's so many you know books for them to read you know, and little things that would interest them would interest me too.

On the basis of the assumption that there is at least an indirect relationship between job interview questions and the job the candidate has applied for, the interviewer's question in this excerpt is indirect, and the interviewer's attempt at restatement – "Any point that you'd like to . . ." – further reinforces this indirectness. What is implied is: "What is there about *working in the library* that interests you *professionally* and which you think you could *do well?*" As is evident in the candidate's response, she missed the nonlexicalized assumptions (italicized above) underlying the question. She interprets the question literally and provides a damaging response about children's books which are, incidentally, not emphasized in a university library.

This conception of going beyond the surface has been the subject of sociological discussion of interview interaction (see, e.g. Selltiz 1964; Denzin 1970; Silverman 1973). Garfinkel (1967:78) characterizes what is involved in discovering the underlying patterns of an utterance as follows:

> The method consists of treating an actual appearance as 'the document of', as 'pointing to', as 'standing on behalf of' a presupposed underlying pattern. Not only is the underlying pattern derived from its individual documentary evidences, but the individual documentary evidences, in their turn, are interpreted on the basis of 'what is known' about the underlying pattern. Each is used to elaborate the other.

What this implies is that interview talk is "never heard *in itself* but as representing or corresponding to some reality routinely available in the world (and of interest to the interviewer) in terms of which it must be decoded" (Silverman 1973:33). In his discussion of Lazarsfeld's principle of tacit assumption, Denzin (1970:118–29) illustrates the problem of underlying patterns in the following terms:

> When a lower class patient says he thinks seeing a psychiatrist would be very likely to help him, does this mean the same thing as when a middle-class patient says it? The response of the patient provides no clear answer; the interviewer must go beyond responses to a question and probe the specific meanings suggested by each person in his answers.

Although Denzin is here taking the point of view of the interviewer in a therapeutic interview, what he says applies to job interviews. The major problem being addressed is that of interpretation and inference. The main issues seem to be: (1) How do we relate surface signs to underlying patterns in order to achieve a successful outcome in interview interaction? (2) What communicative conditions are necessary for effective participation in such interaction or, conversely, (2a) what communicative conditions can lead to miscommunication and negative evaluation? (3) How are interview questions and responses to be evaluated both for purposes of interpretation and assessment? It is to the nature of interview questions and responses that we now turn as part of our initial attempts to answer these questions.

3. Questions and responses

Questions and answers come up in ordinary conversations as part of interactants' attempts to secure and organize information, define topics, and achieve conversational cooperation. Questions are among the most effective devices used by participants in the local management and maintenance of conversational interaction. They are used to secure, allocate, or exit a turn, as well as to open or close topics and whole conversations (Sacks et al., 1974; Sacks and Schegloff 1974; Johnson 1980). In addition, questions are also used by speakers as a self-repair mechanism or as a strategy for modifying their utterances in order to express deference or arrogance, solidarity or power (Ervin-Tripp 1972, 1976). Labov and Fanshel (1977) have also shown how questions can "mitigate" or "aggravate" speech actions. While several studies of the functional use of questions in conversation have concentrated on their role in indicating speakers' weakness, insecurity, and powerlessness (see, e.g., Lakoff 1973, 1975), less attention has been given to the role of questions in the expression of power and authority. Yet this is precisely their role in employment interviews.

One of the few exceptions is provided by Goody (1978) who, among other things, looks at the status implications of questioning. In her attempt to provide "a theory of questions," Goody concludes that questions not only involve asking for information, but also carry a command function, signalling "messages about relationships – about relative status, assertions of status and challenges to status" (p. 39). Unfortunately, however, her anthropological preoccupation with data from a traditional West African society prevented her from looking at the role of questions in modern bureaucratic settings such as the job interview.

The semantico-pragmatic implications and interpretive demands of questions vary with the levels of formality of the encounter, the level of difficulty increasing with the level of formality. That questions can be particularly troublesome in intense conversational engagements is clearly evident in the job interview where questions are formally posed by interviewers in their attempt "to penetrate [interviewees'] private worlds of experience" (Denzin 1970:135). Because of their evaluative orientation, interview questions and the functions they perform differ from those of ordinary conversation in several ways: (1) they are the prerogative of the interviewer, (2) they constitute the focus of communicative activity, (3) they are intended to elicit responses that will be evaluated, and, perhaps most importantly, (4) they are mostly indirect, relying upon the interviewee's ability to infer the type of answer wanted. (Indirectness is used here to refer to the inferential implications of interview questions, e.g., to the fact that "Yes–No" answers may be inappropriate for apparent tag-questions – see Section 7.) This very powerful role of questions no doubt reinforces the structural constraints of the interview situation in generating interviewees' unease.

To the extent that the signalling of intention and interpretive or inferential processes are based on culturally specific discourse conventions, interview questions may be 'wrongly' interpreted where such conventions are not shared between interviewer and interviewee. Besides, several other factors such as experience with formalized (perhaps decontextualized) discourse and the interviewee's network of interpersonal relations may affect inferential processes. (We shall return to these factors later.)

Like the interpretation of interview questions, the evaluation of interviewees' responses is based on culture-specific assumptions. The adequacy of a response is judged relative to stylistic expectations, content, revelation of relevant underlying patterns, and effective interpretation of the question that triggers the response. This means that interviewers often go beyond *what* is said to examine *how* it is said, and to assess which relevant aspects of the respondent's background and qualifications are highlighted in the response.

Since interview questions are mostly indirect, and since interviewers must typically ask questions to seek information that they do not have, the task of relating responses to interview questions is always open to negotiation. Indeed, since identity, role and status are predetermined, much of what is left for negotiation in the job interview is meaning and interactants' intent. The situation is thus not so much of emergent definitions of self (as in ordinary conversation) as of emergent definitions of meaning and intention. The interviewee's ability to go beyond the surface, pick the relevant cues, infer the intended meaning, and effectively negotiate an acceptable relationship between questions and responses is an important measure of his/her success. While individuals vary considerably in such ability, there is no doubt that shared linguistic and cultural backgrounds will normally enhance mutual understanding between interviewer and interviewee and thus promote the latter's success in the interview.

4. Communicative tasks

As in ordinary conversation, certain communicative tasks recur from time to time in the course of interview interaction. Such tasks include narrating, explaining, justifying, emphasizing, arguing, etc. While these are universal discourse tasks, their performance is based on systematic and culturally specific conventions. And within each cultural group, the deployment of such conventions varies from one situation to another.

For example, personal narratives (i.e., stories about personal experience) may be told to entertain, to empathize with the listener, to advise, to inform, to instigate action, to seek praise, admiration, or other kinds of positive evaluation (see Van Dijk 1977; Robinson 1981). Besides, there is considerable variation in audience, context, and setting which necessarily leads to variation in the patterns of communicative choice. Thus different patterns of communicative choice would be employed in narrating the same personal experience to a group of friends at a bar, to a lawyer as part of a lawsuit evidence, or to an interview panel in response to an evaluative question. For example, the form, content, and presentation of personal narratives in job interviews is heavily constrained by the goal orientation of the interaction, by its formal organizational structure, and by the power asymmetry between the participants.

We have selected the narrative task for illustration in this chapter partly because of its frequency of occurrence in our data and partly because it is in the performance of such a task that candidates (unconsciously) reveal much of their personality, job experience, and sociolinguistic background. As a matter of fact, the longest responses to interview questions in our data were elicited when candidates were required to narrate some incident in their previous job experience that would demonstrate certain specified skills or suitability for the job for which they were being interviewed.

Since subcultural groups within the same population may have differing perceptions of the socially appropriate conditions for narrative (Cazden and Hymes 1978, Robinson 1981) there is no doubt that the cultural bias in the structuring of a narrative and the co-occurrence of certain linguistic and prosodic patterns in such a prolonged speech as a narrative can lead to misunderstanding and, hence, negative evaluation when participants do not share similar communicative history.

As pointed out earlier, two of the major differences between a job interview and an ordinary conversation are the former's fixed organizational structure and goal orientation. These structural differences necessarily engender differences of "conversational mode" between the two kinds of encounter. McGuire and Lorch (1968) suggest four conversational modes, each dealing, more or less, with a particular kind of conversation and specifying the nature, mechanics, and goal of that conversation. The four types they propose are (1) the *associational mode* used in casual conversation where the goal is the interaction itself, the mutual exchange of ideas and experiences; (2) the *problem-solving mode* used in goal-oriented interactions; (3) the *interrogation mode* where questions are asked to obtain specific information; and (4) the *clarification-of-misunderstanding mode* where the goal is to determine why misunderstanding has arisen between participants in the conversation. These conversational modes are, of course, not mutually exclusive, as we will illustrate later in our discussion. But, by and large, while casual conversations are carried out primarily in the *associational* mode, interview conversation is governed by the *problem-solving* mode. Robinson has a succinct characterization of the latter:

In this mode, conversation is organized around an exchange of information, whether facts, ideas, or experiences. The topic or theme of the conversation is narrowly defined and dominates verbalization. Each contribution is expected to relate to the problem posed. Since the goal of the conversation is to resolve some problem, there will be a premium on truth-value and plausibility. (1981:79)

Since there is no strict criterion of relevance other than participants' willingness to participate in the conversation, exchanges in the *associational* mode are generally mutual, being based on associative principles. On the other hand, since the focus in interview interaction is not so much on the conversation itself as on the outcome, the *problem-solving* mode emphasizes logical progression. A further complication of interview conversation is that the interviewer predominantly uses a more powerful conversational mode, the *interrogation* mode, while the interviewee is confined, for the most part, to the *problem-solving* mode.

Consequently, while personal narratives in ordinary conversational encounters typically arise out of the ongoing situation, personal narratives in job interviews are typically motivated by specific questions and must be seen as responses-to-questions. Therefore, to produce effective personal narratives in the job interview, narrators must go beyond mere storytelling. They must show the relevance of their story, usually by highlighting relevant aspects of their experience that would attract positive evaluation. Robinson (1981:82) summarizes the essential requirements as follows:

The story told – its subject matter, its point, its purpose, as well as the expressive style employed – must be congruent with the modal qualities of the conversation in which it is embedded.

5. Data and ethnographic background

The texts on which our analysis is based were collected, with the permission of the people involved, in the summer of 1978 in the course of simulated interviews given to selected students at the CETA training center in Oakland, California. The data were collected with the assistance of the CETA training personnel as part of the project on interethnic communication and public negotiation under the supervision of John Gumperz.

Enacted in 1973, the CETA programs have constituted a major share of the Department of Labor's program responsibilities. In addition to job development, classroom and on-the-job training, counselling and job placement, the CETA program also offers assessment training, "interviewing, testing and counselling enrollees to determine 'job-readiness,' aptitudes, abilities, and interests in order to develop a plan to help enrollees get and keep jobs" (US Department of Labor 1973:3). In return for permission to record verbal data and interview trainees, we volunteered to take over the assessment training portion of the course and were allotted four hours a week to discuss communication problems and job interviews. The training period extended over four weeks.

The Oakland CETA training center was chosen for the study mainly because most enrollees in the programs are from minority language and cultural backgrounds and therefore often rely on different patterns of communicative choice whose co-occurrence often leads to misunderstanding, and, therefore, negative evaluation in prolonged, intensive, verbal interaction such as the job interview (see, e.g., Gumperz, Jupp, and Roberts 1979; Jupp, Roberts, and Cook-Gumperz this volume: Chapter 13).

Altogether, twelve students from the Oakland CETA training center took part in our role-play interviews. They all share similar minority linguistic and cultural background and are seeking clerical and semi-professional jobs. They all had high school training and some of them had one or two years of college training. None of them had had more than one or two formal job-interview experiences.

Although our conclusions are based on the results of all the interviews, we have limited our analysis to the performances of two candidates (C_1 and C_2). These two candiates were chosen for purposes of comparison and illustration of our analytical methods. The two candidates contrast in several ways including background experience and performance at the interview.

C_1 is in her early twenties and a single mother living on social welfare funds until she joined the CETA program. She has a high school diploma and worked as assistant librarian while in high school. Before she came to settle in Oakland, she worked as a microfilm operator at the Walgreen Agency in Illinois. She is currently training as a clerk typist and hopes to take employment in a college or university library. She had never had a formal job interview.

C_2 is much older and has had varied work experiences. She is in her late thirties and a single mother with teenage children. Having lived on social welfare funds for several years, she has been involved in several bureaucratic exchanges and is therefore very familiar with bureaucratic language and official procedures, including sustained interviews with social welfare officers. Besides, she has acquired necessary skills for persuasive discourse while working as an Avon representative for several years. Working simultaneously as a cosmetologist, she has also acquired relevant experience in dealing with people and situations. She has a high school diploma and two years of college training. She enrolled in the CETA program to train as a secretary-typist and has been through two formal job interviews.

To compile the ethnographic background materials for the interviews, we had spent several months interviewing personnel officers, employers, and newly hired employees who, from their different perspectives, gave us valuable insights into the nature of the interview process. We also interviewed several established employees holding positions comparable to those for which candidates were interviewed in our role play to elicit information about job content, job conduct, and job retention. Finally, our interview candidates were given adequate job descriptions and were made to go through formal application procedures including the submission of a résumé.

In order to insure the uniformity of the questions posed to the different candidates, we devised a scheme which all interviewers had to follow, regardless of variation in the jobs for which the candidates were interviewed. This standardized scheme was also necessary in controlling for variation in the background and techniques of the participating interviewers, thus emphasizing the characteristic independence of the interview genre. In keeping with interview conventions, the sequence of the interaction was divided into three parts, as the figure shows. The résumé and the role reversal served, respectively, as transition points between (1) the opening and the main interview and (2) the main interview and the closing.

In order to optimize the preparation of the candidates for the interview, we arranged an orientation program in which they listened to talks by career counsellors, established administrative personnel, and professional interviewers. They also watched two video-taped interviews one of which involved a white middle-class candidate who interviewed effectively. The video-taped interviews were analyzed and discussed in an open seminar to assist the candidates in discriminating between effective and noneffective interview strategies.

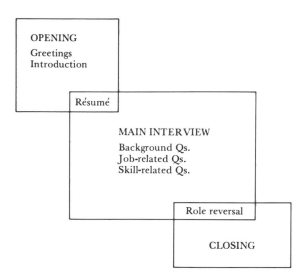

6. Method of analysis

Our analysis involves two comparisons. On the one hand, we compare the performances of two candidates (C_1 and C_2) from the points of view of (1) communicative effectiveness and (2) performance of relevant communicative task – in this case, narrating an experience. On the other hand, we compare the performance of each candidate to the established conventions of interview interaction. Our notion of established interview conventions is based on the comments of white middle-class listeners and professional interviewers to whom we played our tapes of the simulated interview.

We also played the tapes to all participants involved in order to elicit their judgment of the outcome of the encounter. This provided the basis for our interpretation of participants' intent and expectations.

The texts analyzed below are the responses of C_1 and C_2 to a similar set of questions. First we deal with the narrative requirement of the question. Then we move on to analyze the candidates' use of culture-specific paralinguistic features: back channel cuing, vowel lengthening, rhythm, and voice quality.

7. The texts
Text I

Q: Have you had any previous job experience that would demonstrate that you've shown initiative or been able to work independently?

C_1: 1. Well / . . . yes when I / . . . OK / . . . there's this Walgreen's Agency //
2. I worked as a microfilm operator / OK //
3. and it was a snow storm //
4. OK / and it was usually six people / workin' in a group / uhum /
5. and only me and this other girl showed up //
6. and we had quite a lot of work to do /
7. and so the man / he asked us could we / you know //
8. do we / . . . do we thinks we could finish this work /
9. so me 'n' this girl / you know / we finished it all //

Text II

Q: One more question was that ah, this kind of work frequently involves using your own initiative and showing sort of the ability to make independent judgment. Do you have any . . . can you tell me about any previous experience which you think directly show . . demonstrates that you have these qualities?

C_2: 1. Why / . . well / as far as being capable of handling an office, /
2. say if I'm left on my own, / I feel I'm capable I /
3. had a situation where one of my employers that I've been /
4. ah previously worked for / had to go on / a . . / a trip for say / ah
5. three weeks and / he was / . . . I was left alone to . . / handle
6. the office and run it. / And at that time / ah I didn't
7. really have what you would say / a lot of experience. /
8. But I had enough experience to / . . deal with any situations
9. that came up while he was gone, // and those that I couldn't /
10. ah handle at the time, / if there was someone
11. who had more experience than myself / I asked
12. questions / to find out / what procedure I would use, / if
13. something came up / and if I didn't know / who to really
14. go to // I would jot it down / or write it down / on a
15. piece of paper / so that I wouldn't forget that . . / if
16. anyone that / was more qualified than myself / I could
17. ask them about it / and how I would go about solving
18. it. // So I feel I'm capable of handling just about
19. any situation / whether it's on my own / or under supervision //

Although the above questions appear relatively simple, they place a great inferential burden on the candidates because they do not explicitly call for a specific response. This indirectness can lead to a varying number of possible responses such as (R = response):

R_1: Yes.
R_2: Yes, on one of my evaluations, my supervisor once stated that I demonstrated initiative on the job.

None of these responses can be effective in the job interview context since they fail to infer the underlying intent of the interviewer. Although the responses can be varied, the expectation is that an episode be narrated which illustrates relevant job skills. To be effective, such a narrative must be told in the *problem-solving* conversational mode. The narrative must not be seen as an end in itself but as a response-to-question.

8. Analysis and discussion

Here we shall concentrate on the candidates' ethnic style and show how the accretion of culturally specific discourse features can lead to negative evaluation in the interview context.

The narrative structure

A common characteristic of Afro-American narrative structure is the requirement that the storyteller

(a)   establish a scene or setting for the story
(b)   pose the problem to be resolved
(c)   resolve the problem
(d)   close off the story

Both C_1 and C_2 adhere to this structural scheme as shown in Table 1.

Table 1. *Narrative structure*

	C_1	C_2
Setting the scene	1–2	1–5
Posing the problem	3–8	5–7
Resolving the problem	9	8–18
Closing	9	18–19

Afro-Americans generally regard the first task in a narrative to be the setting of the scene. This requires making explicit relevant

information which will later constitute shared background knowledge in the narrative frame.

A. *Scene setting*
At the beginning of her narrative, C_1 makes the following information explicit. In line 1 she states where she worked:

> ... there's this Walgreen's Agency

In line 2 she states what her role was:

> I worked as a microfilm operator

C_2 uses a different strategy in opening her narrative. In lines 1–2
she restates the question in her own terms, which focuses on her
own reference point:

> Why ... well as far as being capable of handling an office, say if I'm
> left on my own

In lines 3–5 she details the scene:

> I had a situation where one of my employers that I've been ah
> previously worked for had to go on a .. trip for say ah three weeks
> and he was ...

In lines 5–6 she states what her role was in the narrative:

> I was left alone to handle the office and run it.

Although both candidates follow the same narrative scheme, we
begin to notice slight stylistic differences. While C_1 goes straight
into her narrative, C_2 begins by setting both the context and
conversational mode in which her narrative is to be told, thus
signalling explicitly that she is telling a narrative as a response-to-
question.

B. *Posing the problem*
C_1's explanation of the problem takes place over lines 3–6 where
she does the following. In line 3 she makes explicit the external
factor which created the problem:

> and it was a snowstorm

In line 4 she makes explicit what the usual work situation is:

> and it was usually six people workin' in a group

In line 5 she relays the problem only after providing additional background information:

> ... and only me and this other girl showed up.

In lines 6–8 she relays additional information which compounds the problem:

> ... and we had quite a lot of work to do and so the man asked us could we you know do we do we thinks we could finish this work

C_2's posing of the problem takes place over lines 5–7:

> I was left alone to handle the office and run it. And at that time ah I didn't really have what you would say a lot of experience.

C. Resolution of the problem

C_1 states the resolution of the problem in the following manner. In line 9 she states that the problem was resolved without explaining *how* it happened:

> So me 'n' this girl we finished it all.

C_2 pays more attention to the resolution of the problem. Although she has relayed that she did not have enough experience, in lines 8–9 she makes explicit what she was able to accomplish with the experience she did have:

> But I had enough experience to deal with any situations that came up while he was gone

In lines 9–17 she makes explicit (1) smaller subsections of the problem and (2) the various options she used to resolve them. For example, in lines 9–10, she states a problem:

> and those that I couldn't ah handle at the time

Lines 10–12 detail the procedure of one possible resolution option:

> if there was someone who had more experience than myself I asked questions to find out what procedure I would use

Lines 12–14 refer to another problem:

> if something came up and if I didn't know who to really go to

In lines 14–18, she outlines the procedure of one possible resolution option:

I would jot it down or write it down on a piece of paper so that I
wouldn't forget that if anyone that was more qualified than myself I
could ask them about it and how I would go about solving it.

D. Closing the scene

In line 9 C_1 closes her narrative prosodically as follows:

we finished it all

C_2 takes a different approach in closing her narrative. In lines
18–19, she provides a summary statement:

So I feel I'm capable of handling just about any situation

Line 19 provides additional supporting information to the summary:

whether it's on my own or under supervision

This evaluation of the two narrative texts requires some assessment of what constitutes an effective response in the context of an
employment interview. Clearly, many of the attributes of casual
face-to-face interaction such as meaning negotiation and establishing a shared body of knowledge are also part of the employment
interview encounter. However, in a formal interview encounter,
questions are designed to elicit responses from the candidate which
are evaluated, and the fact that the outcome of the encounter is
used to settle future decisions sets it apart from casual talk.
Therefore when a candidate responds to an interview question with
a simple explanation s/he reduces the interview encounter to casual
talk.

This point can be illustrated by contrasting the two analyzed
texts. The nature of questioning in the employment interview
requires that a response infer beyond the literal meaning of the
question. This necessitates the ability on the part of the interviewee
to infer the appropriate communicative task and incorporate
outside relevant knowledge which ties the response to the stylistic
expectations of interview interaction. Therefore the first task of any
candidate is to infer and negotiate a shared meaning of speaker's
intent. This establishes boundaries within which the candidate feels
capable of responding to specific questions. The negotiation of this
task can take place in various ways. For example, the candidate can
demand restatement of the question. In most instances the inter-

viewer must then add some additional or clarifying information to the interview question. An example of this is the following:

I: I guess my first question would be what are the particular reasons you're interested in working here at the University?
C_2:   Well ah, I feel that I would . . . excuse me, could you repeat that question?
I: Um, well, what is it about . . . Is there anything about working on campus that particularly appeals to you?

Alternatively, the candidate can restate the question in such a way that it establishes the focus of the response s/he intends to give. For example, in her opening response to the question in Text II, C_2 restates the question in her own terms, thus providing a framework for her narrative:

I: One more question was that ah this kind of work frequently involves using your own initiative and showing sort of the ability to make independent judgments. Do you have any . . . can you tell me about any previous experience which you think directly show . . demonstrates that you have these qualities?
C_2:   Why . . well as far as being capable of handling an office

Once the intended meaning of an interview question is effectively negotiated, the next step is to identify the relevant communicative task and then structure one's information for presentation according to relevant discourse conventions. The above analysis shows that although C_1 and C_2 both have the ability to infer the appropriate communicative task, they differ both in their negotiation of the intended and underlying meanings of the question and in the ways they detail related information within the narrative structure. As we shall soon show, they also differ in their use of paralinguistic cues.

As is evident in the above analysis, the two candidates differ in the ways they open and close their narratives and in the kinds of information they select for emphasis. C_1's failure to begin with a focusing statement is just one example of her inability to distinguish her talk stylistically as interview talk. Similarly, her dependence on culturally specific prosodic cues to signal closure contrasts with C_2's use of a summary statement which ties her narrative back to the frame of focus designated in her opening statement.

We also notice that while C_1 gives considerable attention to detailing the problems to be resolved in her narrative, C_2 pays more attention to the steps taken to resolve the problem, thus highlighting her ability to use her initiative and providing the context for her evaluative summary at the closing of the narrative.

In all, if we compare the overall content of the two responses, we see that C_1 does no more than tell a story, viewing the narrative as an end in itself. This is further confirmed by her use of stylistic cues which presuppose an *associational* rather than a *problem-solving* conversational mode.

Paralinguistic cues
Culturally specific prosodic features are less subject to conscious control than syntactic and other structural features. Where a speaker has not learned to transcend the use of such features in an employment interview, their accretion often increases the chances of misunderstanding and, therefore, of negative evaluation. A comparison of how C_1 and C_2 use prosodic cues will show how the recurrence of certain prosodic patterns affects the evaluation of C_1's responses.

A. *Back channel cuing*
Back channel cuing is one effective and immediate way of noting listener's understanding during the course of conversation. This signalling process can be realized through the use of verbal and/or nonverbal cues. Here the discussion will be limited to verbal cues such as *um hum, um um, yeah*, and *OK*.

The use of back channel cues serves three purposes: to signal (1) reassurance that the speaker is understood, (2) agreement or solidarity with the previous statement, and (3) possible need for further clarification of the previously stated point. During the course of the employment interview it is important that the interviewee be clearly understood. And since most of the interview is normally spent listening to the persuasive style of the interviewee, it is paramount to the exchange that some signalling system of understanding confirmation be negotiated between the interviewee and the interviewer.

Frequently cited in literature as "Call and Response," the use of back channel cuing is an intrinsic part of the discourse mode for Afro-American speakers (Smitherman 1977). In face-to-face interaction, like the employment interview, the successful undertaking of communicative tasks such as the narrative requires that the speaker build upon informational chunks which are utilized to establish shared background knowledge and to make a point effectively. In order for a speaker to rely upon back channel cues as directives, the listener must not play a passive role in the exchange.

Within the text, back channel cuing is used in various ways.

C_1 uses OK in two different ways in her responses. The first OK (line 1) signals that she is ready to begin her narrative. It acts as the announcer: "Now I will begin." The second type of OK occurs in lines 2 and 4 where it ties off informational chunks and sees listener confirmation. A further distinguishing feature of these two different OKs is that the first OK (in line 1) is rhythmically and prosodically marked. It is marked by slowing tempo and vowel lengthening, whereas the information final OKs in lines 2 and 4 have fall-rise intonation. The phrase "you know" in lines 7 and 9 also seek to elicit listener confirmation.

With C_2 there appears to be a lack of back channel cuing throughout the passage.

B. *Vowel lengthening*

Vowel lengthening in Afro-American speaking behavior illustrates the use of the oral ability to transmit information through intonational contouring. The use of vowel lengthening reflects vocal manipulation by a speaker: (1) to mark emphasis stylistically over a word or phrase, (2) to cue a rhythmical transition, and (3) to signal special meaning.

C_1 utilizes vowel lengthening to provide insights into the manipulation of meters and cadences. For instance in lines 2 and 5 the sustained hold acts as a rhythmical transition which sets off two different rhythmically marked phrases. In line 2, C_1 uses vowel lengthening to establish a balance between the phrases "I worked" and "a microfilm operator." A similar sustained style is utilized in line 5; however, the preceding and following phrases are not as rhythmically distinctive as they are in line 2.

A third example of vowel lengthening is in line 7 on the word "ma:n." Vowel lengthening is used here to signal additional meaning. The use of vowel lengthening in such an instance commonly signals the use of inversion like "ba:d," which means

"good." However, in this instance "ma:n," with a lengthened
vowel, is used to refer not simply to the man by gender but also the
boss or supervisor. The use of "ma:n" in this manner signals a
different level of interpretation which requires familiarity with
Afro-American discourse strategies.

The fourth and final use of vowel lengthening is in line 9. Here
the use of "so:" rhythmically establishes the slowing down of
cadence by the speaker. Here the cadence is slowed to effect closure
of the passage.

> so: me 'n' this girl we finished it all

C_2's use of vowel lengthening is not as distinctively marked as C_1's,
therefore her usage does not attract the attention of this analysis.

C. Rhythm

The use of rhythm in the speaking behavior of Afro-Americans
reflects the manipulation of meters and cadence. Rhythm, a universal in all speaking behavior, can be discussed in the following three
ways.

There exists within any string of utterances a general beat
structure, and although cadence can differ from speaker to speaker
what is certain is that all rhythmical shifts utilized in speech return
to this basic beat.

A second kind of rhythmical patterning is a speeding up of
cadence. This can be accomplished in several ways. The use of a
rhythmical tie over a short phrase can aid in effectively speeding up
cadence. Examples of this occur in lines 2 and 4 of C_1's response.

> I worked as a microfilm operator
>
> and it was usually six people workin' in a group

C_2 utilizes moderate rhythmical shifts in lines 5, 6, 13, and 14.
However, rhythm is not as important in her style as in C_1's case.

A third kind of rhythmical patterning is a slowing down of
cadence to build up listener anticipation of a rhythmical shift which
usually occurs over the next passage. In line 4 we have such an
instance in "and it was usually six people workin' in a group." The
opening phrase "and it was usually six people" signals the following rhythmically marked phrase "workin' in a group." C_1 also uses
rhythmical slowdown to signal completion of the passage. In this
case it occurs in line 9 over the phrase: "we finished it all."

D. *Voice quality*

The use of a wide range of vocalizations of the voice is a major characteristic of Afro-American speaking behavior. Used to stylize speech effectively, it can take on the vocal quality of a rasp, growl, falsetto, or whine. Although the use of shifts in tonal voice quality has been cited in the literature as a speaking behavior largely attributed to Afro-American males (Abrahams 1975; Dillard 1972), C_1 utilizes a falsetto voice quality in line 9, over the phrase: "We finished it all." In this case her use of falsetto is demonstrated by elevating voice pitch, reaching its peak on the last syllable.

Though she is Afro-American, C_2 does not manifest these culturally specific prosodic features in her speech. Indeed, until they were told, many evaluators who listened to our tapes had difficulty identifying her as a non-white speaker.

9. Conclusion

Although several researchers have expressed doubts about the reliability and validity of decision making in the employment interview (see Rothstein and Jackson 1980, for a review), there is common agreement that discourse conventions are very crucial to employability (Gumperz, Jupp, and Roberts 1979; Kalin and Rayko 1980; Rey 1977). Consequently, where several candidates have equivalent qualifications, as is often the case in present-day urban settings, candidates who can linguistically match a standard variety and interact within the discourse conventions of the standard language are normally at an advantage (see Jupp, Roberts, and Cook-Gumperz this volume, Chapter 13). Even when the position is explicitly advertised for "minority applicants," candidates are often evaluated on the basis of standardized discourse conventions.

In this study, we have shown how wrong inferences and the recurrence of certain culturally specific prosodic cues can lead to negative evaluation in the job interview. The two candidates discussed in this chapter are not members of the dominant group but as Afro-Americans they are likely to interact on a regular basis with mainstream culture (Abrahams 1975). However, since interaction with mainstream culture depends on several factors such as neighborhood, age, exposure, experience, gender, and social networks, various members of minority groups in mixed populations will have differential access to the cultural and interactional norms of the dominant group. As evident from their own profiles and from subsequent personal interview by one of the investigators, the two candidates discussed here have clearly had differential access to mainstream culture and the rhetorical strategies of bureaucratic discourse.

It is, however, one thing to acquire the rhetorical strategies of bureaucratic discourse, and it is another thing to know *how* and *when* to use such strategies. Such knowledge is necessary for candidates to be able to shift signalling levels, from ordinary conversation to "interview talk," or from *associational* to *problem-solving* conversational mode. A measure of C_2's effectiveness is her ability to shift signalling levels as appropriate, while C_1 fails to make such a shift. This notion of a shift in signalling levels is parallel, in a sense, to the shift that writers must make in order to 'translate' spoken English effectively into written discourse. In a subtle yet very important way, such a shift requires some identity transformation since actors can no longer afford to rely solely on culturally specific discourse strategies; rather, they must use discourse conventions that transcend cultural boundaries.

9

Interethnic communication in committee negotiations

JOHN J. GUMPERZ AND JENNY COOK-GUMPERZ

It took even the Almighty six days to sort out the world's original problems and He was not a committee.

The Economist, May 1980

Committee meetings with their delays, procrastinations, and inconsistencies have long been a favorite source of humor, but, like it or not, committees form an essential and in many ways crucial aspect of the process by which policy is made in industry and public affairs. In modern post-industrial urban societies, institutions of all kinds have become increasingly open to public scrutiny. Regardless of how policies originate, or who proposes them and carries them out, actions of all kinds may ultimately be subject to some public inspection and control of decision making processes. This means that the mechanisms by which policies are adopted must have the visibility of group processes where the evidence for and against is openly debated in ways that are comprehensible to most, regardless of interest and background.

Sociologists of organizational behavior point out that committees are designed to "overcome difficulties in bureaucratic hierarchies caused by jobs needing unfamiliar responsibilities by creating a *super person, a committee*" (Burns 1969). As such superpersons, committees also make decisions that are suprapersonal above and beyond the decision making powers of any member.

Committees act as courts of appeal for what can be acceptable arguments as well as means of sifting information. It is 'in committee' that decision making appears to take place. Even if decisions are made privately off the record, it is the presentation of cases and opinions through the committee process that commits and binds the decision makers in the public record. These decisions are expressed in a nonpersonal language because, above all, relevant information must be put *on record* in the form of written minutes, memoranda, and resolutions. Such written records and the interpretations they reflect, it has been argued, serve as the basis of future actions rather than as a representation of what participants may perceive when in particular interactional situations.

Thus, the procedures of committee meetings, as face-to-face events requiring talk, are a juxtaposition of two rather variant language needs: the requirements of written reports to be clear and precise, in conjunction with interpersonal needs of being persuasive with other committee members. These two communicative needs can appear to be at odds or can make for a special technique of committee talk, which can give the representation of clarity within a developing framework of argumentation that is sufficiently repetitive to give all the members a chance to express opinions or contrary views.

Anyone who has studied bureaucratic proceedings or has otherwise had an opportunity to analyze such public records will agree that these proceedings tend to create communicative conventions of their own. Strategies for putting information into words, for emphasizing, for responding to questions, and for foregrounding and backgrounding arguments tend to arise which may originally have been justified by criteria of public availability but which over time can by themselves constitute criteria for judging appropriate communication in bureaucratic contexts.

However, what students of organizational behavior might use as additional evidence of organizational structuring, the character of the committee talk, can itself be examined as an organizational accomplishment of the committee process. This is the approach we take in exploring how ethnically distinct styles of discourse strategies complicate the accomplishment of committee talk. We will analyse a very lengthy transcript of part of a committee meeting which was tape recorded on the site of a youth club in London.

The meeting in question was between the staff and governing board of The Seventies, a largely West Indian youth club, and officers of the Inner London Education Authority (ILEA), which funds the club. It was called to resolve a staffing and funding problem resulting from the reorganization of the club. Some months earlier, the staff of three full-time workers had resigned. A young West Indian man, who in the past had been active as a volunteer worker in the club and returned from a training course with a diploma in social work, had been appointed to get the club started again. After some time in this new position the young social worker, faced with the task of doing his youth work and simultaneously having to be responsible for managing the club premises and facilities, decided that additional full-time personnel were needed immediately if any progress was to be made in recruiting new members and doing youth work counselling. The ILEA officer in charge of personnel funding seemed to want to delay filling the regularly allotted positions, suggesting that part-time help be employed until the club was more properly established. The club governing committee asked for the meeting to deal with this issue.

Participants in the session were Trent, the young social worker, Lionel, the ILEA officer, several committee members including Clifford, a West Indian social worker and Keith, a West Indian community worker, and two native British professionals from other local agencies, Shirley and Max. Kenneth, the chairman of the ILEA Youth Advisory Board, acted as the presiding officer. The recording on which our analysis is based was made by one of the committee members with the permission of other participants.

Our analysis concentrates on the formal committee proceedings, which were preceded by some informal discussion of issues and possible solutions. In a summary of the meeting's progress we noted the following. Lionel opens the meeting with a statement which sets the scene for what follows by stating the criteria on the basis of which the Education Authority will review the situation. He then goes on to say that the present manager is new, that this puts the club into the category of a new project and that it is customary policy that new projects begin with a trial period before more permanent commitments are made. After some time, if the club comes up to expectations, Lionel argues, the question of further regular staff could be considered.

When asked to comment and present his case, Trent begins with the direct assertion that the arrangement is not feasible. He points out that, apart from part-time helpers who come in the evening, he is the only full-time person in the building, he is forced to spend most of his time on housekeeping duties and he gets very little youth work done. Lionel replies that this is a matter of allocation of working time and not a staffing problem. He suggests that what is needed is better allocation of part-time help.

The chairman then speaks, asking the committee for their opinion. He is followed first by the two West Indians and then by the two native English speakers. None of these individuals contribute new information, they simply seek to clarify the issues and bring out the implications of what Trent has said, using a style of argumentation that is much less direct than Trent's and much closer to the staff officers' style. It is brought out for example that, if Trent has to spend most of his time in the building, he has little time to go out and do the counselling and recruiting that is necessary to get young people off the streets and into the club. There follows some further discussion of what population the club actually serves. Members of the governing board continue to emphasize the need for more meaningful youth work. Finally, when the chairman summarizes by noting the conflict between housekeeping duties on the one hand and counselling on the other, it is agreed that a bona fide case for additional full-time help exists and the meeting concludes.

What is of interest here is that the post factum summary in no way catches the flavor of the actual speeches and the implications and misunderstandings which seem to arise during the progress of the exchanges. The points of view and information given by the two main speakers appear to be interactionally out of synchrony and to fail to establish the basis of a shared perspective from which they can go on to discuss further exchanges. The three subsidiary speakers appear to present positions supportive to the first two speakers and thus to provide some openings for negotiation of a common ground. We could at this level easily conclude that there is a communication problem between the social worker and the ILEA staff officer. The social worker is the person on the spot. It is his professional effectiveness that is at issue. He is the only one with an intimate knowledge of the situation, all others are part-time observers who judge primarily on the basis of what they hear. To win his point he must be able to talk convincingly about what he is doing. Yet when he presents his case his arguments are seen as personal complaints.

What we must ask is: what are the rhetorical strategies used in Trent's statements that lend credibility to Lionel's attempt to treat them in personal terms and therefore as inadequate given the suprapersonal nature of committee proceedings? Why did the chairman ask for additional evidence and why did the committee members merely rephrase Trent's argument? We could perhaps conclude that it is linguistic interference from the social worker's West Indian style that prevents easy communication, but further interactions make this hypothesis unlikely, as the two most effective subsidiary speakers are also West Indians. The explanation must therefore be a more complicated one than the clash of two different ethnic styles of rhetoric.

Committee talk

We begin our analysis by exploring in a little more detail the character of committee talk and how interactants are likely to perceive the needs and constraints of committee talk in relation to their own communicative styles, which may be at variance with those of the majority culture.

Familiarity with the intricacies of this communicative style, both with the content of situational rules and with the organizational structures and rhetorical procedures by which they are put into practice, is essential for anyone wishing to participate in public affairs. Members of urban minorities and any others who have had no experience with the world of public bureaucracy are thus faced with a major problem of translating the persuasive strategies of their home environment into the communicative conventions that determine persuasiveness in public affairs. This problem of translation is at least in part independent of what the linguist would call home language. It is rather a matter of culturally determined rhetorical practices which, although not unaffected by what the linguist calls language differences, are determined by a different range of phenomena, and which tend to appear more clearly in longer interactive sequences than in the production of sentences.

It is a part of the organizational character of committee talk that conventions and acceptable forms of argumentation are presented as if they were culturally and situationally uniform. As we suggested in Chapter 1, what counts in committee talk is the ability to conform to the principle of rhetoric by which effective performance is judged. Our problem in this chapter is to demonstrate how these criteria of effectiveness are communicated and accepted within the interactional setting of any committee meeting. The talk of committee meetings actually persuades in ways opposite to the apparently stated goals and norms of committee talk; that is, while the goal is to present reasoned arguments, the qualities of talk that make an argument appear to be reasoned are not the propositional units as such, but in large part stylistic features of the order, structure, and ways that linkages are created between propositional segments. So that what in one cultural tradition sounds like a reasoned argument may not appear as such in another. That strategies of argumentation are culturally different, we have shown in some of the foregoing chapters. Where these cultural differences come together in face-to-face interactional situations, the predominant style of any interaction will result from a balance achieved from the recognized situational constraints upon the "forms of talk" (Goffman 1981) in conjunction with what results from the progress of the interaction.

The constraint upon the forms of committee talk is that, if in any instance rhetorical strategies were recognized as being subject to cultural variation, then in the actual event the practice of committee speaking leading to decision making would not appear to guarantee uniformity, and discussion would break down. That is, the organizational character of committee talk is such that it must be made to appear to produce common ground from which actions and decisions can be negotiated. Moreover, committee talk is presented as if overriding the caveats to which everyday ordinary language is subject, that is the practical reasoning which allows for any connection between the general rule and the realization to remain implicit. Committee talk is organized as if the arguments and cases were themselves exemplars of the rule. This means that although committee procedures have the appearance of formal rationality, when we look at committee procedures as talk, they are subject to all the indeterminacies, all the 'etcetera' conditions and the 'unless' clauses which sociologists have attributed to everyday practical reasoning (Garfinkel 1967; Zimmerman 1974).

Given these situational constraints, we suggest that the rhetorical strategies of committee talk can perhaps best be characterized by the term *defensible reasoning*. This is a form of reasoning where acceptable arguments rely on establishing a single point of articulation between a rule and the behavior to which it applies. This discourse-created rulefulness then becomes a strategy with which to gain further control or negotiating power. This can be seen in Lionel's opening statement in our transcript.

Example 1

Lionel:

(1) The 'question of the 'method by which the worker wǒrks / is ŏne thing / . . . but the the 'range of 'population with whom he works is anòther / . . or fǒr whom he works . . rather / . . . is anòther //

(2) And as 'far as the IˇLEA is concerned / his responsibilities / ₁are for the five to twenty-one àge range // (3) And that's a / . . ₍ you know⌉ . . 'point we hàve to make // (4) The 'situation as 'I see / the ₁Seventies ₁being in at the mǒment / is virtually / as 'starting ˇalmost / from scṛatch. (5) The 'management committee have acquired / . . "must have acquired / . . a lot of experience from the pa̭st / . . but you 'have / . . you are 'starting again with a něw worker / . . weḷl / . . 'you've 'come back with ₁fresh trǎining, ₁Trent / so you ₁here / . . I know you've had 'some knowledge of the Seventies in the pǎst / . . . but 'really you . . . I 'think / we'd better look at you at the mǒment / as in the nature of a něw worker there / and as 'one would 'do in"any new projeçt / one has to let it grow / at a 'sensible pàce //

As the representative of the funding agency, Lionel here sets out the agency's perspective and argues that these must form the ground rules for the discussion. In utterance (2) he alludes to ILEA policy, according to which the population served constitutes the main criterion in terms of which the performance of the club will be judged. In utterance (4) he then goes on to suggest that, in its present situation, the club should be defined as a beginning venture rather than as an established organization and that allocation of staff positions must reflect this.

Categorizations of events or states of affairs such as are reflected in Lionel's talk form the principal bases of committee debate, which once proposed and left unchallenged constitute the non-negotiable facts to which subsequent arguments, if they are to be effective, should be tied. Speakers violating these principles risk being ruled out of order, or at least having their arguments disregarded.

How are these ground rules established? We will argue that defensible reasoning gains explicative power through the juxtaposition of what, by virtue of its discourse features – or in this case its syntax and prosody – is taken as a rule-like statement and some exemplar of this rule (Pollner 1979). The assumption is that presentation or knowledge of this rule can replace the detailed demonstration and that audiences can supply the necessary logical links on their own. This differs from formal reasoning which requires the establishment of demonstrably cohesive linkages between some set of basic principles and detailed exemplars.

The utterances we referred to above, (2) and (4), have the same basic logical form: (X) believes/holds that (y) is the case. The logical subjects "ILEA" and "I" (i.e., Lionel) moreover appear as constituents of prosodically subordinated topicalizing constructions that end in a rising tune and that are followed by predicate constructions carrying a falling tune. In each, the speaker seems to be raising a rhetorical question which is then answered by what follows, so that the utterance as a whole achieves an air of completeness and definitiveness that eliminates the need for further argument.

Listeners engaged in an oral exchange, who in seeking to understand what is intended must attempt to detect coherence in what is after all a complex argument, are quite likely to respond to such formal similarities. That is, they may very well take both statements as having similar rule-like force, and overlook the basic difference in truth value; that while the first utterance refers to an established ILEA rule, the other merely constitutes a personal interpretation on Lionel's part.

The syntactic and prosodic characteristics of the two utterances moreover are not isolated features. They form an integral part of a complex structure of argumentation which achieves its effect through contextualization cues conveyed at multiple levels of linguistic signalling. Thus, the prosodic structuring of utterance (1) is similar to that of (2) and (4). Utterance (3) is a relatively short semantic elaboration of the second part of (2) and carries a similar falling contour. Utterance (5) opens with a rising tune. There follow several parenthetical comments culminating in: "I think we'd better look at you at the moment as in the nature of a new worker there," which has a falling contour. The concluding two-part sequence, which starts with the conjunction "and," once more has the rise fall pattern. All in all, utterance (5) contains 96 lexical items. It includes several self-corrections and parenthetical remarks, yet at each stage in the argument the listener is guided by strategically placed prosodic markers, rhythmic patterns, hesitation pauses, and interjections. In spite of the lack of overt semantic connections between subsequent phrases, the English listener ends up with the impression that the argument hangs together and that the conclusion follows naturally from what has been said before.

With utterance (6) (example 2), the rhetorical strategy changes. It seems that, having laid down the factual bases for discussion, the speaker now sets out to list the discussibles, or, as he puts it in utterance (10): "whether at this stage we should activate the other two posts, or one or the other of them or both." He then goes on to suggest what types of arguments should be made in discussing the issue.

Example 2
    Lionel contd:
    (6) Now one thing I want to dispel is any question um of our having withdrawn, if you like, the other two posts, which are part of the establishment. (7) um . .. That could be a matter for discussion later on, if the project really failed to come up to expectations in the future. (8) But at the moment, what we're talking about, I think, is asking to see for the chairman's sake a broad description of the way you see things going. (9) I don't ask for uh a detailed day-to-day term paper, but I would like to see a broad description of the way things are going. (10) And I think on the basis of that I should be able to come to a conclusion of what to confirm . . . whether at this stage we would activate the other two posts, or one or other of them or both, or possibly follow the suggestion made earlier. (11) I'd like to hear from Trent um whether he thinks my first suggestion (personally) is feasible at this stage or what else do you think how he sees it.

The difference between this and the preceding passage is most apparent at the lexical level. Individual utterances continue to follow the basic two-part structure, but the initial topic setting clauses are now marked by phrases like: "I want to dispel" (6); "what we're talking about" (8); "I think . . . I should be able to" (10). Such expressions which have the surface form of personal appeals or opinions are completely absent from the preceding passage. Only two instances of "I" occur and these are rhetorically not very salient, since they occur in side comments or as part of complex topicalizing phrases. This does not mean that the initial passage does not reflect personal opinion, but the point is that preferences are signalled indirectly through prosody and sequential ordering of component clauses; they are not overtly lexicalized. In utterance (1), for example, two alternatives are presented, but the utterance final position and the falling contour of the second imply that the second alternative is to be preferred. Let us now turn to Trent's strategy:

Example 3

Trent:

(1) No // . . your 'first suggestion isn't // . . it's possibly feasible // . .
but as 'far as 'I'm concerned / ⌐it's to put it crude / . . it's just not on //
(2) Because at / _ _ ⌐for the 'past 'two "weeks / ⌐I've been ₁starting at
Seventies / at 10 PM // _ _ ⌐"10 AM // . . and leaving the Seventies /
around 10.15 / 10.30 // (3) which ₁means / it's 'just a 'case of
'Seventies 'sleep / and 'Seventies 'again // (4) ⌐Sure I've "got 'some
'part-timers // . . and they in ₁turn can only start up at six o'clock //
right // ⌐Which just isn't on as far as I'm concerned / (5) because / I've
been 'wearing a 'number of hats / over the 'past 'three weeks //
⌐These ₁hats has ₁been / ⌐general repairman, 'cant'een 'management /
'youth / . . a bit . . no 'very little youth work / unfortunately // . .
⌐because it's me on 'my own // (6) And ⌐you know / . . ⌐I would 'like
to 'see another 'full-time worker //

Lionel:

Here . . here again I think um your management isn't being fair to

you if it's expecting you to do all those functions uh general

repairman uh . . .

Following the methods outlined in other similar studies (Gumperz 1982), native speakers of English of professional or academic background, with some experience in public meetings, were asked to discuss or evaluate these and the succeeding passages in terms of their overall quality. They generally characterize the staff officer's talk as calm, factual, and reasoning. While some object to the overly bureaucratic tone, it was nevertheless agreed that the points are well made and the argument hangs together. Trent's performance, by contrast, tends to be judged as abrupt, impulsive, and perhaps somewhat rude. Some judges comment that, while some of his metaphors are quite apt, his statement as a whole lacks clear connections.

West Indian audiences who were similarly interviewed react primarily to what they see as the excessive stiffness and redundancy of Lionel's statements. They point to what they call the condescending tone with which the audience is being addressed in the second passage. Trent's statement is characterized as typical of West Indian argumentative style, direct but not at all impolite. It is argued that he simply says what he means, making clear how he himself feels without beating around the bush, as the staff officer does, and that his reasoning is quite clear.

How can we explain such different evaluations? What is it about Trent's performance that justifies Lionel's opinion that Trent is making a personal complaint which can be dealt with by reallocation of responsibilities among the existing staff, as well as the conflicting West Indian interpretation?

Trent's response begins with a direct assertion that the proposed solution is not feasible and cannot be carried out. He makes no attempt to justify his position either by challenging Lionel's interpretation of the rules or by reference to the day-to-day workings of the club. Instead he gives what sounds like a list of statements about how long he's been working, his lack of help, and the many functions that he has had to fill. He caps his presentation with: "I'd like to see another full-time worker" which, although presented as if it followed logically from a preceding argument, has the surface form of a personal request.

A closer look at content shows that Trent's argument does present some justifications for his position. At the end of utterance (5), which lists the many functions he has to fulfil, the phrase "very little youth work, unfortunately" is followed by "because it's me on my own" spoken in a lowered pitch register. What seems to be implied here is that, because he has to do all the other jobs, the speaker is unable to devote sufficient time to youth counselling which is his primary function. To draw these inferences, however, the listener must rely on outside knowledge of youth club work. No verbally explicit rationale is presented.

Other committee members in fact devote much time to explaining the bases of Trent's line of reasoning. Here are Kenneth's (the chairman's) comments:

Example 4
> Kenneth:
> There's also the fact and this is what Mr. Jackson is reinforcing. Um. I understand his position entirely. All of us who are full-time leaders, voluntary or paid leaders . . . all do this . . . we all get the screwdriver out . . . we all put the piece of glass in the window or fix the locks because if we didn't it would take a long time and cost too much to do it . . . but whilst he is doing that . . . and this is the problem I think the area (Youth Focus) is mainly concerned about . . . whilst he is doing that . . . he is not doing the things which jointly he is being paid to do . . . um . . . and I gather from his point of view that he feels that these are items which are restricting him from his work . . . and . . . this is the point that has to be made to (a . . .) We don't feel that enough attention has been given to that side of it. Uh. We regret I'm sure as much as you do that uh Mr. Jackson finds that this sort of thing is happening. Now . . we all know he's got to do it. He wouldn't be a good leader if he didn't. But we want to hear from the Committee about how he is going to be relieved of this so he can . . .

This passage is somewhat similar in rhetorical structure to the opening statement. The presentation starts with basic facts about what is involved in working at the club. These are then developed to provide a rationale for Trent's statements. Finally, other committee members are called upon to give their views on how the issues raised by Lionel can be resolved.

The next speaker, Keith, a West Indian community worker, presents further, more specific, arguments to illustrate the functions that the social worker must fulfil and to show why it is that one person cannot possibly do it all.

Example 5
> Keith:
> Well that's the again I think from the point of view . . . because you see this is how . . this is . . . where Mr. Jackson is gonna tell us. You

see because the position is if . . . as repairs have been coming in to do things the only way the repairman is going to get in is if Trent lets him in at 10 o'clock when the repairman comes to take care of the job. 'Cause Trent has been phoning me and saying things like . . uh . . . uh . . . "Will you uh (treat the) spending big sums of money on so and so. Yes." But it means that he has got to be there. And what you can't say . . . what I can't say . . . is that he shouldn't be there at that particular time . . . otherwise the man can't get in . . and this is precisely I think what he's saying. Rather than the other way around that he's doing the the sort of things that are stopping him from doing his job. So what I'm saying is that he's in a position at the moment where he has to be a . . uh . . a sort of thing called Dog's Body. And this . . . you know . . . a dog's body . . . and it . . it seems to me that what is likely to happen is that he can remain a perpetual dog's body. You know . . . and this is what he doesn't want to do. He wants to get on with youth work. And to get on with youth work . . . it seems to me um . . . what he's saying is that it is necessary to have other personnel with him.

Shirley, a native English professional who is called on next, provides yet more support for Trent's position.

Example 6
Shirley:
Thank you. yes. Um . . . I feel very much that as we all do that um Trent does need to have the strongest possible support . . and I think it's a situation where it's quite impossible for one person to do the job effectively. I think he's made it very clear just the hours he has to keep . . . and he really needs at least two people just on those terms. Um . . I appreciate Mr. Cox's point about the possibility of seeing how things (going) would be . . you keeping perhaps one post (on us a bit) and using up the sessions part times . . have more part-time sessions for the time being. But I would certainly . . uh . . give every support to . . . in fact I'll really feel very badly about it if he doesn't get a second worker. And somebody who he helps to choose. Very silly.

The next speaker, Max, another committee member, attempts to change the subject to ask about the population served:

Example 7
Max:
I wonder, Mr. Chairman, if I could just come in here, seeking information really. Um . . I . . I . . I don't want to (drop) in. But I've heard mention in rough terms . . . this'd only be rough terms . . . the number of older people . . i.e. say over 21 . . uh who attend the coffee

bar and the number of young people under 21. [. . .] Yes. You see . . .
what concerns me is with an establishment of three part-time . . . uh
full-time workers . . . that is extremely high.

Trent: hmmm.

Max contd:
I I I'm conscious of the problem being (   ) and I'm conscious of the
youngsters you're dealing with . . . but uh for three full-timers that
does strike me as a very high establishment . . . I mean . . uh . .
thinking of other clubs (certainly . . .) where there are three
full-timers they've got very large numbers to deal with.

Clifford, the second West Indian professional, responds to Max's
arguments by mentioning his and Trent's plans for contacting
neighborhood schools and points out that such outreach work will
not be possible unless the permanent staff is increased.

Example 8
Clifford:
Uh . . . do you mind me coming in (   ) yes. Um you're talking about
reassurance that you can take back to the Youth Committee about
um (   ). If we are to think in terms of of forward planning . . . for
instance Trent and I have been uh discussing various schemes we
would like to to get off the ground. One is um for us to go into the
schools in the neighborhood . . . and to to talk with the teachers
because they have been coming to us and inviting us in. Now um at
the present moment . . . it would be difficult for Trent to run the
coffee bar . . . um on on on his own . . . and to do this as well. Um
there are things with with employers careers . . . uh and things like
that. Now I don't see anybody . . . planning to do these things to
develop these links after having made them uh without knowing
what your complement would do.

These final remarks seem to carry the day because soon afterwards the chairman intervenes to suggest that a case has been made
and it is decided to activate one additional position.

Note that, apart from Trent, all speakers take care to build a
foundation for what they have to say, either by referring to a
previous speaker's remarks or to the basic issues defined by the first
speaker. Conclusions are justified with reference to the already
established frame of reference. Trent is alone in relying on listeners'
knowledge of how the club works and on their ability to read his
indirect contextualization cues to carry his argument. A look at the
prosodic features of what he says in example 3 shows why this

strategy is likely to be ineffective with native English listeners who are not attuned to his cultural background and his point of view. The prosody of Trent's speech in example (3) is clearly distinct from that of the native English speakers. The passage is segmented into what seems an unusually large number of tone groups. The average number of words per tone group is four, versus six for the other speakers. Tone groups moreover are separated by many more major or utterance final boundaries. Accented words for the most part carry a falling tune. The incidence of rising tunes is very low, and complex fall rises and rise falls do not occur at all. Many tone groups do have several highly stressed syllables as for example in: "For the past two weeks"; "It's just a case of Seventies sleep and Seventies again."

The interpretive import of these differences becomes clear if we look at the signalling of discourse coherence. Consider the utterance "No . . your first suggestion isn't," which is incomplete and ends in a low fall. It is followed by "it's possibly feasible" with an extra loud low fall (here indicated by doubling the accent mark). "I've been starting at Seventies at 10 PM" is followed by "10 AM" with an extra high and extra loud fall. In both these examples extra loudness seems to be used to correct a preceding assertion. Compare this with the way Lionel, in example 1, signals self-correction in "with whom he works is another or for whom he works . . rather . . . is another." In the English system self-corrections carry a fall rise and they are, if anything, lower in pitch and less loud. Loudness is associated with rude or assertive corrections of what someone else says, not with self-corrections. As used here, Trent's utterance sounds inexplicably odd or rude. Now consider utterance (4): "Sure I've got some part-timers" where "got" has the extra loudness reminiscent of the second part of the preceding utterance. By analogy with the first two utterances one might infer that the first point is implied but not overtly verbalized, so that the utterance could be understood as equivalent to "You may say I already have some additional help and I do have some part timers." This is in fact the interpretation that the West Indian listeners do make. But to make this interpretation a listener needs to be familiar with the relevant communicative convention. Those who are not are unlikely to recognize the strategy as meaningful.

Beginning with "I've been wearing a number of hats," (utterance

(5)) the rhythm slows and the number of stressed syllables per tone group decreases. The qualifying phrase "over the past three weeks," which native English speakers would expect to be less prominent, has the same rhythmic pattern. There follows the listing of more functions: "general repairman, canteen manager, youth . . a bit . .''; then after a very slight pause the rhythm speeds up and the pitch register is lowered on the last clause of "very little youth work, unfortunately, because it's me on my own." The concluding utterance "I would like to see another worker" then reverts to the higher pitch register and the slower, more highly stressed rhythm.

If shifts in rhythm and pitch register carry signalling value, then Trent's point about not having much time for youth work is indeed being set off from what proceeds, and given some prominence. The fact that it is heard as part of the list of work functions is merely due to English speakers' lack of familiarity with the relevant signalling cues. It seems that the very contextualization conventions that enable us to see Lionel's talk as logically coherent lead us to see Trent's performance as incoherent or even rude.

A detailed description of the systematic features of Trent's system would require considerably more analysis than can be given here. Our own preliminary examinations of other conversational exchanges indicate that Trent's limited use of tune, his tone grouping practices, his use of loudness for emphasis and correction, his reliance on alternating rhythmic patterns, frequent pitch register shifts and vowel elongation are regular features of West Indian talk.

Keith and Clifford, who follow the rhetorical strategies of the other English-speaking committee members, also show a number of these features. Let us look once more at the beginning part of Keith's comment in example 5.

Example 5

    Keith:

(1) This is how . . this is . . . 'where / Mr. Jackson is gonna tell us // (2) You see because / the position is if / . . . ₗas repairs have been coming in / to ₗdo things / (3) the 'only way the 'repairman is going to get in / is if Trent lets him in at ten o'clock / when the repairman comes / to take care of the job //

This passage starts with slow stressed rhythm. Utterance (1) ends with an overly loud "tell us." Then with (2) the rhythm speeds up and slows again on "to do things." Acceleration sets in once more with "if Trent" and is followed by another slowing on "when the repairman . . ."

The first part of example 9 is taken from a portion of Clifford's comments not previously cited. The second reproduces the beginning of his speech in example 8.

Example 9a

Clifford:

(1) Now / you ˌneed ⌐someˌbody to . . to / um / . . in order to really

'function / to do this work / (2) you ⌐need someone the:re / whose

role ⌐specifically / . . . I mean / ˌapart from doin' other things /

ˌwho um / can provide this ˌkind of service //

Example 9b

(1) uh . . . do you ⌐mind me coming in ( ) // 'yes // um / you're talking

ˌabout reassurance /that you can ˌtake ˌback to the 'Youth

Committee / about um ( ) //

Example 9 begins with slow stressed rhythm. In the first tone group of utterance (1) "somebody" is picked out by a rise in the pitch register and stress on both syllables of "body." The same is true for both syllables of "function" in the next full tone group. In the following short tone group, both "do" and "work" are accented. Utterance (2) begins with "you need someone there" with a rise in pitch register on "need" and vowel elongation on "there." Then the aside, "I mean apart from doing other things" is accelerated and the rhythm slows again with the last phrase "who can provide . . ."

In 9b Clifford claims the floor, speaking very softly at normal speed with the phrase "you're talking about reassurance." The rhythm slows and there is a stress on "about" and the two last syllables of "reassurance" after which the tempo increases to normal.

It seems clear that at a purely phonetic level Keith and Clifford employ many of the same signalling cues as Trent. But the discourse functions for which these are used differ. To begin with, note the high incidence of meta comments such as "you can't say"; "and this is precisely"; "the fact is"; "what I'm saying is"; "I mean." Rhythmic and pitch register shifts seem to be used primarily for two functions: (a) to mark clauses identified by those comments, such as for example asides, qualifying statements and the like, and (b) to mark prominent portions of a clause. In other words, those signs have functions which are equivalent to accent placement and tune, and pitch register shift in native English speech. This is quite different from Trent, who seems to use these signs to mark larger discourse segments and whose conventions seem to conflict with native English speakers' expectations about how interclausal relations are to be marked.

Trent's situation is illustrative of the communicative issues that affect professionals in industrial societies. To be effective, an individual must compete for scarce resources under conditions where decision making processes need to be put on record and made available for outside scrutiny. While Trent is a non-native speaker of English and a member of an economically depressed minority group, his problem cannot simply be described as one of learning a new language or adapting to a new culture. Our analysis shows that grammar and accent as such are not at issue, nor is it simply a matter of acculturation or learning to make a logical argument. Both Keith and Clifford have strong accents, their talk is full of hesitation pauses and incomplete sentences, yet they are very effective communicators.

Understanding in oral exchanges is always significantly affected by perception of discourse salience and by inferential processes that rest on unverbalized presuppositions. The very constraints under which individuals communicate favor the emergence of strategies governing what is to be put in words, how it is to be made salient and what can be left unsaid. Over time, these strategies tend to be conventionalized and to become part of the standards by which effectiveness is judged. Such conventions can be learned only through face-to-face interaction. Ethnic differences in communicative strategies affect the contextual and interpretive conditions that make this type of learning possible.

10

Fact and inference in courtroom testimony

JOHN J. GUMPERZ

In August 1978, a sixteen-month-old child was brought to the emergency room of a large US Navy hospital in Southern California for treatment of burns. The personnel present were the emergency room nurse, a physiotherapist, a medical corpsman and Dr. A, the Navy physician in charge. Dr. A is one of many medical officers, natives of the Philippines, who are attached to various Navy units currently stationed at the base. Unofficial sources state that about 40% of the junior physicians who are the primary care providers in this and other US Government hospitals in the Western United States, and who come into most direct contact with patients, are speakers of Philippine and other Asian languages. To the extent that this is true, this case raises communicative issues that have considerable importance for health care delivery in this region.

Dr. A speaks Aklan as his native tongue and in addition is fluent in Tagalog, the national language, and in English. His career pattern is similar to that of many other American physicians of South-East Asian background. He had been admitted to the University of California after secondary school training at home, where he was educated in English and Tagalog. Upon completion of a BA course in science, he enlisted in the US Navy, serving three years as a clerk at various bases in the United States and abroad, including Vietnam. Having decided to seek medical training, he applied to schools in the United States and the Philippines, but for financial reasons he was forced to take his medical training at the University of the Philippines. After a year's internship in the Philippines, he returned to the United States. He spent a year in the Los Angeles area, applying for admission to internship programs until he secured a second internship appointment at a US Public

Health Service hospital in the East. Subsequently he received a
commission as a medical officer with a Navy mobile construction
battalion. By August 1978 he had been with this unit about a year,
partly in California and partly in Okinawa. Dr. A had thus had
many years of work experience in English-speaking settings. His
professional goal is to specialize in radiology and a few months
after the incident which forms the subject of this paper, he was in
fact transferred to a major Navy radiology facility in the Eastern
United States.

On the day of the incident, Dr. A was serving in the emergency
room as part of the regular rotating tour of duty, which he shared
with all other medical officers at the base. The nurse who called
him into the examination room had informed him that the child's
parents, who were both present at the examination, claimed that
the child was suffering from sunburn as a result of having been left
uncovered in the open. Dr. A's diagnosis, submitted in a report
written in excellent English, cites evidence of first and second
degree burns in the front and back of the child's upper trunk. He
writes that at the time of the examination the child was alert and in
no respiratory distress. Skin color, eyes, temperature, and pulse
were judged normal. There was thus no evidence of shock. The
customary treatment for secondary burns was prescribed. While
treatment was being administered in the adjoining room, Dr. A
questioned the parents, who told him that the child had been eating
and taking her formula normally. He then released the child in the
parents' care, recommending that she be given plenty of fluids and
be brought in once a day for treatment until the burns were healed
and that the hospital be notified immediately if her condition
worsened.

Approximately six hours later, in the early evening, the same
child was brought back to the emergency room. A second Navy
doctor and a civilian physician employed by the Navy, who by then
had relieved Dr. A, now determined that the child was suffering
from severe dehydration and was covered with third degree burns.
She was immediately sent to a nearby civilian hospital for treatment
at a proper burn centre, but died on her way there.

Dr. A was informed of the child's death by phone later on the
same evening. In retrospect he states that he had been terribly upset
at the news and had at first been unable to understand what had

happened. When he returned to the hospital the next morning, everyone seemed concerned. It was obvious by then that the burns had been intentionally inflicted, yet the unexpected death seemed difficult to explain given the fact that the initial symptoms did not seem serious. The previous evening's local radio news broadcast had focused attention on the incident and negligence in the emergency room had been suggested as a possible cause of death. In the course of the morning, Dr. A was called away from his duties to be interviewed by the FBI agent charged with investigating the case. The interview lasted for not more than fifteen minutes and was interrupted at least twice while Dr. A left the room to deal with patients. Part of the interview time, moreover, was consumed with questions about Dr. A's background. Except for a brief interchange in the hospital corridor with the physician who had examined the child on her second visit, Dr. A did not take part in any professional discussion of the case in the days immediately after the incident.

The FBI agent's handwritten record of the interview, which is part of the trial documents, consists of a total of twelve brief numbered notes. No verbatim transcript exists. Here are some samples.

1. Nurse takes vital signs. Parents say due to sunburn.
4. Suspicious of child abuse, because burn pattern, but feels he must take parent story at face value.

Clearly these are no more than mnemonic notations, summarizing the agent's own understanding of what Dr. A said. Item 12 on the sheet ends with the phrase "very positive evidence" which is set off from the text and put in quotes presumably to suggest that these were the actual words used.

As a result of the investigation, the child's father, who, as was later determined, was actually the stepfather not the natural parent, was indicted on a charge of first degree murder. Dr. A testified for the prosecution. In his testimony, which agreed with the substance of his written diagnosis, he stated that the symptoms as they appeared during the first examination were not severe enough to warrant immediate hospitalization and that at the time there had been no reason to question the parents' sunburn story. Dr. A's testimony was supported by that of the emergency room nurse and a medical corpsman who assisted him. The trial ended in a conviction of second degree manslaughter and a sentence of four years imprisonment for the father. The leniency of this sentence caused considerable public criticism.

Sometime after the trial, Dr. A, who by then had already taken up his new Eastern post in radiology, was called back to California to face an indictment of perjury. A written FBI report, which formed the basis for this indictment, contained considerably more detail about the emergency room incident than the original hand-written notes. Among other things, the report states that medical personnel who had seen the child on her second visit had expressed suspicions that the earlier treatment had been negligent, that Dr. A in his interview with the investigating agent had admitted that, given the location of the burns, he had suspected child abuse all along, but that he had disregarded these suspicions in spite of the fact that the risk to the child was severe enough to warrant hospitalization. Dr. A is furthermore reported as saying that he had had problems in facing parents suspected of child abuse on another occasion, and that it was his personal philosophy not to become involved in child abuse accusations until he was a hundred percent certain that he had "positive evidence" for such a conclusion. The phrase "positive evidence" which appears in the agent's handwrit-ten notes, is here again put in quotes. But it is now embedded in the narrative text in such a way as to give the impression that the entire section of the FBI report, not just the one phrase, reflects Dr. A's own words. The district attorney's indictment relies on this second report in charging that Dr. A's sworn testimony in the child abuse trial directly conflicted with what he had admitted to the FBI agent and that he had therefore perjured himself to cover up his own negligence.

The perjury indictment attracted considerable public attention, both locally and in the California Filipino community. Relations between the Navy base and local residents had long been tense and the case could be regarded as still another indication of the poor quality of patient care at the hospital. The presence of the large Filipino community in this conservative suburban area was another complicating factor. Local papers, as well as the Filipino commun-ity Press, gave the trial day-by-day coverage. Members of the Filipino community accused the district attorney of racism, of trying to make Dr. A the scapegoat to cover up his own failings in prosecuting the child abuse case. A number of Filipinos kept up a daily silent vigil in the courtroom to remind the general public of their concern.

The Press reports made much of the prosecution medical evidence describing the severity of the burns, which by then were known to be due to thermal fluid. Color photographs of the child's horribly disfigured body, taken about six hours after death, had been blown up to poster size and remained hung up in the courtroom for most of the trial. The child's mother, aged twenty-two, who by then had divorced the stepfather, her second husband, and had again remarried, testified for the prosecution. She had been present during the first examination and had at the time neither contradicted the sunburn story, nor asked that the child be hospitalized. Yet her detailed description of her child's gradually deteriorating condition and her expression of hatred and contempt for her ex-husband, as well as for Dr. A, were given detailed coverage. The FBI agent also testified extensively about what Dr. A had admitted to him. Finally, the prosecuting attorney in the child abuse case, who never interviewed Dr. A except on the witness stand, was quoted as stating emphatically that he felt sure, on the basis of the trial record, that Dr. A had perjured himself.

In attempting to counter this sort of evidence, the defense faced three distinct problems: the medical question of the severity of the burns, the conflict between Dr. A's testimony and the FBI report, and Dr A's decision not to hospitalize the child. Pediatric specialists familiar with child abuse cases were called in to show that it is quite possible for third degree burns not to appear on the skin until several hours after exposure. The experts showed 'before and after' pictures of similar burn cases to counter the prosecution's photographic evidence and to demonstrate how the surface symptoms of third degree burns can gradually spread over the body in the hours after the initial injury. There were therefore no compelling medical reasons to invalidate the original diagnosis. While a seasoned pediatrician, familiar with modern American conditions, might have suspected child abuse right away, an emergency room physician, particularly someone trained in the Philippines where such cases are rare, would not ordinarily have the experience to do so.

The second and third problems were more difficult to deal with. At first glance, the matter seemed to be simply one of who was telling the truth: the physician or the FBI agent. This is how the case was generally viewed. The fact that Dr. A's testimony was supported by the other medical personnel who had assisted him did not count for too much, since they could also be accused of trying to avoid blame. Given the publicity that the case had received moreover, and the known conservative attitudes of the judge and jury, it seemed like a dangerous strategy simply to question the veracity of the official reports.

It was at this stage that one of the defense attorneys noted what he termed as Dr. A's "funny" use of pronouns on certain occasions. He agreed that Dr. A speaks English well and for the most part has only a very slight foreign accent, but there seemed to be something about the way he talked at times that struck him as strange and that frequently seemed to make it difficult for him to follow Dr. A's argument. A linguist was called in as an expert to go over the evidence and look into the issue of comprehensibility. The remainder of this paper will illustrate the nature of the analysis employed, and discuss what the findings imply for our knowledge of the interplay of cultural and linguistic presuppositions in interpreting conversations on the one hand, and for our understanding of some key problems of social interaction in modern multiethnic societies on the other.

The communicative issues arising from the case can be summarized as follows. How can we explain the many factual discrepancies between the agent's report and what Dr. A claims to have said and done? How can we defend the view that someone who, like Dr. A, has almost perfect command of English can nevertheless fail to communicate what at first glance seem like relatively simple facts: namely, whether or not he had always suspected child abuse, or why he had not questioned the parents' story. What solutions can linguistic analysis offer to deal with these problems?

Ultimately it will have to be shown that something in Dr. A's cultural and communicative background may at times create difficulties in interaction with English monolinguals. Yet the linguistic problem is too complex to be described simply as a matter of discovering evidence for what students of second language acquisition call interference: the transfer of grammatical features from the speaker's native language to the second language. Established methods for determining interference rely on direct comparison between the grammatical systems of the two languages in order to isolate points of difference, and on tests to determine individual speakers' ability to comprehend and produce grammatical sentences in the two languages. In the present case, however, the problem is not one of abstract competence in sentence grammar. Grammatical oddities appear only in some contexts, not in others, so that one could argue that the speaker might merely be pretending not speak well when it suits his purposes. This was in fact the rationale the prosecuting attorney attempted to use when questioning the defense comprehensibility argument in court.

A more promising approach is to focus directly on empirical evidence, i.e., to search for specific conversational exchanges or texts which exemplify relevant communicative difficulties and then to rely on interpretive analysis to discover differences in the actual processes of conversational inference through which interpretations are made. Once this is done, one can go on to determine whether or not variant interpretations can be explained in terms of participants' linguistic and sociocultural background (Gumperz 1975). A number of such texts are available. Apart from Dr. A's written diagnosis, the agent's notes and the formal FBI report, we have verbatim transcripts of Dr. A's testimony at the child abuse trial as well as the transcripts of an extensive Navy hearing held to explore both Dr. A's background and the circumstances surrounding Dr. A's diagnosis at the first examination.

These materials provide an initial basis for discovering possible sociolinguistic sources of communication problems. Additional oral talk was recorded in the course of an informal discussion in a university setting. Participants included Dr. A, his lawyer, and two Filipino acquaintances, a physician practicing in Northern California and a local real estate agent, as well as a native American, married to a Filipino nurse, who had taken an interest in the case. Both Filipino Americans were native speakers of Aklan. The aim of this session was to obtain samples of Dr. A's natural speech, talking to other Filipinos and to English monolinguals. The linguist guided the discussion, shifting topics so as to generate a variety of speech styles ranging from casual exchanges to discussions approximating the formality of an official hearing.

Analysis began with an examination of the written transcripts of the Navy hearing and the child abuse trial, totalling about 150 typed pages, to discover oddities of language usage which, when they occur in face-to-face encounters, might cause difficulties either in sentence comprehension or in following the speaker's line of reasoning. Several distinct types of verbal exchange are represented, as in the following examples (Q = question; A = answer).

(A) Brief answers to questions:
1. Q. On the textbooks, were they in English?
2. A. Yes.
3. Q. And were the textbooks American textbooks or European textbooks?
4. A. As far as I can recall, most of them are written by American authors.
5. Q. Do you recall the names of some of the textbooks that dealt with burns?
6. A. Well, I don't remember having a textbook exclusively on burns, but most of the topics on burns are incorporated within the main topic, usually surgery.

(B) Simple narrative passages:
1. A. Well, first thing, I saw some skin . . some dead
2.   skin on the border, especially on the left scapular
3.   area, and so I . . seeing the dead tissue . . it's
4.   very important to remove the dead tissue, which is
5.   a source of infection, so that it was the first
6.   procedure to do. And, since the child was crying,
7.   Miss Terrel suggested *to do* a whirlpool, *although*
8.   I had in mind to cut around the edges, but since
9.   she suggested that it might be better for the child
10.   to do a whirlpool, *as far as* areadment [sic], then I
11.   consented to it, just to minimize the crying of the
12.   child. So I told her just to bring the child to
13.   the whirlpool.
14. Q. After whirlpool treatment was begun, what did you
15.   recommend as a treatment?
16. A. Then I recommended application of sulphurmilon
17.   [sic], *of which* I was familiar with, *as far as*
18.   the ointment, but Miss Terrel again suggested
19.   *to use* Pherasein [sic] because she told me that
20.   it's less painful *in applying*, so I walked to
21.   the medical cabinet and read the label and it
22.   says 'indicated for second and third degree burns',
23.   and then with that I said, "Well, okay go ahead
24.   and try it."

Dr A's speech in both sections is near native in style, with the possible exception of the italic phrases, which present no comprehension problems. The bulk of available transcripts are similar to examples A and B so that American readers are unlikely to encounter difficulties in following the testimony as a whole. However, the incidence of linguistic oddities increases as we go to cognitively more complex passages, particularly those where the speaker is asked to describe the academic content of the courses he took, or explain medical symptoms to lay audiences who are not familiar with technical terminology. Sections C and D illustrate this type of situation.

(C)　1. A. The only experience I had *as far as actual manage-*
　　2. *ment of the cases* that we see as we were working in
　　3. the emergency room during our clerkship and intern-
　　4. ship. We manage minor burns *from kerosine* burns or
　　5. from . . . specially during New Year's or New Year's
　　6. Eve *where they* usually have a lot of firecrackers,
　　7. we got a lot of burns *from them* and so we'll manage
　　8. *them* with, or I can remember we always *wash them*
　　9. and apply *them* with sulfamylon and dressings. That's
　　10. the standard that *we were lectured on for usually*
　　11. first and second degree burns. *As far as* the
　　12. actual management of extensive burns like the
　　13. third and second, more than . . these *were*
　　14. cases that *have* to be hospitalized. We don't have
　　15. a chance to . . .

(D)　1. A. Respiratory distress is a sign or symptom where the
　　2. patient has difficulty breathing *which* could be
　　3. secondary to obstruction of the airway; obstruction,
　　4. *secondary again, it could* be a foreign body, it could
　　5. also have secondary to fluids into the pleural cavity,
　　6. *hence* causing collapse of the lung, *or* you could
　　7. have also within the pleural *cavity air* . . .

These examples differ significantly from the first two. The former involve short answers to questions or narrative accounts detailing temporal sequences of events that recount incidents which must have been discussed many times before. In the second set of passages, by contrast, the speaker must either recall several separate incidents exemplifying a single theme, locate each incident in time and space, show how each relates to the topic at hand, and tie them all into a cohesive sequence, or, as in D, give a single definition to cover and relate a complex set of symptoms.

It is in fact the speaker's use of linguistic forms to indicate the relevant cohesive links, his choice of conjunctions, pronouns, noun or verb complements, and other connecting or qualifying phrases that seem to create comprehension difficulties for the native English listener. Some typical instances are: the only experience I had *as far as* actual management of the cases that we see as we were working . . . (C1–2); *as far as* the actual management of extensive burns (C11–12); we manage burns *from* kerosine (C4); that's the standard that *we were lectured on for usually* first and second degree burns (C9–11); obstruction, *secondary again, it could* be a foreign body (D3–4); where the patient has difficulty breathing which could be secondary to obstruction of the airway (D2–3); it could also *have secondary* to fluids into the pleural cavity, *hence* causing collapse of the lung, *or* you could have also within the pleural *cavity air* (D4–7). In C7 and C8 the same pronoun *them* appears three times in succession, first to refer to firecrackers and then to burns, but the text itself contains no surface indication of what the intended referent is.

Communication difficulties can and do of course also affect monolingual encounters. Speakers regularly correct themselves or are corrected by others and in the heat of an exchange, important information may sometimes be lost. This is especially true for situations of stress, when, for whatever reasons, participants are uncertain of what persuasive strategies to employ. The problem might therefore simply be a matter of individual performance. In the Navy hearing, and to a lesser extent in the court testimony, the witness frequently shifts topic in mid-sentence and starts anew or fails to complete a clause altogether. Lines 4 and 8 in example C show instances of this phenomenon. Yet the passages in question tend to be marked in the transcript by dots or are otherwise semantically identifiable by abrupt, unprepared for topic shifts or topic recycling. No such signs of conversational repair occur with the grammatical oddities listed above. The witness seems to be unaware of the fact that what he says may not be clear to others.

Grammatical oddities, moreover, do of course also occur in conversations among native English speakers who share the same background. What is special about the present case is that the same expressions are repeatedly found in similar discourse environments. Odd uses of *as far as*, for example, occur in at least ten instances;

which is repeatedly used in place of a conjunction like *and*; *it* very frequently appears where we would expect a new clause starting with *this is* or *that is*. It is quite unlikely that such regularities reflect isolated errors. A more likely explanation is that we are dealing with an established style of English, used in informal situations by Filipino-English bilinguals. Like South Asian English, this speech variety has grammatical characteristics of its own that ultimately derive from local languages such as Tagalog and Aklan. We can then explain the intermingling of grammatical oddities with long, native English-like passages by assuming that the former reflect instances of style or code switching triggered by the interview situation.

Independent evidence for the existence of such a variety of Filipino English and for the claim that its use in public settings may be misunderstood by native English-speaking Americans comes from a linguistic study of another court trial (Naylor 1980). The case, which arose out of occurrences at a large Midwestern Veterans Administration hospital, shows a number of similarities to the present one. An unusually large number of instances of respiratory arrest that could not be attributed to specific ailments had occurred in the intensive care unit. Computer studies revealed that one or the other of two Filipino nurses had been on duty when the incidents occurred. The two nurses were subsequently indicted for conspiracy and murder. They were charged with injecting a poison, Pavulon, into the patients through the intravenous tubing attached to the patient's arm, thus causing death through asphyxiation. Apart from the claim that the nurses had done what they were accused of doing in order to protest working conditions at the hospital, no definite criminal motive was established. Nor was any direct evidence presented to link the nurses to the supposed crime. The prosecution's case was entirely circumstantial and hinged on the credibility of the nurses' testimony as compared with that of the experts.

In discussing the linguistic issues involved, Naylor points to contrastive grammatical studies (Schachter and Otanes 1972) which reveal significant differences between the Tagalog and English verb tense and aspect systems, and goes on to cite extracts from courtroom testimony suggesting how these differences could affect the witness's credibility. She writes:

Tagalog verbs operate on a system of aspectual distinctions and tense is not
marked on the verb as it is in English verb forms. For example, in the
following representation of the Tagalog aspect system, *is eating* and *was
eating* are not differentiated in the Tagalog verb form. Similarly, *ate, have
eaten* and *had eaten* are not differentiated and are expressible by one and
the same Tagalog verb form.
　　－ Begun: kakain 'will eat'
　　＋ Begun: － completed: kumakain 'eats/is eating/was eating'
　　　　　　　＋ completed: kumain 'ate/has eaten/had eaten'
It is no surprise, therefore, that the most frequently occurring form of
interference in the testimonies of the two nurses, whose native language is
Tagalog, was the wrong choice of tense form of the verb in English. They
were constantly using present tense forms when past tense forms were
called for. For example:
　　Q. Would you say that the two of you were close friends during that
　　　　period of time?
　　A. I would say that we are good friends but we are really not that
　　　　close because I don't know her and we don't know each other that
　　　　much.
While this answer might have been true in the past, the fact is that she had
earlier testified that they had become very close friends in the course of
going through together and sharing the same ordeal. Therefore, phrased in
the present tense, the statement was false and apparently a contradiction of
earlier testimony.

Our transcripts reveal many similarly odd uses of tense. The
question and answer sequences of the Navy hearings, moreover,
illustrate the interpretive problems that can result:

(E)　　1. Q. Then I am to understand that you were really not
　　　　2.　　aware at the time that you were working at Port
　　　　3.　　Hueneme that a list of rules, or what we call the
　　　　4.　　Navy Instructions existed governing the day to
　　　　5.　　day conduct and operation of the hospital?
　　　　6. A. *I'm* not aware.
　　　　7. Q. You weren't aware of that?
　　　　8. A. Maybe they have, but I was not told where to find
　　　　9.　　it or where I could find it.

The next extract from Dr. A's testimony at the child abuse trial
reflects the kind of evidence that led to the perjury indictment.

(F)　　1. Q. At the end when you released the child to the parents,
　　　　2.　　did you feel that the cause of the injuries was
　　　　3.　　sunburn or thermofluid burn?
　　　　4. A. I still feel it was due to sunburn.
　　　　5. Q. Did you suspect that it was thermofluid burn?

6. Mr. Davidson: Objection, your Honor, it's been asked and
7. answered.
8. The Court: Sustained.

In both these examples a past tense question receives a present tense reply. The questioner then repeats the question using a past tense verb, presumably because he is unsure of how to interpret the switch to the present tense.

Given that the question in F refers to the initial diagnosis, a listener who understands the witness's perspective might argue that what he really meant to say was something like: "I still feel that at the time I was justified in concluding that it was due to sunburn." Yet the present tense verb *feel* here makes it appear as if Dr. A claimed he still believed the sunburn explanation in spite of subsequent developments and in spite of what he himself has said on other occasions. Taken by itself, the answer certainly sounds contradictory.

Since the two unconnected court cases show communicative problems attributable to similar linguistic sources, we have a prima facie case for arguing that language differences may affect the non-native speakers' treatment in court. But in newspaper accounts of such cases, as well as in many linguists' descriptions, the difficulties are identified in general rhetorical terms as relating to the 'credibility' of a witness's testimony. Dr. A's case suggests that the issue is more complex than that. If we look at the hearing in its entirety, we find that he is quite an effective witness. Particularly in the relatively informal Navy hearing, where he is given scope in formulating his statements, his explanations are on the whole quite convincing. What he is accused of is perjury. The indictment charges that his courtroom testimony conflicts with specific statements he made to the FBI agent concerning the time he first suspected child abuse and concerning his reasons for accepting the parents' account of what caused the child's burns. The question we must therefore ask is: how can different inferences of what it is that a speaker intends to convey in any one point in time arise? This will require a somewhat broader sociolinguistic treatment of interpretive processes than the linguist's contrastive grammatical analysis can provide.

Consider the following three additional examples from the Navy hearing:

(G)		1.	Q.	It's the testimony by Lieutenant Commander Gilbert
		2.		that you did not attend the briefing.
		3.	A.	*Yes.*
		4.	Q.	You did attend it?
		5.	A.	No.
		6.	Q.	Why didn't you attend that lecture?

(H)		1.	Q.	Did you check to determine if dehydration
		2.		was present?
		3.	A.	Yes.
		4.	Q.	What steps did you take to determine that? If it
		5.		was there or absent?
		6.	A.	When the child came, I initially examined the patient
		7.		and I noted the moistness of the tongue, sunken eyes,
		8.		the skin color, and everything was okay.
		9.	Q.	Are you suggesting that there were no sunken eyes?
		10.	A.	*No.*
		11.	Q.	I think we better slow down a little bit more and make
		12.		sure the record . . . did you observe sunken eyes?
		13.		No.

(I)		1.	Q.	Now, you indicated that you informed the nurse. Why did
		2.		you inform the nurse?
		3.	A.	Because I didn't know who to call in cases like that.
		4.	Q.	Now that indicates that you must have had some prior
		5.		knowledge of having to report cases where there is
		6.		apparent or suspected child abuse. What is the basis
		7.		for your – that understanding?
		8.	A.	*No I don't have* – I don't think I was aware that I had
		9.		to report it but I just wanted. The reason that I
		10.		referred to Dr. Gilbert was a confirmation of my
		11.		suspicions.
		12.	Q.	Let me back up. Let me turn back the record a bit.
		13.		You indicated you knew you had to report a suspected
		14.		child abuse – child abuse cases – isn't that correct?
		15.	A.	To report?
		16.	Q.	Yes.
		17.	A.	No.
		18.	Q.	Okay. Let's go back.
		Captain Biehl, senior member:
		19.		My understanding of the witness's testimony is that he
		20.		was seeking consultation on a case of child abuse that
		21.		he suspected. A medical consultation. Not reporting
		22.		requirements.

Here we find clear indications that listeners have problems in determining what is intended. In line H9 the examiner seems unaware as to what the child's symptoms were. His question: "Are you suggesting there were no sunken eyes?" received a brief ambiguous "No." The uncertainty is cleared up only when the question is once more rephrased in the positive.

Dr. A's narrative account of previous experiences with child abuse in example I evokes a series of queries probing for conflicts with earlier testimony concerning his acquaintance with official regulations governing reporting of child abuse. His reply to these queries creates further uncertainties. The "No I don't have" in line 18 could simply be a false start. The dashes in the transcript suggest that the court reporter noticed signs of hesitation. But the surface form is typical of certain kinds of English replies. As such it could refer to the main question or the earlier introductory portions in lines 14–5. A reader who has the leisure to examine the text at length might conclude, as the senior member did in line 119, that what Dr. A intended to say was that he called in his colleague only for a medical consultation. But the listener whose on-the-spot interpretation is subject to the time constraints of oral exchanges is likely to be put off by the fact that Dr. A's reply does not have the form one would expect of an answer to the main question.

Similar difficulties occur in response to a complex question concerning a third person's testimony in G3. Given the way the question is phrased, American audiences might expect a more explicit reply such as "that's right, I did not." As it stands the "yes" is ambiguous, since it could refer either to Lt. Com. G's testimony or to Dr. A's attendance at the briefing. The follow-up question about the briefing is then again answered with a simple "no," which at first glance sounds contradictory. Without further analysis it is difficult to determine in these cases whether it is the questioner who fails to understand or whether the witness is simply being evasive, or both.

At issue in these examples are variant perceptions of coherence or ways of integrating items of information into consistent themes or lines of reasoning. How do these affect interpretation and what is their relationship to interactants' linguistic background? If we could isolate linguistic environments where certain morphological or syntactic relationships are regularly and predictably realized in ways that reflect native language patterns, we could have clear evidence of the influence of linguistic background. But, as our discussion of the first four examples indicates, the incidence of linguistic oddities in our transcripts, while clearly detectable, is relatively low and related to the interactive setting and the cognitive complexity of the discourse task rather than to linguistic environment as such. Many of the ungrammatical expressions that do occur, moreover – constructions such as "lack of oxygen at the tissues," "because of that basis," "it also has different approaches as far as that treatment," "I applied to the medical school for enquiry of how to complete my medical requirements" – do not cause comprehension difficulties. Grammatical analysis by itself therefore cannot account for interpretive differences. We must examine how grammar interacts with other kinds of interactive signs.

Coherence judgments are matters of conversational inference, which like grammatical rules involve automatic processes not readily subject to conscious control. Yet interpretation at this level of discourse is subject to a far greater degree of optionality than grammaticality judgments. While utterances in isolation are either acceptable (i.e., grammatical or appropriate) or not, what counts as coherent in discourse depends on the range of interpretive options interactants recognize, on the frames of reference they adopt, and on how they use them to select among possible interpretations and eliminate sources of ambiguity.

In negotiating interpretive frames participants rely on contextualization of linguistic cues in interaction with other types of contextual and social background knowledge. The process is hierarchically ordered in such a way that higher order inferences form part of the input to more specific lower order judgments. Inferencing begins with determination of what the basic interactive goal and likely outcomes are. The resulting expectations are then either confirmed or revised by more local inferences that control turn taking, speech act sequencing, maintenance of thematic continuity, and similar aspects of discourse management. At any one point in the interaction, therefore, interpretation of intent is dependent on logically prior relational decisions on how utterance segments fit into what precedes and on what is likely to follow. It is this process of reconciling levels of signalling, and the extent to which participants in an interaction can jointly negotiate interpretive frames rather than the mere evaluation of utterances, in relation to some a priori standard of appropriateness or context-free grammatical rules, that determine the effectiveness of an interaction. When contextualization conventions are not shared, miscommunication may occur, and this may lead to pejorative judgment or conversational breakdown.

It is evident from both the proceedings of the Navy hearing and the perjury trial that all participants agree on higher level interactive expectations. However, when it comes to reconciling these expectations with utterance level relational signs, listeners frequently encounter problems. Note for example that the "no" in H10 could be read as "no, that's not what I am suggesting" or "no, there were no symptoms of sunken eyes." Such inherent ambiguities are often resolved by culturally specific discourse conventions which in interethnic settings can lead to misunderstandings. Dr. A, throughout his testimony, tends to use brief yes and no answers in place of more explicit replies such as "yes that's right" or "no I don't," which suggests that he may not be aware of the potential ambiguity in his replies.

The reply "I initially examined the patient and I noted the moistness of the tongue, sunken eyes, the skin color, and everything was okay" in lines H6–8 illustrates the additional semantic issues. The witness has been maintaining all along that the child did not show any serious symptoms apart from the actual burns; but the phrase "sunken eyes," here used as an object of "note," seems to imply that the child did in fact show sunken eyes. The concluding phrase "and everything was okay," however, contradicts this inference, so that the utterance as a whole is ambiguous and can be taken as a sign of inconsistency. Since his testimony is otherwise quite clear and consistent, it is unlikely that this effect was intended. Observe that the first and the third of the three complements of the verb "note" do not presuppose a preexisting condition. This suggests that there may be interpretative problems. The past participle qualifier "sunken" carries a secondary connotation of reference to an already existing condition. This is not the case with noun qualifiers such as "moistness." In Tagalog or Aklan, the ambiguity would not have arisen. We can assume that presuppositions based on native language syntax are here carried over into English so that Dr. A was most probably unaware that his choice of the qualifier "sunken" could be misinterpreted as carrying

temporal connotations by listeners who do not share these presuppositions.

The next passage reveals additional insights into the role of
grammar in inference:

(J)   1. Q. Any other sources of burns that you've observed?
        2. A. Occasionally from gasoline and kerosine burn because as
        3.   far as the situation there, most of the house don't have
        4.   any natural gas or electric or stove as here. They use
        5.   kerosine instead as a means of fuel for cooking. The
        6.   reason why I'm saying this is because this hospital
        7.   where I had my training is a government hospital, so
        8.   most of the patients that go there are the poverty
        9.   stricken patients, *unlike* you going to a medical center,
       10.   it's usually the middle class who go where you don't
       11.   have this problem.

In this and other portions of the Navy hearing which deal with
his medical training in the Philippines, the witness repeatedly
compares the situation there with American conditions. He makes
such a contrast in the first part of his answer to the question about
burns, and, from the way he begins the second part, we would
assume that a similar strategy is intended. Yet his words in lines
8–11 are difficult to fit into this frame. We do not know whether
poverty-stricken patients are being compared with middle-class
patients or whether government hospitals in the Philippines are
compared with medical centers in the United States. Given the
overall context, the second possibility is the more likely one, but
there is little in the surface structure of the utterances used that
confirms that this is what is meant.

Note that for someone reading it for the first time the passage is
clearly too long to be processed as a whole. It must first be chunked
into relevant information units. In doing this kind of chunking we
rely on our knowledge of both syntax and prosody (i.e., intonation,
stress, and rhythm), sounding out the words to try alternative
groupings. An English speaker following this strategy will have
serious difficulty in assigning the "*unlike*" in line J9 to any one
clause. If "unlike" is treated as part of the preceding clause, i.e., as
part of a noun phrase complement "unlike you", the rest of the
passage makes no sense. The alternative is to treat it as introducing
a new clause "unlike you going to the medical center." This would
be in line with what the context indicates that he intends to say. But

the resulting clause lacks a subject phrase specifying what it is that is being compared.

To discover how a native speaker might understand this sentence, a Filipino linguist was asked to read and diagram it. She provided the following analysis ([= major utterance boundary; (= clause boundary; | = side comment):

> [most of the patients that go there are the poverty-stricken patients) unlike (you going to a medical center) | it's usually the middle class who go | (where you don't have this problem)

and commented that the English "unlike" is used here like a Tagalog equational marker which functions to tie together two independent clauses but is independent of either. English has no equivalent for such construction. The closest English translation would be a clause like "this is unlike."

To understand the passage in the way it was intended, a listener would have to assume that the subject of this clause was not overtly expressed.

Now such syntactically and semantically incomplete clauses present no problem with inferences like "maybe they have" in E8, which is readily understood to mean "maybe they have a list of rules." We assume that in these cases listeners, relying on English rules of anaphoric deletion, search their memory of previous talk to find a phrase that is both coreferential and fills the incomplete syntactic frame. The actual words used in E3–4 are "a list of rules . . . existed." But this is sufficiently close to fit. In the present example, however, there is no single noun phrase which fits the syntactic frame. Contextual expectations suggest that the entire preceding passage beginning with line J5 is being referred to so that what is meant is something like "this is unlike you going to a medical center." But according to English syntax "this is" would not have been subject to anaphoric deletion. Tagalog differs from English in that it follows different principles of clause structure (Foley 1980).

To summarize our argument so far, we assume that the colloquial style regularly used by speakers of Philippine languages when talking to others of similar background follows taken-for-granted contextualization conventions patterned on those of their native languages. The effect is most noticeable in the principles of interclausal syntax involved in ellipsis, in the signalling of sententiality and of given and new information as well as in the discourse conventions which determine the semantic range of responses in verbal exchanges. When used in public settings with native American monolinguals these conventions can lead to communication problems. Having been trained in the United States, Dr. A has good control of expository English and for the most part his testimony is effective. But formal interrogation – where testimony is challenged, statements must be justified, and precise definitions adhered to – presents special problems, as Danet has shown (1980) and as Bresnahan's work on the Philippine nurses' case discussed above confirms (1981). It is well known from our studies of language acquisition that, in such situations of stress and cognitive complexity, first language influences are most likely to affect performance in the second language.

The principles of interclausal syntax we have referred to are not ordinarily dealt with in sentence level grammatical analyses and as a result tend not to be covered in standard contrastive grammars. But our hypothesis that syntactic presuppositions lead to different discourse processing strategies can be tested directly with informants. When native speakers of Tagalog were asked to read the "unlike" passage in example J, they tended to identify "unlike" as part of the following clause and their oral reading confirmed this. The hypothesis concerning "sunken eyes" could not be tested with English data, since informants' responses in elicitation situations tend to be determined by what they know of native English norms. But when the passage was translated into Tagalog, one informant suggested that, while the phrase judged in isolation presupposes a preexisting condition, this presupposition does not hold for the sentence as a whole.

Many other features in the testimony which strike native American speakers as odd can be explained by differences in the grammatical mechanisms for signalling interclausal and interphrasal linkages and in the degree of sententiality of particular syntactic constructions. The phrases "as far as a readment. . ." in B10, "as far as the ointment . . ." in B17–18, "as far as actual management of the cases . . ." in C1–2 all function as independent clauses and are readily integrated into the text if we supply the predicate filler "is concerned." The phrases "burns from kerosine" in C4 and "burns from them" become clearer if we insert the verb form "caused." In D2 the text reads: ". . . the patient has difficulty breathing which could be secondary to obstruction . . ." An English speaker would be inclined to interpret the "which" as referring to breathing rather than to the entire preceding clause. Similar odd uses of "which" are found throughout. The following segment: "Obstruction, secondary again, it could be a foreign body" in C4 becomes more readily interpretable if we resegment and supply fillers as follows: (this) secondary obstruction could again be a foreign body . . ."

The view of grammar as guiding the way we segment the stream of talk, keep track of information, tie message elements into a thematic whole, and as suggesting what additional, nonverbalized information needs to be brought in to make judgments of communicative intent, provides a useful perspective for examining the role of the other more commonly discussed grammatical distinctions in communication. In a recent grammatical analysis of pronouns in Samal, a Southern Philippine language that resembles Tagalog in this aspect of grammar, Geoghegan (1981) argues that the system can be fully described in terms of the following three abstract semantic oppositions: speaker included (S) vs. speaker excluded (S̄); hearer included (H) versus hearer excluded (H̄); and singular versus plural.

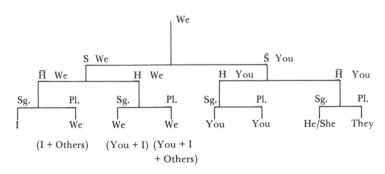

The lowest level of the taxonomy above gives a paradigmatic representation of Samal pronouns in terms of these dimensions and their English translation equivalents. This same structure obtains for Tagalog. We note that English lacks terms for many of the categories in this system. Samal and Tagalog, on the other hand, have no words to correspond to the gender distinction in the English third person singular pronouns.

Such paradigmatic representations cannot, however, directly account for the semantics and pragmatics of language use. There are more abstract, subtle interlanguage differences, which, like those discussed before, go beyond what is actually expressed in words, but have more direct communicative import.

Taxonomies, as anthropologists have shown, reflect complex, hierarchically arranged clusters of semantic features. These have the property of permitting terms at higher levels of the hierarchy, in appropriate contexts, to be employed to refer to information that in other contexts would be signalled by more specific or more highly marked lower level terms. As Frake (1969) points out, we might use the phrase "would you like some food" in offering someone a ham sandwich, relying on our knowledge that a ham sandwich is a kind of food. Geoghegan notes that Samal speakers commonly elevate some of the lower level terms given in Fig. 1 to less marked, more general uses in situations where speakers, for politeness or similar reasons, seek to distance themselves from the message or minimize personal involvement. Extending this line of reasoning to pronoun usage, we can ask whether in Tagalog an equivalent of English "we" can, apart from its specific usage, be used either as a general cover term for "I" and "we," or at the highest taxonomic level to mean something like the English "one" in "one cannot tell." Such a strategy may be at work in the following example from Dr. A's testimony:

(K)   1. Q. Okay. For the record, would you please describe that
        2.   one case you observed.
        3. A. I cannot exactly recall the kind or the month, but the
        4.   case is a three-year-old black boy who was brought in by the
        5.   mother for a fractured femur. Now I cannot recall whether
        6.   it was the left or the right. I cannot remember. A
        7.   fracture of the midshaft of the femur. And the boy was
        8.   – *we* had it X-rayed and *we* documented the fracture and
        9.   while the boy was sitting on the –
Captain B. senior member:
        10. Q. One clarification, "*we*"?
Counsel for the party:
        11. Q. Who do you mean by "*we*" doctor? When you said *we* doc-
        12.   umented the fracture –

13. A. I mean – I'm sorry – I stand corrected. I docu-
14. mented the fracture by sending him to X-ray and *we* saw
15. a converse fracture.

The witness here shifts to "we" in the midst of his first person narrative, in connection with the X-ray examination. When asked to clarify, he corrects himself but then, in the very next sentence, he once more reverts to "we" to talk about X-ray findings. It seems evident that this pronoun shift is not a matter of conscious choice, but rather an automatic grammar-like reaction. Perhaps, as Geoghegan's discussion of marked and unmarked pronouns would imply, the underlying motive is to signal personal distance and to distinguish descriptions of impersonal laboratory procedures from statements about personal opinions or self-initiated actions.

The issue here is that grammatical categories often reflect more than one underlying semantic dimension. These dimensions are hierarchically ordered, but their ordering differs across languages, so that when more specific or marked terms are used at higher taxonomic levels, listeners' perceptions of what the underlying ordering of semantic categories is may lead to different surface interpretations of what a term refers to. For example, a Filipino's use of "we" to refer to a single person in this case is a matter of the personal dimension having more saliency than the plurality dimension. This can be misunderstood by native English speakers, for whom plurality has priority.

A. L. Becker's recent study of person in Kawi, or Old Javanese, the member of the Austronesian family for which we have the most complete historical records and to which Tagalog also belongs, supports this hypothesis (1980). By means of a subtle and elegant analysis of language in context, Becker shows that personal distance constitutes a semantic dimension, which in one form or other underlies the grammatical categories as well as the lexical systems of most Austronesian languages and which, for speakers of these languages, is more basic than number and tense categories so prominent in Western European languages.

A similar discourse perspective also helps to clarify the interpretive import of grammatical contrasts in the verb system. The fact that Tagalog is an aspect language and that aspect systems are structurally distinct from tense systems should not be taken to mean that Tagalog speakers do not signal temporal distinctions and

English speakers do not indicate duration. Utterances in any language, if they are to be understood at all, must be locatable in time and space. At the level of discourse there are other signalling options, apart from morphology, to accomplish this, through adverbs, qualifiers, or indirectly through lexical choice. Nonetheless, the grammar of a language, as Roman Jakobson (1971) has pointed out, distinguishes between what is obligatorily coded in surface structure and what is optionally signalled and/or encoded by indirect means. From the perspective of conversational inference, one could by extension argue that a grammar sets interpretive priority on what will be distinguished, rather than simply forces polar semantic contrasts. Having aspect verbal systems, then, means that Philippine languages predispose speakers and hearers to attend to whether or not actions are begun and completed, as an interpretive priority, with less focus on time per se. English speakers, by contrast, only secondarily indicate aspectual matters, giving priority instead to locating actions in time. Dr. A's tendency to answer past tense English questions with such nominally present tense expressions as "I'm not aware" (E6) and "I still feel" (F4), accordingly, can be seen to be a function of the fact that time is not inflected in Tagalog verbs – with time as a lower interpretive priority, it is as if it is all the same to him, relatively speaking, whether he uses an English past or present verb form. In effect, this can then 'free up,' so to speak, the English present/past alternates for interpretive use as indicators of greater or lesser personal distance from the message, by analogy with the pronoun examples above. Present tense forms in Philippine English, under this view, possibly stand in unmarked, hierarchical relation to present/past forms which have literal time reference at the lower taxonomic level. A native speaker of English, approaching such messages with interpretive priority on time designations, will correspondingly miss any personal distance meanings and instead hear time designations which are inconsistent with what is already known about the action in question – and thus attribute more general inconsistency, if not also lack of credibility, to his utterances, intentions, veracity, and the like.

We have argued that, while there is no one-to-one relationship between grammar and interpretation, grammar enters into inference both at the clause level and at the level of interclausal relations. At this latter level however it is only one of several factors that serve to convey information on such matters of conversational management as semantic scope, sententiality, utterance focus, given and new contrasts, aspect modality, and others that inter into our perceptions of coherence. Apart from higher level discourse conventions, prosody also plays a crucial role in these signalling processes. To show how this works we now turn to an analysis of tape recorded materials from the informal group discussion in the university office.

The passages in question come from the latter part of the discussion after the general aspect of the case had been talked about and the linguist had explained and illustrated his approach to miscommunication with examples from the written materials. Participants had come to know each other somewhat by that time and the atmosphere was relaxed, so that issues that had been introduced quite formally before could now be brought up again in a more informal, personalized manner. The talk turns around what is likely to happen in the trial and what the prosecution's goals are.

Our prosodic transcription marks major and minor tone group boundaries, accent placement within a tone group, salient aspects of tempo, relative pitch register of the tone group, hesitation pauses, and conversational overlap.

(L) 1. A. Of course my .. lawyer will be there / on his toes /

2.   to make sure those questions are .. ⌈   / properly /

3. Q.   ⌊yea

4. A. asked / and ah .. so on ... ⌈// but .. ah ... / ⌈those

5. Q.   ⌊ya ya know

6. A. things / I .. I was ah / .. answering it / ⌈when I was a

7.   witness // then he turns around and .. / file a perjury

8.   case against me // ᵃᶜᶜapparently the ah .. / my former

9.   lawyer said / had they gotten / a first degree

10.   murder / in this case / ᵃᶜᶜthis perjury case / ⌈wouldn't

11.   even been brought up //

12. Q. Ah bec .. Why is that? Because then the district

13.   attorney would have been happy?

14. A. ⌐yèa

15. Q. ⌊⋅This is like

16. A. (   ) ⌐ˢᵉᵉ they were after / ⌐for a

17.   first degree murder / and he only got a manslaughter //

18. Q. How much?

19. A. Only a maximum of / ⌐four years // and then / ⌐after that /

20.   three months later / ʰᵉ turns around and file a perjury

21.   case against me they said that . . . / my testimony / was

22.   so crucial / ⌐to the case / that the jury / could not

23.   give him / a first degree mùrder //

24. Q. Well, that's not your business.

25. A. ⌐Yèa

26. Q. Its

27. A. ⌊ⁱⁿ the first place / ⌐he boobooed the case / because

28.   he only established / ⌐one set of burn // ᵈᵉᶜ had he brought

29.   up / ᵈᵉᶜ the possibility / of second burning / then that

30.   would . . / be a good . . / a good . . / basis / ⌐for first

31.   degree / ⌐or even second degree / because . . . / yè

32.   know . . / there's a premeditated ⌈ah . . . / ⌐element there

33. Q.   ⌊yea

34. A. but . . // they said / it's all the same / and therefore /

35.   because of that basis . . / I committed perjury / ⌐just

36.   to cover myself // ⌐but it's not the càse / because . . /

37.   ⌐what was mòtive // since I only saw // that much of buŕn //

38. Q. Yea what . . you didn't know the people

39. A. Nò

40. Q. Did they ever say anything about motives? Why should

41.   you perjure yourself?

42. A. Well that's their mo . . / the district attorney/

43.   assùme . . / that it is / ⌐one set of burn // ⌐you saw

44.   the picture / ⌐right //

45.   Q.   yea but ⌈uh . .

46.   A.   ⌊now / ⌈if

47.   you saw that picture . . / at the time / at twelve

48.   o'clock . . .// there's no question about it // that it

49.   is a case of child abuse / ⌈but I did not / ⌈I have

50.   nothing to cover up / because I did not see / those

51.   pictures / I mean those . . / extensiveness of burn /

52.   ⌈at twelve o'clock . . . / right //⌈now if they assume . . /

53.   that that burn / or those burns / were . . there / at

54.   twelve o'clock . . // and I missed it . . . // and that's

55.   their theory / that they're working on // therefore I

56.   was . . / I I I ah / covered myself to commit perjury //

57.   but . . the fact that / ⌈I did not see it . . / as

58.   confirmed by the nurses . . / and the physical therapist /

59.   ⌈what is my motive //

Monolingual Americans, noting that the English is near native, are likely to interpret the talk in terms of their own prosodic system. In this system, an intonational clause or tone group, i.e., a stretch of speech bounded by an intonation contour, carries one or more accentual peaks, each located on a specific syllable. The placement of accents within a tone group, the tune or direction of the pitch change which marks the accent (i.e., falling or rising) as well as the relationship of accents within and across tone groups, all play a role in signalling thematic continuity. So that the listeners' interpretive strategies concentrate on locating accented syllables and on evaluating the semantic import of perceived relationships among accented items in relation to information signalled through grammar and lexicon (see Gumperz 1982, chapter 5).

Anyone approaching what Dr. A says with these presuppositions will notice a number of oddities. While many of the utterances show what seem like normal contours, there are many places where the stream of talk is divided into an unusually large number of tone groups. These tone groups separate sequences which on semantic grounds we might consider as part of the same information unit.

For example in "had they gotten a first degree murder in this case" (L9–10), in "because he only established one set of burn" (L27–8), and in "had he brought up the possibility of second burning" (L28–9), verb and verb complement and noun and noun complement constructions are separated by tone group boundaries. Elsewhere, as in "he turns around and file a perjury case against me they said that" (L20–1), what seem like more than one information units are run together into a single tone group, and the tempo accelerates.

Only two types of stress are heard for the most part: low falling and high falling. Except in one or two idiomatic expressions we find no instances of the rising or complex rising–falling and falling–rising contours which are so characteristic of American and British English. If, following American English convention, we interpret perceived stress as accent, we will find that accent placement is quite different from what we would expect. The phrase "perjury case" occurs on three separate occasions, each time with the accent on "case." In American English such unexpected accent placement carries contrastive connotations, such as in "I mean perjury accusation, not perjury case." On the other hand in the sentence "I committed perjury just to cover myself" (L35–6), where the context would lead us to expect a contrastive accent either on "my" or the verb "cover" or on both, only "self" is accented.

The interpretive problems are compounded when we examine interclausal relations in longer sequences. In lines L6–8 Dr. A states that the testimony he gave on the witness stand led to the perjury indictment. Here "answering it" and "perjury case" are items of new information which we would expect to be foregrounded; instead it is the word "witness" which carries the major stress. In line L10 the phrase "in this case" qualifies the preceding phrase "a first degree murder" and we would expect it to be deaccented. Instead it is this qualifying phrase which we hear as carrying the main stress. Similarly in "they were after for a first degree murder and he only got a manslaughter" (L16–17), the last phrase is the punch line which gives the main point, yet the entire passage is divided into three short tone groups each carrying relatively strong stress, of which the second seems highest. In lines L21–3 we have a similar sequence of short accented tone groups.

The above features lend the passage a prosodic monotony which at times makes it difficult for listeners relying on American English strategies to determine what is being emphasized and where the argument is going. A detailed examination of Dr. A's prosodic system and its relation to that of Philippine languages is beyond the scope of this paper. But the passage does show enough regularities to suggest that this is not simply idiosyncratic. Rather than relying on accent placement and on accentual contouring of syllables within a group, Dr. A seems to treat the tone group as a prosodic whole. Emphasis and interclausal connections are signalled by varying the pitch, register, and tempo of an entire group and by increasing the number of tone group boundaries, while the accent placement seems constrained by syntactic and lexical structure and does not convey pragmatic information. Preliminary investigations show that these patterns are sufficiently similar to those used by other speakers of Philippine English, and to Tagalog, to suggest that they are not simply idiosyncratic but can be regarded as systematic features learned through previous communicative experience.

The last portion of the passage in lines L43–58 illustrates how grammatical presuppositions can interact with prosodic signals to heighten the likelihood of actual misunderstanding. Dr. A here is referring to the enlarged photos of the horribly disfigured corpse taken in the night, about six hours after the child's death – that is about 12 hours after the first emergency room examination, which had taken place at noon. These are the photos that had been displayed in the courtroom throughout the trial. What he intends to convey – and the context is quite clear on this – is that the symptoms he and his emergency room team saw when they first examined the child were quite different from those that appear in the photo enlargements. Both Dr. A and his audience know that no photographs of the child's burns as they appeared on the first examination were ever taken.

Now consider lines L43–8. In the initial question, "picture" is accented. There are no qualifying phrases so that the listener must infer what picture is being referred to. In line L47 "picture" is once more stressed and in the following line "o'clock" and "question" are stressed. The casual American listener here is most likely to assume that there was indeed a picture which had been taken at 12 o'clock. In fact American audiences who have listened to this portion of the tape and who were then asked "was there a picture which was taken at 12 o'clock?" generally answer "yes, there was." But then, beginning in line L49, Dr. A goes on to deny that he saw the picture. In line L50 he intends to say "they assume that there were severe burn symptoms at 12 o'clock and that I failed to see this" but what is stressed is "I missed it" while the following phrase, "that's their theory that they are working on," which is new information, is destressed. Finally in the last two lines he once more emphasizes that he did not observe any severe burn symptoms and then adds the new information that other team members have confirmed his diagnosis. Yet this important new information is again destressed prosodically. Moreover neither here nor elsewhere are the relevant sentences topicalized syntactically in a way that would make the information stand out.

Note that the passage deals with a matter he must have rehearsed many times in the year since the incident occurred. Yet, when faced with the need to be specific about causative and temporal events and when the topic is emotionally stressful, he automatically reverts to the discourse conventions with which he is most familiar. The impression this conveys to the casual listener is one of inconsistency, as if the speaker were hedging to try to keep from admitting the truth.

To illustrate the distinction between native American interpretation and what we – given what we know about Dr. A's background and contextualization conventions – could infer he really intended to say, we present another rendering of the last portion of the preceding passage in ordinary English punctuation. Our own interpretations of what he intended to say are given in italics within braces, either above the relevant item or, in the case of insertions, on the line.

1.   A. You saw the picture, right?

2.   Q. Yea

3.   A. Now if $\left\{{one \atop you}\right\}\left\{{had\ seen \atop saw}\right\}\left\{{such\ a \atop that}\right\}$ picture $\left\{{and\ it\ had\ been\ taken \atop at\ the\ time}\right\}$

4.   at twelve o'clock, there $\left\{{would\ have\ been \atop is}\right\}$ no question

5.   about it that it $\begin{Bmatrix} was \\ is \end{Bmatrix}$ a case of child abuse. But I

6.   did not, I have nothing to cover up. Because I did

7.   not see $\begin{Bmatrix} any\ such \\ those \end{Bmatrix}$ pictures .. I mean $\begin{Bmatrix} that \\ those \end{Bmatrix}$ extensiveness

8.   of burn at twelve o'clock, right? Now if they

9.   assume that $\begin{Bmatrix} those \\ that \end{Bmatrix}$ burns, or those burns, *were* there

10.   at twelve o'clock, and I missed it, and that's their theory

11.   that they are working on, therefore {*they assume*}

12.   I was I I I $\begin{Bmatrix} committed\ perjury\ to\ cover\ myself \\ covered\ myself\ to\ commit\ perjury. \end{Bmatrix}$

13.   But the fact {*is*} that I $\begin{Bmatrix} had \\ did \end{Bmatrix}$ not $\begin{Bmatrix} seen \\ see \end{Bmatrix}$ $\begin{Bmatrix} such\ burns \\ it, \end{Bmatrix}$

14. $\begin{Bmatrix} this\ was \\ as \end{Bmatrix}$ confirmed by the nurses, and the physical

15.   therapist {*so*} what $\begin{Bmatrix} was \\ is \end{Bmatrix}$ my motive?

The bulk of the changes we have made can be justified in terms of the features of Philippine English and of Tagalog which we have discussed in this paper. Thus "one" (line 3) counts as the unmarked equivalent of "you." The several alternations in verb forms reflect the distinctions between tense and aspect systems. Substitutions of indefinite articles for definite articles are motivated by the fact that Philippine languages do not have to distinguish between definite and indefinite articles. The "they assume" in lines 8–9 reflects differences in deletion conventions like those discussed in the 'unlike" passage (see p. 181). Similarly in lines 3 and 4 we have inserted verbal phrases in places where tone group boundaries in the oral message yield what in American English sound like syntactically incomplete clauses. Finally the phrase "covered myself to commit perjury" is one which occurs in several other places in the oral transcript, and which involves possible systematic differences which lead English speakers to hear this as a causative statement.

Apart from the problem of miscommunication, there remains the further issue of why it was that Dr. A did not question the parents' explanation of what caused the sunburn. Recall that, even though the initial burn symptoms were not severe, the pattern of burns was such that an American pediatrician, experienced with burn injuries, would probably have questioned the parents' explanation from the outset. But Dr. A was an emergency room physician, not a specialist in pediatrics. Moreover neither he nor other physicians trained in the Philippines have had much experience with child abuse cases. The FBI agent in his report argued that it was Dr. A's personal philosophy not to question parents' explanations of their children's symptoms. He connects this with the claim that Dr. A had had previous problems with parents over child abuse, as if to say he acted as he did to avoid further difficulties with patients.

Dr. A's acceptance of the parents' statements in the emergency room examination was discussed in some detail during the group discussion in the university office. All Filipinos present there agreed that child abuse is almost unknown in the Philippines. There is in fact no word for child abuse in Philippine English or in the native languages. It was argued that if child abuse did occur it would most probably go unreported, since those actually involved would not be likely to admit it. Outsiders would not report it because of local norms against any action that could be interpreted as interference with others' personal or family life. It is interesting to note that Dr. A as well as his Filipino friends repeatedly employed expressions such as "I personally believe" when talking about such matters. When asked to explain, their explanations referred to "what we were taught" or "what was expected of us in the Philippines." Thus they seemed to be using "personally" in connection with differences in social norms rather than to refer to individual preferences.

Questions of individual versus group identity and of non-interference in family affairs are treated in some detail in the anthropological literature on interpersonal behavior in the Philippines, which emphasizes the closeness of family bonds, and the extent to which individuals identify with their family in relations with outsiders. As Guthrie and Azores (1961) put it, "the success or disgrace of one member is felt by all." Moreover, a great deal of value is placed on social acceptance, and overt criticism counts as a denial of social acceptance (Lynch 1973). A public official would therefore be especially hesitant to question any one person's statement concerning family matters. To do otherwise would risk causing 'hiya' which as Lynch points out is the discomfort resulting from jeopardizing one's social acceptance by criticizing family practice. The FBI agent's interpretation of Dr. A's statements as indicating a personal motive is therefore merely an instance of the kind of cross-cultural misunderstanding that frequently leads us to misread others' motives.

We have demonstrated that many aspects of Dr. A's behavior can be explained by his linguistic and cultural background. The features in question are automatic and not readily subject to conscious control. They do not affect his written performance, yet they are likely to recur whenever he is faced with complex oral communicative tasks, so that, in spite of the fact that he speaks English well, he is more likely than native speakers of English to be misunderstood in such situations. This does not of course constitute proof that he was actually misunderstood. In the relatively informal Navy hearing where he was represented by his own counsel and questions were rephrased whenever problems arose, there clearly was no miscommunication. On the contrary his testimony was quite effective. But given the nature of the FBI interview, given the fact that only 15 minutes were allotted to obtaining the information, that part of the meeting was taken up with questions about background, and that there was hardly any time at all to go into details, check out initial impressions, and clear up possible misunderstandings, the likelihood that misunderstanding did occur is very high.

The miscommunication argument was a major plank in the defense attorney's argument in the perjury trial. The argument was accepted by the majority of the jurors and ultimately led to the dismissal of the perjury charges.

But the case is of more than mere local importance. During the last decade professionals of Asian background have come to occupy an increasingly important role in health care as well as in industry and in other areas of public affairs. Difficulties that may arise in their contacts with Americans under such conditions as we have described can be a major factor in interethnic tensions. Although the problems we have described are communicative in nature, the question is not one of appropriate discourse styles. Misunderstandings are mutual and they are as much due to the nature of the situations in which interactions take place, and to the standards by which words are evaluated, as to linguistic or cultural facts as such.

11

A cultural approach to male–female miscommunication

DANIEL N. MALTZ AND RUTH A. BORKER

Introduction

This chapter presents what we believe to be a useful new framework for examining differences in the speaking patterns of American men and women. It is based not on new data, but on a reexamination of a wide variety of material already available in the scholarly literature. Our starting problem is the nature of the different roles of male and female speakers in informal cross-sex conversations in American English. Our attempts to think about this problem have taken us to preliminary examination of a wide variety of fields often on or beyond the margins of our present competencies: children's speech, children's play, styles and patterns of friendship, conversational turn-taking, discourse analysis, and interethnic communication. The research which most influenced the development of our present model includes John Gumperz's work on problems in interethnic communication (1982) and Marjorie Goodwin's study of the linguistic aspects of play among black children in Philadelphia (1978, 1980a, 1980b).

Our major argument is that the general approach recently developed for the study of difficulties in cross-ethnic communication can be applied to cross-sex communication as well. We prefer to think of the difficulties in both cross-sex and cross-ethnic communication as two examples of the same larger phenomenon: cultural difference and miscommunication.

The problem of cross-sex conversation

Study after study has shown that when men and women attempt to interact as equals in friendly cross-sex conversations they do not play the same role in interaction, even when there is no apparent element of flirting. We hope to explore some of these differences, examine the explanations that have been offered, and provide an alternative explanation for them.

The primary data on cross-sex conversations come from two general sources: social psychology studies from the 1950s such as Soskin and John's (1963) research on two young married couples and Strodbeck and Mann's (1956) research on jury deliberations, and more recent sociolinguistic studies from the University of California at Santa Barbara and the University of Pennsylvania by Candace West (Zimmerman and West 1975; West and Zimmerman 1977; West 1979), Pamela Fishman (1978), and Lynette Hirschman (1973).

Women's features
Several striking differences in male and female contributions to cross-sex conversation have been noticed in these studies.

First, women display a greater tendency to ask questions. Fishman (1978:400) comments that "at times I felt that all women did was ask questions," and Hirschman (1973:10) notes that "several of the female–male conversations fell into a question–answer pattern with the females asking the males questions."

Fishman (1978:408) sees this question-asking tendency as an example of a second, more general characteristic of women's speech, doing more of the routine "shitwork" involved in maintaining routine social interaction, doing more to facilitate the flow of conversation (Hirschman 1973:3). Women are more likely than men to make utterances that demand or encourage responses from their fellow speakers and are therefore, in Fishman's words, "more actively engaged in insuring interaction than the men" (1978:404). In the earlier social psychology studies, these features have been coded under the general category of "positive reactions" including solidarity, tension release, and agreeing (Strodbeck and Mann 1956).

Third, women show a greater tendency to make use of positive minimal responses, especially "mm hmm" (Hirschman 1973:8), and are more likely to insert "such comments throughout streams of talk rather than [simply] at the end" (Fishman 1978:402).

Fourth, women are more likely to adopt a strategy of "silent protest" after they have been interrupted or have received a delayed minimal response (Zimmerman and West 1975; West and Zimmerman 1977:524).

Fifth, women show a greater tendency to use the pronouns "you" and "we," which explicitly acknowledge the existence of the other speaker (Hirschman 1973:6).

Men's features
Contrasting contributions to cross-sex conversations have been observed and described for men.

First, men are more likely to interrupt the speech of their conversational partners, that is, to interrupt the speech of women (Zimmerman and West 1975; West and Zimmerman 1977; West 1979).

Second, they are more likely to challenge or dispute their partners' utterances (Hirschman 1973:11).

Third, they are more likely to ignore the comments of the other speaker, that is, to offer no response or acknowledgment at all (Hirschman 1973:11), to respond slowly in what has been described as a "delayed minimal response" (Zimmerman and West 1975:118), or to respond unenthusiastically (Fishman 1978).

Fourth, men use more mechanisms for controlling the topic of conversation, including both topic development and the introduction of new topics, than do women (Zimmerman and West 1975).

Finally, men make more direct declarations of fact or opinion than do women (Fishman 1978:402), including suggestions, opinions, and "statements of orientation" as Strodbeck and Mann (1956) describe them, or "statements of focus and directives" as they are described by Soskin and John (1963).

Explanations offered
Most explanations for these features have focused on differences in the social power or in the personalities of men and women. One variant of the social power argument, presented by West (Zimmerman and West 1975; West and Zimmerman 1977), is that men's dominance in conversation parallels their dominance in society. Men enjoy power in society and also in conversation. The two levels are seen as part of a single social-political system. West sees interruptions and topic control as male displays of power – a power

based in the larger social order but reinforced and expressed in face-to-face interaction with women. A second variant of this argument, stated by Fishman (1978), is that while the differential power of men and women is crucial, the specific mechanism through which it enters conversation is sex-role definition. Sex roles serve to obscure the issue of power for participants, but the fact is, Fishman argues, that norms of appropriate behavior for women and men serve to give power and interactional control to men while keeping it from women. To be socially acceptable as women, women cannot exert control and must actually support men in their control. In this casting of the social power argument, men are not necessarily seen to be consciously flaunting power, but simply reaping the rewards given them by the social system. In both variants, the link between macro and micro levels of social life is seen as direct and unproblematic, and the focus of explanation is the general social order.

Sex roles have also been central in psychological explanations. The primary advocate of the psychological position has been Robin Lakoff (1975). Basically, Lakoff asserts that, having been taught to speak and act like 'ladies,' women become as unassertive and insecure as they have been made to sound. The impossible task of trying to be both women and adults, which Lakoff sees as culturally incompatible, saps women of confidence and strength. As a result, they come to produce the speech they do, not just because it is how women are supposed to speak, but because it fits with the personalities they develop as a consequence of sex-role requirements.

The problem with these explanations is that they do not provide a means of explaining why these specific features appear as opposed to any number of others, nor do they allow us to differentiate between various types of male–female interaction. They do not really tell us why and how these specific interactional phenomena are linked to the general fact that men dominate within our social system.

An alternative explanation: sociolinguistic subcultures
Our approach to cross-sex communication patterns is somewhat different from those that have been previously proposed. We place the stress not on psychological differences or power differentials, although these may make some contribution, but rather on a notion

of cultural differences between men and women in their conceptions of friendly conversation, their rules for engaging in it, and,
probably most important, their rules for interpreting it. We argue
that American men and women come from different sociolinguistic
subcultures, having learned to do different things with words in a
conversation, so that when they attempt to carry on conversations
with one another, even if both parties are attempting to treat one
another as equals, cultural miscommunication results.

The idea of distinct male and female subcultures is not a new one
for anthropology. It has been persuasively argued again and again
for those parts of the world such as the Middle East and southern
Europe in which men and women spend most of their lives spatially
and interactionally segregated. The strongest case for sociolinguistic subcultures has been made by Susan Harding from her research
in rural Spain (1975).

The major premise on which Harding builds her argument is that
speech is a means for dealing with social and psychological
situations. When men and women have different experiences and
operate in different social contexts, they tend to develop different
genres of speech and different skills for doing things with words. In
the Spanish village in which she worked, the sexual division of
labor was strong, with men involved in agricultural tasks and
public politics while women were involved in a series of networks
of personal relations with their children, their husbands, and their
female neighbors. While men developed their verbal skills in
economic negotiations and public political argument, women became more verbally adept at a quite different mode of interactional
manipulation with words: gossip, social analysis, subtle information gathering through a carefully developed technique of verbal
prying, and a kind of second-guessing the thoughts of others
(commonly known as 'women's intuition') through a skillful monitoring of the speech of others. The different social needs of men and
women, she argues, have led them to sexually differentiated
communicative cultures, with each sex learning a different set of
skills for manipulating words effectively.

The question that Harding does not ask, however, is, if men and
women possess different subcultural rules for speaking, what
happens if and when they try to interact with each other? It is here
that we turn to the research on interethnic miscommunication.

Interethnic communication

Recent research (Gumperz 1977, 1978a, 1978b, 1979; Gumperz and Tannen 1978) has shown that systematic problems develop in communication when speakers of different speech cultures interact and that these problems are the result of differences in systems of conversational inference and the cues for signalling speech acts and speaker's intent. Conversation is a negotiated activity. It progresses in large part because of shared assumptions about what is going on.

Examining interactions between English-English and Indian-English speakers in Britain (Gumperz 1977, 1978a, 1979; Gumperz et al. 1977), Gumperz found that differences in cues resulted in systematic miscommunication over whether a question was being asked, whether an argument was being made, whether a person was being rude or polite, whether a speaker was relinquishing the floor or interrupting, whether and what a speaker was emphasizing, whether interactants were angry, concerned, or indifferent. Rather than being seen as problems in communication, the frustrating encounters that resulted were usually chalked up as personality clashes or interpreted in the light of racial stereotypes which tended to exacerbate already bad relations.

To take a simple case, Gumperz (1977) reports that Indian women working at a cafeteria, when offering food, used a falling intonation, e.g. "gravy," which to them indicated a question, something like "do you want gravy?" Both Indian and English workers saw a question as an appropriate polite form, but to English-English speakers a falling intonation signalled not a question, which for them is signalled by a rising intonation such as "gravy," but a declarative statement, which was both inappropriate and extremely rude.

A major advantage of Gumperz's framework is that it does not assume that problems are the result of bad faith, but rather sees them as the result of individuals wrongly interpreting cues according to their own rules.

The interpretation of minimal responses

How might Gumperz's approach to the study of conflicting rules for interpreting conversation be applied to the communication between men and women? A simple example will illustrate our basic approach: the case of positive minimal responses. Minimal re-

sponses such as nods and comments like "yes" and "mm hmm" are
common features of conversational interaction. Our claim, based
on our attempts to understand personal experience, is that these
minimal responses have significantly different meanings for men
and women, leading to occasionally serious miscommunication.

We hypothesize that for women a minimal response of this type
means simply something like "I'm listening to you; please continue," and that for men it has a somewhat stronger meaning such
as "I agree with you" or at least "I follow your argument so far." The
fact that women use these responses more often than men is in part
simply that women are listening more often than men are agreeing.

But our hypothesis explains more than simple differential frequency of usage. Different rules can lead to repeated misunderstandings. Imagine a male speaker who is receiving repeated nods
or "mm hmm"'s from the woman he is speaking to. She is merely
indicating that she is listening, but he thinks she is agreeing with
everything he says. Now imagine a female speaker who is receiving
only occasional nods and "mm hmm"'s from the man she is
speaking to. He is indicating that he doesn't always agree; she
thinks he isn't always listening.

What is appealing about this short example is that it seems to
explain two of the most common complaints in male–female
interaction: (1) men who think that women are always agreeing
with them and then conclude that it's impossible to tell what a
woman really thinks, and (2) women who get upset with men who
never seem to be listening. What we think we have here are two
separate rules for conversational maintenance which come into
conflict and cause massive miscommunication.

Sources of different cultures

A probable objection that many people will have to our discussion
so far is that American men and women interact with one another
far too often to possess different subcultures. What we need to
explain is how it is that men and women can come to possess
different cultural assumptions about friendly conversation.

Our explanation is really quite simple. It is based on the idea that
by the time we have become adults we possess a wide variety of
rules for interacting in different situations. Different sets of these
rules were learned at different times and in different contexts. We

have rules for dealing with people in dominant or subordinate social positions, rules which we first learned as young children interacting with our parents and teachers. We have rules for flirting and other sexual encounters which we probably started learning at or near adolescence. We have rules for dealing with service personnel and bureaucrats, rules we began learning when we first ventured into the public domain. Finally, we have rules for friendly interaction, for carrying on friendly conversation. What is striking about these last rules is that they were learned not from adults but from peers, and that they were learned during precisely that time period, approximately age 5 to 15, when boys and girls interact socially primarily with members of their own sex.

The idea that girls and boys in contemporary America learn different ways of speaking by the age of five or earlier has been postulated by Robin Lakoff (1975), demonstrated by Andrea Meditch (1975), and more fully explored by Adelaide Haas (1979). Haas's research on school-age children shows the early appearance of important male–female differences in patterns of language use, including a male tendency toward direct requests and information giving and a female tendency toward compliance (1979:107).

But the process of acquiring gender-specific speech and behavior patterns by school-age children is more complex than the simple copying of adult "genderlects" by preschoolers. Psychologists Brooks-Gunn and Matthews (1979) have labelled this process the "consolidation of sex roles"; we call it learning of gender-specific 'cultures.'

Among school-age children, patterns of friendly social interaction are learned not so much from adults as from members of one's peer group, and a major feature of most middle-childhood peer groups is homogeneity; "they are either all-boy or all-girl" (Brooks-Gunn and Matthews 1979). Members of each sex are learning self-consciously to differentiate their behavior from that of the other sex and to exaggerate these differences. The process can be profitably compared to accent divergence in which members of two groups that wish to become clearly distinguished from one another socially acquire increasingly divergent ways of speaking.[1]

Because they learn these gender-specific cultures from their age-mates, children tend to develop stereotypes and extreme versions of adult behavior patterns. For a boy learning to behave in a masculine way, for example, Ruth Hartley (1959, quoted in Brooks-Gunn and Matthews 1979:203) argues that:

both the information and the practice he gets are distorted. Since his peers have no better sources of information than he has, all they can do is pool the impressions and anxieties they derived from their early training. Thus, the picture they draw is oversimplified and overemphasized. It is a picture drawn in black and white, with little or no modulation and it is incomplete, including a few of the many elements that go to make up the role of the mature male.

What we hope to argue is that boys and girls learn to use language in different ways because of the very different social contexts in which they learn how to carry on friendly conversation. Almost anyone who remembers being a child, has worked with school-age children, or has had an opportunity to observe school-age children can vouch for the fact that groups of girls and groups of boys interact and play in different ways. Systematic observations of children's play have tended to confirm these well-known differences in the ways girls and boys learn to interact with their friends.

In a major study of sex differences in the play of school-age children, for example, sociologist Janet Lever (1976) observed the following six differences between the play of boys and that of girls: (1) girls more often play indoors; (2) boys tend to play in larger groups; (3) boys' play groups tend to include a wider age range of participants; (4) girls play in predominantly male games more often than vice versa; (5) boys more often play competitive games, and (6) girls' games tend to last a shorter period of time than boys' games.

It is by examining these differences in the social organization of play and the accompanying differences in the patterns of social interaction they entail, we argue, that we can learn about the sources of male–female differences in patterns of language use. And it is these same patterns, learned in childhood and carried over into adulthood as the bases for patterns of single-sex friendship relations, we contend, that are potential sources of miscommunication in cross-sex interaction.

The world of girls
Our own experience and studies such as Goodwin's (1980b) of black children and Lever's (1976, 1978) of white children suggest a

complex of features of girls' play and the speech within it. Girls play in small groups, most often in pairs (Lever 1976; Eder and Hallinan 1978; Brooks-Gunn and Matthews 1979), and their play groups tend to be remarkably homogeneous in terms of age. Their play is often in private or semi-private settings that require participants be invited in. Play is cooperative and activities are usually organized in noncompetitive ways (Lever 1976; Goodwin 1980b). Differentiation between girls is not made in terms of power, but relative closeness. Friendship is seen by girls as involving intimacy, equality, mutual commitment, and loyalty. The idea of 'best friend' is central for girls. Relationships between girls are to some extent in opposition to one another, and new relationships are often formed at the expense of old ones. As Brooks-Gunn and Matthews (1979:280) observe, "friendships tend to be exclusive, with a few girls being exceptionally close to one another. Because of this breakups tend to be highly emotional," and Goodwin (1980a:172) notes that "the non-hierarchical framework of the girls provides a fertile ground for rather intricate processes of alliance formation between equals against some other party."

There is a basic contradiction in the structure of girls' social relationships. Friends are supposed to be equal and everyone is supposed to get along, but in fact they don't always. Conflict must be resolved, but a girl cannot assert social power or superiority as an individual to resolve it. Lever (1976), studying fifth-graders, found that girls simply could not deal with quarrels and that when conflict arose they made no attempt to settle it; the group just broke up. What girls learn to do with speech is cope with the contradiction created by an ideology of equality and cooperation and a social reality that includes difference and conflict. As they grow up they learn increasingly subtle ways of balancing the conflicting pressures created by a female social world and a female friendship ideology.

Basically girls learn to do three things with words: (1) to create and maintain relationships of closeness and equality, (2) to criticize others in acceptable ways, and (3) to interpret accurately the speech of other girls.

To a large extent friendships among girls are formed through talk. Girls need to learn to give support, to recognize the speech rights of others, to let others speak, and to acknowledge what they say in order to establish and maintain relationships of equality and

closeness. In activities they need to learn to create cooperation
through speech. Goodwin (1980a) found that inclusive forms such
as "let's," "we gonna," "we could," and "we gotta" predominated
in task-oriented activities. Furthermore, she found that most girls in
the group she studied made suggestions and that the other girls
usually agreed to them. But girls also learn to exchange information
and confidences to create and maintain relationships of closeness.
The exchange of personal thoughts not only expresses closeness but
mutual commitment as well. Brooks-Gunn and Matthews
(1979:280) note of adolescent girls:

> much time is spent talking, reflecting, and sharing intimate thought.
> Loyalty is of central concern to the 12- to 14-year old girl, presumably
> because, if innermost secrets are shared, the friend may have 'dangerous
> knowledge' at her disposal.

Friendships are not only formed through particular types of talk,
but are ended through talk as well. As Lever (1976:4) says of 'best
friends,' "sharing secrets binds the union together, and 'telling' the
secrets to outsiders is symbolic of the 'break-up'."

Secondly, girls learn to criticize and argue with other girls
without seeming overly aggressive, without being perceived as
either 'bossy' or 'mean,' terms girls use to evaluate one another's
speech and actions. Bossiness, ordering others around, is not
legitimate because it denies equality. Goodwin (1980a) points out
that girls talked very negatively about the use of commands to
equals, seeing it as appropriate only in role play or in unequal
relationships such as those with younger siblings. Girls learn to
direct things without seeming bossy, or they learn not to direct.
While disputes are common, girls learn to phrase their arguments in
terms of group needs and situational requirements rather than
personal power or desire (Goodwin 1980a). Meanness is used by
girls to describe nonlegitimate acts of exclusion, turning on someone, or withholding friendship. Excluding is a frequent occurrence
(Eder and Hallinan 1978), but girls learn over time to discourage or
even drive away other girls in ways that don't seem to be just
personal whim. Cutting someone is justified in terms of the target's
failure to meet group norms and a girl often rejects another using
speech that is seemingly supportive on the surface. Conflict and
criticism are risky in the world of girls because they can both

rebound against the critic and can threaten social relationships. Girls learn to hide the source of criticism; they present it as coming from someone else or make it indirectly through a third party (Goodwin 1980a, 1980b).

Finally, girls must learn to decipher the degree of closeness being offered by other girls, to recognize what is being withheld, and to recognize criticism. Girls who don't actually read these cues run the risk of public censure or ridicule (Goodwin 1980). Since the currency of closeness is the exchange of secrets which can be used against a girl, she must learn to read the intent and loyalty of others and to do so continuously, given the system of shifting alliances and indirect expressions of conflict. Girls must become increasingly sophisticated in reading the motives of others, in determining when closeness is real, when conventional, and when false, and to respond appropriately. They must learn who to confide in, what to confide, and who not to approach. Given the indirect expression of conflict, girls must learn to read relationships and situations sensitively. Learning to get things right is a fundamental skill for social success, if not just social survival.

The world of boys

Boys play in larger, more hierarchically organized groups than do girls. Relative status in this ever-fluctuating hierarchy is the main thing that boys learn to manipulate in their interactions with their peers. Nondominant boys are rarely excluded from play but are made to feel the inferiority of their status positions in no uncertain terms. And since hierarchies fluctuate over time and over situation, every boy gets his chance to be victimized and must learn to take it. The social world of boys is one of posturing and counterposturing. In this world, speech is used in three major ways: (1) to assert one's position of dominance, (2) to attract and maintain an audience, and (3) to assert oneself when other speakers have the floor.

The use of speech for the expression of dominance is the most straightforward and probably the best-documented sociolinguistic pattern in boys' peer groups. Even ethological studies of human dominance patterns have made extensive use of various speech behaviors as indices of dominance. Richard Savin-Williams (1976), for example, in his study of dominance patterns among boys in a summer camp uses the following speech interactions as measures of dominance: (1) giving of verbal commands or orders, such as "Get up," "Give it to me," or "You go over there"; (2) name calling and other forms of verbal ridicule, such as "You're a dolt"; (3) verbal threats or boasts of authority, such as "If you don't shut up, I'm gonna come over and bust your teeth in"; (4) refusals to obey orders; and (5) winning a verbal argument as in the sequence: "I was here first" / "Tough," or in more elaborate forms of verbal duelling such as the 'dozens.'[2]

The same patterns of verbally asserting one's dominance and challenging the dominance claims of others form the central element in Goodwin's (1980a) observations of boys' play in Philadelphia. What is easy to forget in thinking about this use of words as weapons, however, is that the most successful boy in such interaction is not the one who is most aggressive and uses the most power-wielding forms of speech, but the boy who uses these forms most successfully. The simple use of assertiveness and aggression in boys' play is the sign not of a leader but of a bully. The skillful speaker in a boys' group is considerably more likeable and better liked by his peers than is a simple bully. Social success among boys is based on knowing both how and when to use words to express power as well as knowing when not to use them. A successful leader will use speech to put challengers in their place and to remind followers periodically of their nondominant position, but will not browbeat unnecessarily and will therefore gain the respect rather than the fear of less dominant boys.

A second sociolinguistic aspect of friendly interaction between boys is using words to gain and maintain an audience. Storytelling, joke telling, and other narrative performance events are common features of the social interaction of boys. But actual transcripts of such storytelling events collected by Harvey Sacks (Sacks 1974; Jefferson 1978) and Goodwin (1980a), as opposed to stories told directly to interviewers, reveal a suggestive feature of storytelling activities among boys: audience behavior is not overtly supportive. The storyteller is frequently faced with mockery, challenges and side comments on his story. A major sociolinguistic skill which a boy must apparently learn in interacting with his peers is to ride out this series of challenges, maintain his audience, and successfully get to the end of his story. In Sacks's account (1974) of some teenage boys involved in the telling of a dirty joke, for example, the narrator is challenged for his taste in jokes (an implication that he doesn't know a dirty joke from a non-dirty one) and for the potential ambiguity of his opening line "Three brothers married three sisters," not, as Sacks seems to imply, because audience members are really confused, but just to hassle the speaker. Through catches,[3] put-downs, the building of suspense, or other interest-grabbing devices, the speaker learns to control his audience. He also learns to continue when he gets no encouragement whatever, pausing slightly at various points for possible audience response but going on if there is nothing but silence.

A final sociolinguistic skill which boys must learn from interacting with other boys is how to act as audience members in the types of storytelling situations just discussed. As audience member as well as storyteller, a boy must learn to assert himself and his opinions. Boys seem to respond to the storytelling of other boys not so much with questions on deeper implications or with minimal-response encouragement as with side comments and challenges. These are not meant primarily to interrupt, to change topic, or to change the direction of the narrative itself, but to assert the identity of the individual audience member.

Women's speech

The structures and strategies in women's conversation show a marked continuity with the talk of girls. The key logic suggested by Kalčik's (1975) study of women's rap groups, Hirschman's (1973) study of students and Abrahams's (1975) work on black women is that women's conversation is interactional. In friendly talk, women are negotiating and expressing a relationship, one that should be in the form of support and closeness, but which may also involve criticism and distance. Women orient themselves to the person they are talking to and expect such orientation in return. As interaction, conversation requires participation from those involved and back-and-forth movement between participants. Getting the floor is not seen as particularly problematic; that should come about automatically. What is problematic is getting people engaged and keeping them engaged – maintaining the conversation and the interaction.

This conception of conversation leads to a number of characteristic speech strategies and gives a particular dynamic to women's talk. First, women tend to use personal and inclusive pronouns, such as 'you' and 'we' (Hirschman 1973). Second, women give off and look for signs of engagement such as nods and minimal response (Kalčik 1975; Hirschman 1973). Third, women give more extended signs of interest and attention, such as interjecting comments or questions during a speaker's discourse. These sometimes take the form of interruptions. In fact, both Hirschman (1973) and Kalčik (1975) found that interruptions were extremely common, despite women's concern with politeness and decorum (Kalčik 1975). Kalčik (1975) comments that women often asked permission to speak but were concerned that each speaker be allowed to finish and that all present got a chance to speak. These interruptions were clearly not seen as attempts to grab the floor but as calls for elaboration and development, and were taken as signs of support and interest. Fourth, women at the beginning of their utterances explicitly acknowledge and respond to what has been said by others. Fifth, women attempt to link their utterance to the one preceding it by building on the previous utterance or talking about something parallel or related to it. Kalčik (1975) talks about strategies of tying together, filling in, and serializing as signs of women's desire to create continuity in conversation, and Hirschman (1973) describes elaboration as a key dynamic of women's talk.

While the idiom of much of women's friendly talk is that of support, the elements of criticism, competition, and conflict do occur in it. But as with girls, these tend to take forms that fit the friendship idiom. Abrahams (1975) points out that while 'talking smart' is clearly one way women talk to women as well as to men, between women it tends to take a more playful form, to be more indirect and metaphoric in its phrasing and less prolonged than similar talk between men. Smartness, as he points out, puts distance in a relationship (Abrahams 1975). The target of criticism, whether present or not, is made out to be the one violating group norms and values (Abrahams 1975). Overt competitiveness is also disguised. As Kalčik (1975) points out, some stories that build on preceding ones are attempts to cap the original speaker, but they tend to have a form similar to supportive ones. It is the intent more than the form that differs. Intent is a central element in the concept of 'bitchiness,' one of women's terms for evaluating their talk, and it relates to this contradiction between form and intent, whether putting negative messages in overtly positive forms or acting supportive face to face while not being so elsewhere.

These strategies and the interactional orientation of women's talk give their conversation a particular dynamic. While there is often an unfinished quality to particular utterances. (Kalčik 1975), there is a progressive development to the overall conversation. The conversation grows out of the interaction of its participants, rather than being directed by a single individual or series of individuals. In her very stimulating discussion, Kalčik (1975) argues that this is true as well for many of the narratives women tell in conversation. She shows how narrative "kernels" serve as conversational resources for individual women and the group as a whole. How and if a "kernel story" is developed by the narrator and/or audience on a particular occasion is a function of the conversational context from which it emerges (Kalčik 1975:8), and it takes very different forms at different tellings. Not only is the dynamic of women's conversation one of elaboration and continuity, but the idiom of support can give it a distinctive tone as well. Hannerz (1969:96), for example, contrasts the "tone of relaxed sweetness, sometimes bordering on the saccharine," that characterizes approving talk between women, to the heated argument found among men. Kalčik (1975:6) even goes so far as to suggest that there is an "underlying esthetic or organizing principle" of "harmony" being expressed in women's friendly talk.

Men's speech

The speaking patterns of men, and of women for that matter, vary greatly from one North American subculture to another. As Gerry Philipsen (1975:13) summarizes it, "talk is not everywhere valued equally; nor is it anywhere valued equally in all social contexts." There are striking cultural variations between subcultures in whether men consider certain modes of speech appropriate for dealing with women, children, authority figures, or strangers; there are differences in performance rules for storytelling and joke telling; there are differences in the context of men's speech; and there are differences in the rules for distinguishing aggressive joking from true aggression.

But more surprising than these differences are the apparent similarities across subcultures in the patterns of friendly interaction between men and the resemblances between these patterns and those observed for boys. Research reports on the speaking patterns of men among urban blacks (Abrahams 1976; Hannerz 1969), rural Newfoundlanders (Faris 1966; Bauman 1972), and urban blue-collar whites (Philipsen 1975; LeMasters 1975) point again and again to the same three features: storytelling, arguing and verbal posturing.

Narratives such as jokes and stories are highly valued, especially when they are well performed for an audience. In Newfoundland, for example, Faris (1966:242) comments that "the reason 'news' is rarely passed between two men meeting in the road – it is simply not to one's advantage to relay information to such a small audience." Loud and aggressive argument is a second common feature of male–male speech. Such arguments, which may include shouting, wagering, name-calling, and verbal threats (Faris 1966:245), are often, as Hannerz (1969:86) describes them, "debates over minor questions of little direct import to anyone," enjoyed for their own sake and not taken as signs of real conflict. Practical jokes, challenges, put-downs, insults, and other forms of verbal aggression are a third feature of men's speech, accepted as normal among friends. LeMasters (1975:140), for example, describes life in a working-class tavern in the Midwest as follows:

It seems clear that status at the Oasis is related to the ability to "dish it out" in the rapid-fire exchange called "joshing": you have to have a quick retort, and preferably one that puts you "one up" on your opponent. People who can't compete in the game lose status.

Thus challenges rather than statements of support are a typical way for men to respond to the speech of other men.

What is happening in cross-sex conversation

What we are suggesting is that women and men have different cultural rules for friendly conversation and that these rules come into conflict when women and men attempt to talk to each other as friends and equals in casual conversation. We can think of at least five areas, in addition to that of minimal responses already discussed, in which men and women probably possess different conversational rules, so that miscommunication is likely to occur in cross-sex interaction.

(1) There are two interpretations of the meaning of questions. Women seem to see questions as a part of conversational maintenance, while men seem to view them primarily as requests for information.

(2) There are two conventions for beginning an utterance and linking it to the preceding utterance. Women's rules seem to call for an explicit acknowledgment of what has been said and making a connection to it. Men seem to have no such rule and in fact some male strategies call for ignoring the preceding comments.

(3) There are different interpretations of displays of verbal aggressiveness. Women seem to interpret overt aggressiveness as personally directed, negative, and disruptive. Men seem to view it as one conventional organizing structure for conversational flow.

(4) There are two understandings of topic flow and topic shift. The literature on storytelling in particular seems to indicate that men operate with a system in which topic is fairly narrowly defined and adhered to until finished and in which shifts between topics are abrupt, while women have a system in which topic is developed progressively and shifts gradually. These two systems imply very different rules for and interpretations of side comments, with major potential for miscommunication.

(5) There appear to be two different attitudes towards problem sharing and advice giving. Women tend to discuss problems with one another, sharing experiences and offering reassurances. Men, in contrast, tend to hear women, and other men, who present them with problems as making explicit requests for solutions. They respond by giving advice, by acting as experts, lecturing to their audiences.[4]

Conclusions

Our purpose in this paper has been to present a framework for thinking about and tying together a number of strands in the analysis of differences between male and female conversational styles. We hope to prove the intellectual value of this framework by demonstrating its ability to do two things: to serve as a model both of and for sociolinguistic research.

As a model *of* past research findings, the power of our approach lies in its ability to suggest new explanations of previous findings on cross-sex communication while linking these findings to a wide range of other fields, including the study of language acquisition, of play, of friendship, of storytelling, of cross-cultural miscommunication, and of discourse analysis. Differences in the social interaction patterns of boys and girls appear to be widely known but rarely utilized in examinations of sociolinguistic acquisition or in explanations of observed gender differences in patterns of adult speech. Our proposed framework should serve to link together these and other known facts in new ways.

As a model *for* future research, we hope our framework will be even more promising. It suggests to us a number of potential research problems which remain to be investigated. Sociolinguistic studies of school-age children, especially studies of the use of speech in informal peer interaction, appear to be much rarer than studies of young children, although such studies may be of greater relevance for the understanding of adult patterns, particularly those related to gender. Our framework also suggests the need for many more studies of single-sex conversations among adults, trying to make more explicit some of the differences in conversational rules suggested by present research. Finally, the argument we have been making suggests a number of specific problems that appear to be highly promising lines for future research:

(1) A study of the sociolinguistic socialization of 'tomboys' to see how they combine male and female patterns of speech and interaction;

(2) An examination of the conversational patterns of lesbians and gay men to see how these relate to the sex-related patterns of the dominant culture;

(3) An examination of the conversational patterns of the elderly to see to what extent speech differences persist after power differences have become insignificant;

(4) A study of children's cultural concepts for talking about speech and the ways these shape the acquisition of speech styles (for example, how does the concept of 'bossiness' define a form of behavior which little girls must learn to recognize, then censure, and finally avoid?);

(5) An examination of 'assertiveness training' programs for women to see whether they are really teaching women the speaking

skills that politically skillful men learn in boyhood or are merely
teaching women how to act like bossy little girls or bullying little
boys and not feel guilty about it.

We conclude this paper by reemphasizing three of the major
ways in which we feel that an anthropological perspective on
culture and social organization can prove useful for further research on differences between men's and women's speech.

First, an anthropological approach to culture and cultural rules
forces us to reexamine the way we interpret what is going on in
conversations. The rules for interpreting conversation are, after all,
culturally determined. There may be more than one way of
understanding what is happening in a particular conversation and
we must be careful about the rules we use for interpreting cross-sex
conversations, in which the two participants may not fully share
their rules of conversational inference.

Second, a concern with the relation between cultural rules and
their social contexts leads us to think seriously about differences in
different kinds of talk, ways of categorizing interactional situations,
and ways in which conversational patterns may function as
strategies for dealing with specific aspects of one's social world.
Different types of interaction lead to different ways of speaking.
The rules for friendly conversation between equals are different
from those for service encounters, for flirting, for teaching, or for
polite formal interaction. And even within the apparently uniform
domain of friendly interaction, we argue that there are systematic differences between men and women in the way friendship is defined and thus in the conversational strategies that
result.

Third and finally, our analysis suggests a different way of
thinking about the connection between the gender-related behavior
of children and that of adults. Most discussions of sex-role
socialization have been based on the premise that gender differences are greatest for adults and that these adult differences are
learned gradually throughout childhood. Our analysis, on the other
hand, would suggest that at least some aspects of behavior are most
strongly gender-differentiated during childhood and that adult
patterns of friendly interaction, for example, involve learning to
overcome at least partially some of the gender-specific cultural
patterns typical of childhood.

NOTES

1. The analogy between the sociolinguistic processes of dialect divergence and genderlect divergence was pointed out to us by Ron Macaulay.
2. In the strict sense the term, 'dozens' refers to a culturally specific form of stylized argument through the exchange of insults that has been extensively documented by a variety of students of American black culture and is most frequently practiced by boys in their teens and pre-teens. Recently folklorist Simon Bronner (1978) has made a convincing case for the existence of a highly similar but independently derived form of insult exchange known as 'ranking', 'mocks', or 'cutting' among white American adolescents. What we find striking and worthy of note is the tendency for both black and white versions of the dozens to be practiced primarily by boys.
3. 'Catches' are a form of verbal play in which the main speaker ends up tricking a member of his or her audience into a vulnerable or ridiculous position. In an article on the folklore of black children in South Philadelphia, Roger Abrahams (1963) distinguishes between catches which are purely verbal and tricks in which the second player is forced into a position of being not only verbally but also physically abused as in the following example of a catch which is also a trick:

    A: Adam and Eve and Pinch-Me-Tight
    Went up the hill to spend the night.
    Adam and Eve came down the hill.
    Who was left?
    B: Pinch-Me-Tight
    [A pinches B]

What is significant about both catches and tricks is that they allow for the expression of playful aggression and that they produce a temporary hierarchical relation between a winner and loser, but invite the loser to attempt to get revenge by responding with a counter-trick.
4. We thank Kitty Julien for first pointing out to us the tendency of male friends to give advice to women who are not necessarily seeking it and Niyi Akinnaso for pointing out that the sex difference among Yoruba speakers in Nigeria in the way people respond verbally to the problems of others is similar to that among English speakers in the U.S.

12

Ethnic style in male–female conversation
DEBORAH TANNEN

This chapter focuses on indirectness in male–female discourse, seen as a feature of conversational style. The present analysis investigates social, rather than individual, differences in the context of conversation between married partners; however, the phenomena elucidated operate in individual style as well. Investigation of expectations of indirectness by Greeks, Americans, and Greek-Americans traces the process of adaptation of this conversational strategy as an element of ethnicity.

Misunderstandings due to different uses of indirectness are commonplace among members of what appear to (but may not necessarily) be the same culture. However, such mixups are particularly characteristic of cross-cultural communication. There are individual as well as social differences with respect to what is deemed appropriate to say and how it is deemed appropriate to say it.

It is sharing of conversational strategies that creates the feeling of satisfaction which accompanies and follows successful conversation: the sense of being understood, being "on the same wave length," belonging, and therefore of sharing identity. Conversely, a lack of congruity in conversational strategies creates the opposite feeling: of dissonance, not being understood, not belonging and therefore of not sharing identity. This is the sense in which conversational style is a major component of what we have come to call ethnicity.

As has been shown in earlier chapters in this volume, conversational control processes operate on an automatic level. While it is commonly understood that different languages or different dialects have different words for the same object, in contrast, ways of signalling intentions and attitudes seem self-evident, natural, and real.

Much recent linguistic research has been concerned with the fact that interpretation of utterances in conversation often differs radically from the meaning that would be derived from the sentences in isolation. Robin Lakoff (1973) observes that sociocultural goals, broadly called *politeness*, lead people to express opinions and preferences in widely varying linguistic forms. Lakoff's (1979) recent work demonstrates that characteristic choices with respect to indirectness give rise to personal style, and that an individual's style is a mixture of strategies which shift in response to shifting situations. Ervin-Tripp (1976) has shown the great variation in surface form which directives may take in American English. Brown and Levinson (1978) argue that the form taken by utterances in actual interaction can be seen as the linguistic means of satisfying the coexisting and often conflicting needs for *negative face* (the need to be left alone) and *positive face* (the need to be approved of by others). As a result, people often prefer to express their wants and opinions *off record* – that is, indirectly.

Indirectness is a necessary means for serving the needs for *rapport* and *defensiveness*, associated respectively with Brown and Levinson's positive and negative face. *Rapport* is the lovely satisfaction of being understood without explaining oneself, of getting what one wants without asking for it. *Defensiveness* is the need to be able to save face by reneging in case one's conversational contribution is not received well – the ability to say, perhaps sincerely, "I never said that," or "That isn't what I meant." The goals of rapport and defensiveness correspond to Lakoff's politeness rules "Maintain camaraderie" and "Don't impose."

An individual learns conversational strategies in previous interactive experience, but chooses certain and rejects other strategies made available in this way. In other words, the range of strategies familiar to a speaker is socially determined, but any individual's set of habitual strategies is unique within that range. For example, research has shown that New Yorkers of Jewish background often use overlap – that is, simultaneous talk – in a cooperative way; many members of this group talk simultaneously in some settings without intending to interrupt (Tannen 1979, 1981). This does not imply that all New Yorkers of Jewish background use overlap cooperatively. However, a speaker of this background is more likely to do so than someone raised in the Midwest. And it is even more unlikely that such simultaneous talk will be used by an Athabaskan raised in Alaska, according to the findings of Scollon (forthcoming), who has shown that Athabaskans highly value silence and devalue what they perceive as excessive talk.

The present analysis and discussion seeks to investigate social differences in expectations of indirectness in certain contexts by Greeks, Americans, and Greek-Americans, tracing the process of adaptation of this conversational strategy as an element of ethnicity. The research design is intended to identify patterns of interpretation, not to predict the styles of individual members of these groups.

A Greek woman of about 65 told me that, before she married, she had to ask her father's permission before doing anything. She noted that of course he never explicitly denied her permission. If she asked, for example, whether she could go to a dance, and he answered,

(1)   An thes, pas. (If you want, you can go.)

she knew that she could not go. If he really meant that she could go, he would say,

(2)   Ne. Na pas. (Yes. You should go.)

The intonation in (1) rises on the conditional clause, creating a tentative effect, while the intonation in (2) falls twice in succession, resulting in an assertive effect. This informant added that her husband responds to her requests in the same way. Thus she agrees to do what he prefers without expecting him to express his preference directly.

This example is of a situation in which interlocutors share expectations about how intentions are to be communicated; their communication is thus successful. To investigate processes of indirectness, however, it is useful to focus on interactions in which communication is not successful (Gumperz and Tannen 1979). Such sequences are the discourse equivalents of starred sentences in syntactic argumentation. They render apparent processes which go unnoticed when communication is successful.

The present chapter focuses on communication between married partners. Interactions between couples reveal the effects of differing uses of indirectness over time. People often think that couples who live together and love each other must come to understand each other's conversational styles. However, research has shown that repeated interaction does not necessarily lead to better understanding. On the contrary, it may reinforce mistaken judgments of the other's intentions and increase expectations that the other will behave as before. If differing styles led to the earlier impression that the partner is stubborn, irrational, or uncooperative, similar behavior is expected to continue. This has been shown for group contact among Greeks and Americans (Vassiliou et al. 1972) and can be seen in personal relations as well. Misjudgment is calcified by the conviction of repeated experience.

Systematic study of comparative communicative strategies was made by asking couples about experiences in which they become aware of differing interpretations of conversations. It became clear that certain types of communication were particularly given to misinterpretation – requests, excuses, explanation: in short, verbalizations associated with getting one's way. One couple recalled a typical argument in which both maintained that they had not gone to a party because the other had not wanted to go. Each partner denied having expressed any disinclination to go. A misunderstanding such as this might well go undetected between casual acquaintances, but, between couples, ongoing interaction makes it likely that such differences will eventually surface.

In this case, the mixup was traced to the following reconstructed conversations:

(3)   Wife: John's having a party. Wanna go?
       Husband: OK.
       (Later)
       Wife: Are you sure you want to go to the party?
       Husband: OK, let's not go. I'm tired anyway.

In this example the wife was an American native New Yorker of East European Jewish extraction. It is likely that this background influenced her preference for a seemingly direct style. (This phenomenon among speakers of this background is the focus of analysis in Tannen 1979, 1981.) In discussing the misunderstanding, the American wife reported she had merely been asking what her husband wanted to do without considering her own preference. Since she was about to go to this party just for him, she tried to make sure that that was his preference by asking him a second time. She was being solicitous and considerate. The Greek husband said that by bringing up the question of the party, his wife was letting him know that she wanted to go, so he agreed to go. Then when she brought it up again, she was letting him know that she didn't want to go; she had obviously changed her mind. So he came up with a reason not to go, to make her feel all right about getting her way. This is precisely the strategy reported by the Greek woman who did what her father or husband wanted without expecting him to tell her directly what that was. Thus the husband in example 3 was also being solicitous and considerate. All this considerateness, however, only got them what neither wanted, because they were expecting to receive information differently from the way the other was sending it out.

A key to understanding the husband's strategy is his use of "OK." To the wife, "OK" was a positive response, in free variation with other positive responses such as "yes" or "yeah." In addition, his use of *anyway* is an indication that he agrees. Finally, the husband's intonation, tone of voice, and nonverbal signals such as facial expression and kinesics would have contributed to the impact of his message. Nonetheless, the wife asserted that, much as she could see the reasoning behind such interpretations in retrospect, she still missed the significance of these cues at the time. The key, I believe, is that she was not expecting to receive her husband's message through subtle cues; she was assuming he would tell her what he wanted to do directly. To the listener, a misunderstanding is indistinguishable from an understanding; one commits to an interpretation and proceeds to fit succeeding information into that mold. People will put up with a great deal of seemingly inappropriate verbal behavior before questioning the line of interpretation which seems self-evident. Direct questioning about how a comment was meant is likely to be perceived as a challenge or criticism.

This example demonstrates, furthermore, the difficulty of clearing up misunderstandings caused by stylistic differences. In seeking to clarify, each speaker continues to use the very strategy that confused the other in the first place. In this way, interaction often results in increasing divergence rather than convergence of style. That is, each partner's characteristic style leads the other to apply increasingly extreme forms of the conflicting strategy. In example 3, the wife's strategy for clarifying was to go 'on record,' through a direct question, as inquiring about her husband's preference, and to ask her husband to go on record about his preference. Since the husband did not expect preferences to be directly expressed, his wife's second question seemed to him an even more recondite hint. He responded with an even more subtle use of indirectness: to allow her to get her way and to offer a reason of his own in justification. And so it goes. Expectations about how meaning will be communicated are so compelling that information intended in a different mode is utterly opaque.

A key parameter here is setting. Does a participant define an interaction as one in which it is appropriate to hint? Numerous discussions triggered by the presentation of these findings have suggested possible male–female differences among Americans in this regard. An audience member commented, "When I first started going out with my boyfriend, we never had misunderstandings about where we should go and what we should do. Now that we've been going together for two years, it seems to happen all the time. How come?" My hypothesis is that, at the beginning of their acquaintance, both partners deemed it appropriate to watch out for the other's hints, to give options. However, as the relationship was redefined, the woman expected increased use of indirectness, reasoning, "We know each other so well, you will know what I want without my telling you." The man, on the other hand, expected less indirectness, reasoning, "We know each other so well that we can tell each other what we want." As the context of their relationship changed, they differed in how they expected their communicative strategies to change. In addition, when partners interact over time, they become more rather than less likely to react, perhaps negatively, to each other's subtle cues, as repeated experience leads them to expect such behavior.

Another example of a reported conversation between a married couple follows.

(4)   Husband: Let's go visit my boss tonight.
        Wife: Why?
        Husband: All right, we don't have to go.

Both husband and wife agreed that the husband's initial proposal was an indication that he wanted to visit his boss. However, they disagreed on the meaning of the wife's question, "Why?" The wife explained that she meant it as a request for information. Therefore she was confused and frustrated and couldn't help wondering why she married such an erratic man who suddenly changed his mind only a moment after making a request. The husband, for his part, explained that his wife's question clearly meant that she did not want to go, and he therefore rescinded his request. He was frustrated, however, and resentful of her for refusing. In discussion, the wife, who was American, reported that she systematically confronted this strange reaction to her asking "Why?" Certainly, the use of this question can be either a request for information or an indirect way of stalling or resisting compliance with a perceived request. The key here is which meaning of "why" is likely to be used in this context.

In order to determine to what extent cross-cultural differences are operating in patterns of interpretation of indirectness, further systematic questioning of Greeks, Americans, and Greek-Americans was undertaken. The remainder of this chapter reports results of that research.

The Greek sample was taken from native Greeks living in the Bay Area of California. Most were young men who had come to the United States for graduate study or women contacted through church organizations. Therefore the age and educational levels differed sharply for men and women. In all cases, Greek respondents had been exposed to American communicative systems. That differences emerged nonetheless is a testament to the reality of the effect.

Greek-Americans were contacted in New York City because it was not possible to find California Greek-Americans who had grown up in distinctly Greek communities. The fact that Greek-Americans from New York are compared with Americans from California is now seen as a weakness; subsequent research (Tannen 1979) has indicated that New Yorkers are less likely to expect indirectness than Californians. Again, the fact that differences do emerge is testimony to the effect of ethnicity. Finally, Americans with Greek-born parents and grandparents are lumped together in this study. There is some indication that those with Greek parents

Table 1. *Respondents choosing 1–I*

Greeks (27)	Greek-Americans (30)	Americans (25)
48%	43%	32%
(13)	(13)	(8)

show the effect of ethnicity more strongly than do those of Greek grandparents and American-born parents.

A questionnaire was designed to present the Greek, American, and Greek-American respondents with the conversation about going to a party. The questionnaire elicited their interpretations by presenting paraphrase choices and then asked for explanations of those choices in order to identify the interpretive strategies motivating them. The first part of the questionnaire reads:

(5)   A couple had the following conversation:
      Wife: John's having a party. Wanna go?
      Husband: OK.
      Wife: I'll call and tell him we're coming.
      Based on this conversation only, put a check next to the statement which you think explains what the husband really meant when he answered "OK."
      [1–I] My wife wants to go to this party, since she asked. I'll go to make her happy.
      [1–D] My wife is asking if I want to go to a party. I feel like going, so I'll say yes.
      What is it about the way the wife and the husband spoke, that gave you that impression?
      What would the wife or husband have had to have said differently, in order for you to have checked the other statement?

The first choice, here referred to as 1–I (Indirect), represents roughly what the Greek husband reported he had meant by "OK." 1–D (Direct) represents what the American wife reported she had thought he meant. A comparison of the percentage of respondents in the three groups who opted for Paraphrase 1–I turns out looking much like a continuum, with Greeks the most likely to take the indirect interpretation, Americans the least likely, and Greek-Americans in the middle, somewhat closer to Greeks (see Table 1).

In example 5, and throughout the present discussion, I refer to one interpretation as direct and the other as indirect. These labels reflect the two possible functions of the question: as a request for information (its literal sense) and as an off-record show of resist-

Table 2. *Male respondents choosing 1–I*

Greeks (10)	Greek-Americans (9)	Americans (11)
50%	44%	27%
(5)	(4)	(3)

Table 3. *Female respondents choosing 1–I*

Greeks (17)	Greek-Americans (21)	Americans (14)
47%	43%	36%
(8)	(9)	(5)

ance (an indirect speech act). This is not to imply, however, that anyone's conversational style is categorically direct. In a sense, all interpretation in context is indirect. What are variable are the modes of indirectness – when and how it is deemed appropriate to hint, that is, to signal unstated contextual and interpersonal information.

It has been suggested (Lakoff 1975) that American women tend to be more indirect than American men. As seen in Tables 2 and 3, percentages of respondents taking the indirect interpretation are more or less the same for Greek men and women and for Greek-American men and women, while, for Americans, separating male and female respondents yields quite different percentages, with fewer men and more women choosing Paraphrase 1–I. If these samples are representative, they are intriguing in suggesting a stylistic gulf between American men and women which does not exist between Greek men and women.

The second part of the questionnaire presents the second part of the conversation, followed by paraphrase choice and questions about interpretive strategies. It reads:

(6)   Later, the same couple had this conversation:
       Wife: Are you sure you want to go to the party?
       Husband: OK, let's not go. I'm tired anyway.

Based on *both* conversations which you read, put a check next to the statement that you think explains what the husband really meant when he spoke the second time:

[2–I] It sounds like my wife doesn't really want to go, since she's asking about it again. I'll say I'm tired, so we don't have to go, and she won't feel bad about preventing me from going.

[2–D] Now that I think about it again, I don't really feel like going to a party because I'm tired.

What is it about the way the husband or wife spoke that gave you
that impression?
What would they have had to have said differently, in order for you
to have checked the other statement?

The two paraphrases presented in the second part of the questionnaire represent the respective interpretations reported by the
Greek husband (the one here labelled 2–I, Indirect) and the
American wife (here labelled 2–D, Direct) in the actual interchange.
This also highlights an aspect of the questionnaire which is different
for male and female respondents. Women and men are both asked
to interpret the husband's comments, while it is likely that women
identify with the wife and men with the husband. Furthermore, the
indirect interpretation is favored by the fact that the husband's
response indicates that he took that interpretation.

The choice of both 1–I and 2–I reveals the most indirect interpretive strategy, by which both the wife's questions are taken to
indicate her hidden preferences – or at least that the husband's
reply is taken to show that he interprets them that way. Again,
results fall out on a continuum with Greeks the most likely to take
the indirect interpretation, Americans the least likely, and Greek-
Americans in between, slightly closer to the Greeks (see Table 4).

Quantitative results, then, tended to corroborate the impression
that more Greeks than Americans opted for the indirect interpretation of questions, and that Greek-Americans were in between,
slightly closer to Greeks. However, the pilot study questionnaire
was not designed primarily to yield quantitative data. The main
function of the paraphrase choices was to serve as a basis for short
answers and extended discussion about the patterns of interpretation which prompted one or the other choice, and the linguistic and
contextual factors influencing them. Results of the short answer
and interview/discussion components follow.

Patterns of interpretation emerged from respondents' explanations of their choice of paraphrase and from alternative linguistic
forms they reported would have led them to the other choice.
Following paraphrase choices, the questionnaire asked, "What is it
about the way the wife and the husband spoke, that gave you that
impression?" and then, "What would the wife or husband have had
to have said differently, in order for you to have checked the other
statement?" Differences in explanations of interpretations were

Table 4. *Respondents choosing 1–I and 2–I*

Greek (27)	Greek-American (30)	American (25)
26%	20%	12%
(7)	(6)	(3)

systematic in reference to two aspects of the conversation: the wife's asking of questions, and the form of the husband's responses. Paraphrase 1–I indicates that the wife's question means she wants to go to the party. The reasoning reported by Greeks to explain their choice of 1–I is that if the wife didn't want to go, she would not have brought it up in the first place. Greeks, Americans, and probably members of any cultural group are capable of interpreting a question either as a request for information or as an expression of some unstated meaning. However, members of one culture or another may be more likely to interpret a question in a particular context in one way or another. Much recent research in pragmatics has elaborated on the indirect speech act function of questions as requests for action, or commands. Esther Goody (1978:40) set out to discover why natives of Gonja do not ask questions in teaching and learning situations. She concluded that Gonjans are "trained early on to attend above all to the command function of questioning. The pure information question hasn't got a chance!" Similarly, I suggest, in the context under consideration, natives of Greece are more disposed to attend to the indirect request function of questions.

Respondents' comments explaining why they chose one or the other paraphrase often focused on the husband's choice of OK. Americans who thought the husband really wanted to go to the party explained that "OK" = "yes" (24% of the Americans said this). But if they thought the husband was going along with his wife's preference, the Americans still focused on "OK" as the cue. In this case they explained that "OK" lacks enthusiasm (20% of the Americans said this).

The expectation of enthusiasm was stronger for Greeks than for Americans. Whereas 24% of the Americans pointed to the affirmative nature of "OK," not a single Greek did so. In contrast, fully half of the Greeks who explained their choices referred to the fact that "OK" (in Greek, *endaxi*) was an unenthusiastic response. This is more than double the percentage of Americans (20%) who said this. The *enthusiasm constraint* is in keeping with findings of Vassiliou, Triandis, Vassiliou and McGuire (1972), who conclude that Greeks place value on enthusiasm and spontaneity (as opposed to American emphasis on planning and organization). Vassiliou et al. observe that such differences in "subjective culture" may contribute to the formation of ethnic stereotypes.

Related to the enthusiasm constraint – perhaps another aspect of it – is the *brevity effect*. Many respondents referred to the brevity of the husband's response when they explained their paraphrase choices. However, if Americans made reference to his brevity, it was in explanation of their choice of paraphrase 1–D, the direct interpretation. Their reasoning was that brevity evidenced informality, casualness, and hence sincerity. This explanation is based on a strategy which assumes that people will express preferences directly in this context. More than a quarter (28%) of the American respondents took this approach. In stark contrast, any Greeks who mentioned the brevity of the husband's answer "OK" (*endaxi*), pointed to it as evidence that he was reluctant to go to the party. To them, brevity is a sign of unwillingness to comply with another's perceived preference. This interpretation presupposes that resistance to another's preference, in this context, will not be verbalized directly; 20% of Greek respondents took this approach.[1]

The explanations given by Greek-Americans for their paraphrase choices were a blend of typical Greek and typical American explanations. They explained that brevity reveals lack of enthusiasm, whereas no Americans did, and they explained that brevity is casual, whereas no Greeks did, in roughly the same proportions (23% and 20% respectively). Only two (7%) said that "OK" = "yes," whereas no Greeks and 24% of Americans said this. Thus Greek-Americans were closer to Greeks than to Americans in their interpretive style.

Further corroborative results came in the form of comments volunteered by respondents following their completion of the questionnaire; the suggestion that Greeks tend to be more indirect in the context of an intimate relationship 'rang true' for respondents.

What are the implications of such differences for cross-cultural communication? It is possible that a good bicultural, like a good bilingual, sees both possibilities and code-switches. For example, an American-born woman of Greek grandparents said that she had to check both paraphrases on the questionnaire. She explained that if she projected herself into the position of the wife, she would take the indirect interpretation, but if she imagined her non-Greek husband asking, she would take the direct paraphrase. In other words, she was aware of both possible strategies. She commented that she tends to be indirect because she picked it up from her mother, who was influenced by her own mother (i.e., the grand-mother born in Greece). In the same spirit, another Greek-American woman laughed when she read paraphrase 2–I, saying, "That sounds just like my grandmother."

It is far from certain, however, that awareness of the existence of differences in communicative strategies makes them less trouble-some, since their operation remains unconscious and habitual. Again, a personal testimony is most eloquent: that of a professional man living in New York City, whose grandparents were from Greece. He seemed fully assimilated, did not speak Greek, had not been raised in a Greek neighborhood, and had few Greek friends. In filling out the questionnaire, he chose paraphrase 1–I, the initial indirect interpretation. In later discussion he said that the notion of indirectness "rang such a bell." He commented, ". . . to a great extent being Greek implies a certain feeling of differentness with regard to understanding others which I have some trouble with." He elaborated on what he meant: "I was trying to get at the idea of . . . this very thing that we talked about [indirectness] and I see it as either something heroically different or a real impediment . . . Most of the time I think of it as a problem. And I can't really sort it out from my family and background . . . I don't know if it's Greek. I just know that it's me. And it feels a little better to know that it's Greek."

Conclusions
These results indicate how respondents report they would interpret a conversation. In actual interaction, intonation, facial expression, past experience with these and other speakers, and a myriad other factors influence interpretation. Moreover, whenever people com-municate, they convey not only the content of their message, but an image of themselves (Goffman 1959). Thus respondents must have

referred for their answers not only to their interactive experience but also to their notion of social norms.

Eventually such an approach must be combined with tape-recording and video-taping of actual interaction, to determine not only what speakers expect but what they do.

Conversational style – the ways it seems natural to express and interpret meaning in conversation – is learned through communicative experience and therefore is influenced by family communicative habits. As the Greek-American quoted above put it, one "can't really sort it out from . . family and background." In other words, conversational style is both a consequence and indicator of ethnicity. Conversational style includes both how meaning is expressed, as seen in patterns of indirectness, and what meaning is expressed, as in how much enthusiasm is expected. All of these conversational strategies create impressions about the speaker – judgments which are made, ultimately, not about how one talks but about what kind of person one is. Conversational style, therefore, has much to do with the formation of ethnic sterotypes.

Conversational style is more resistant to change than more apparent marks of ethnicity such as retention of the parents' or grandparents' language. Seaman (1972:204) demonstrates that the modern Greek language is "practically extinct" among third generation Greek-Americans and will be "totally extinct in the fourth generation." However, those very third generation Greek-Americans who have lost the Greek language may not have lost, or not lost entirely, Greek communicative strategies. Understanding these strategies, and the patterns of their retention or loss, can offer insight into the process of cultural assimilation at the same time that it provides insight into discourse processes in a heterogeneous society.

NOTE

1. An earlier study (Tannen 1976) presented two different versions of this conversation with a rating-scale questionnaire. The two English versions differed in that one presented the husband's first response as "OK," while the other presented it as "yeah." The two Greek versions, administered in Athens, differed in that one presented the husband's first response as "OK" (*endaxi*), while the other presented it as the informal Greek "yes" (*ne*). Whereas I had expected the shift to "yes/yeah" to produce more choices of the direct interpretation among both Greeks and Americans, I found that the substitution of "yeah" for "OK" made no difference in American responses, while the substitution of "yes" (*ne*) for "OK"

(*endaxi*) did yield fewer choices of the indirect interpretation by Greeks. In other words, "OK" and "yeah" turned out to be equivalents for English, whereas "OK" and "yes" did not turn out to be equivalents for Greeks. This difference may be explained in part by the "yes/yeah" distinction in English, but I believe it is also attributable in part to the greater expectation among Greeks that objections will not be directly expressed, so one must attend to the indirect interpretation of "OK."

13

Language and disadvantage: the hidden process

T. C. JUPP, CELIA ROBERTS, AND
JENNY COOK-GUMPERZ

General introduction

In the 1950s and 1960s, many major urban areas of Britain which
had been relatively monolingual and monocultural became multiethnic for the first time. A similar process of transformation
occurred in many large industrialized cities of the world and for a
similar reason: the need to fill unskilled, unsocial or poorly paid
jobs which could not be filled locally. Generally, therefore, the jobs
of the newly settled immigrants have not been determined by their
qualifications, skills, and experience, but by gaps in local labor
markets. So the primary cause of immigration was the needs of
workplaces, and now many workplaces are, in turn, a reflection of
the new multiethnic pattern of urban life which has resulted from
this labor market immigration. But the particular circumstances
and pattern of this immigration have varied significantly between
different countries as has the pattern of settlement of families and
dependants during the 1970s. Britain is different in some respects
from the rest of Western Europe, and both are quite different from
the United States, Canada and Australia.

Multiethnic workplaces are among those strategic research sites
referred to in Chapter 1 which exemplify the problems of intergroup communication in modern industrial society. This paper
arises from observation, analysis, and training programs related to
communication in such multiethnic workplaces, particularly where
numbers of South Asian people are employed. The first part of this
chapter provides empirical background to some of the case studies
in this volume and places them in a socioeconomic perspective.
From participant observation, we describe some of the social
conditions of such workplaces particularly in terms of interpersonal

relations, instances of key speech events and the role of language. We point out how the long-term attitudinal consequences of interethnic contact are often rooted in people's experience of such communicative environments. We then go on to discuss the processes and difficulties of adult language socialization for minority ethnic groups in these communicative environments. Finally, we describe how the research perspective exemplified in the rest of this book can be employed in the development and use of materials and training methods which can create an awareness and acceptance of the facts and consequences of linguistic diversity.

The largest group of post-war settlers in Britain is of South Asian origin, having come from North India, Pakistan, East Africa, and Bangladesh. There is also a large group of West Indian origin, and there are smaller groups from different parts of the Mediterranean basin and from South-East Asia. This chapter largely refers to people of South Asian origin, particularly from North India and East Africa. By the 1980s, this group was well settled with grown or growing families. The original social and economic backgrounds of this group of people are diverse and include widely different educational levels, expectations of life in Britain, experience of British institutions, as well as differences in the degree of fluency in English. However, one common factor is Britain's former colonial relationship with their countries of origin. This has provided a significant historical dimension to expectations and stereotypes both amongst the white British and amongst the immigrants themselves whatever their particular backgrounds. Another aspect of this historical connection was the relative freedom of entry to Britain from former colonial territories during the 1950s and early 1960s. This historical connection and the entry procedures made immigration appear attractive for some well-educated and professional people.

A small but significant group of South Asian immigrants came to Britain with a university education in India or Pakistan through the medium of English and based upon British traditions. These people naturally considered themselves well prepared educationally and linguistically for their life in Britain. However, British authorities were sceptical of the value of their qualifications and often refused to recognize them. The majority of such educated immigrants found that their opportunities also were confined to low-status gaps in various areas of the labor market. This group is one example of the differences between Britain and other parts of Western Europe in terms of the background and experience of minority ethnic groups even though the broad economic factors behind immigration have been the same.

The events of the past two decades provide abundant evidence that the integration of these groups into the social and economic life of Britain has by no means been smooth. Open interethnic and interracial conflict, rather than becoming less evident, has in fact increased over time. The primary cause of this is the unequal distribution of social power, with ethnic minorities clustered in socially weaker roles. Other overt causes of tension include prejudice and intergroup stereotypes, lack of knowledge, and linguistic and cultural differences. In the case of South Asians, differences of language background, in terms of both their mother tongue and their use of English, have resulted in a perceived difference in communicative power compared to white British people, which can be seen to have been of real importance in the continued disadvantage and discrimination they experience. This communicative dimension cannot be understood on the basis of a simple view of a 'language deficit,' which is implied in the phrase 'poor speaker of English.' If communicative problems only arose from a 'language deficit,' increased ability in English would be matched by increased communicative and social power. However, many South Asian speakers of English with extensive lexical and grammatical knowledge do not succeed communicatively in speech events of key significance to them.

Many of the factors in ethnic and race conflict and disadvantage go beyond a study of communication processes. But discrimination has a linguistic dimension, and individuals' interaction can *reinforce* distance, difference, and stereotype, or it can *alleviate* these factors. How this works is largely a "hidden process' as other chapters in this volume also show.

The social position of South Asian workers

South Asian immigrants tended to settle in areas and to find jobs where they were not in competition with local workers. This pattern of South Asian employment is reflected in general studies of the position of immigrant workers in Europe and Britain which show that they have occupied a position as an employment 'buffer zone' between local workers and low-status jobs (Peach 1968; Castles and Kosack 1973; Moore 1975). This conclusion in turn fits well with the theory of a two-tier labor market (Doeringer and Piore 1971). According to this theory, it is normal in industrial society for two distinct labor markets to develop. Rex and Tomlinson (1979) have suggested that immigrants in post-war Britain provided an especially important and alienated element in the lower labor market. They characterize one labor market as open to candidates who have contacts (indeed it may not strictly speaking be a market at all, but simply a system of internal promotion within an organization) and who, when appointed, have long tenure, a great measure of trade union protection, welfare benefits, high wages, and also some degree of humanization of their relations with their employers. In the other labor market, all the opposite conditions hold. There is frequent rotation of employees, much short-term and part-time employment, little in the way of welfare benefits, poor trade union protection, and a tendency for work to be regarded purely as a means of earning money to be used in more significant life contexts.

Studies of the pattern of employment of ethnic minorities in Britain (Department of Employment 1974; Smith 1977) and analysis from field work in multiethnic workplaces (National Centre for Industrial Language Training 1977) have found that only a few manufacturing and service industries account for most of the employment of South Asians. The position is set out in Chart 1. Once an immigrant worker entered these employment categories in the new society, the negative cycle of social class and ethnicity began to operate. Social class became quickly fixed and reinforced by the nature of the immigrant's work. In a long-established industrialized class society such as Britain, it is an immigrant's current labor market position which determines social class membership not educational achievements and social position from the society of origin.

A closer examination of each of the employment categories in Chart 1 confirms the marginal nature of the minority ethnic group workers' positions in the type of lower level labor market described. We can see that the main areas of employment were in jobs where skills are minimal: either in jobs which are semi-automated

Chart 1. *Major employment categories of South Asians*

> (a) semi-automated industries which expanded rapidly in the fifties and sixties and required additional unskilled labor, but were located in areas of labor shortage in, for example, food processing, plastics manufacture and mass-production engineering.
> (b) traditional industries which were deskilled, reorganized, and had an insecure market such as textiles, clothing and foundries.
> (c) service industries with labor shortage in some parts of the country, particularly Greater London, in, for example, transport, hospitals, and hotels and catering.
> (d) clerical and routine administrative jobs in the Civil Service and nationalized service industries.
> (e) certain low-status professional jobs in medicine and in education.

and routine, or in the lower levels of service industries. Many of the jobs in employment category (a) have also been characterized by marked fluctuations in demand for the industries' products and by substitution of further new technology for labor. The position of workers has been even more insecure in category (b) because these have been deskilled and dwindling industries in Britain for the last twenty years, or industries which can only survive by offering very poor working conditions. In employment categories (a) and (b), the human environment is marked by close supervision, machine discipline, and often by shift work and by the concentration of ethnic minorities in particular work sections.

The jobs in category (c) are rather different and more diverse in character. They are usually marked by low pay, unsocial hours, or both. However, although the job tasks are relatively simple, the need for communication and understanding with clients may arise in some of these jobs – for example, transport workers and cafeteria service staff.

The rise of mass unemployment in Britain during the late 1970s has affected South Asian workers in categories (a) and (b) particularly harshly. Many of them have been made redundant by a combination of closures and automation, and have experienced increased competition from the white majority group for the remaining jobs and for service industry jobs in category (c) Consequently, many South Asian workers can no longer depend on the labor market for low-status and unskilled, but available, jobs. Instead they have had to seek training and jobs on a wider basis than in the past, and at a time when discrimination and a cluster of disadvantages operate more damagingly on their chances (Jupp 1981). They have, therefore, had to turn increasingly to the official employment and welfare services for help in coping with unemployment and in seeking work and training. South Asians are thus becoming more dependent on the bureaucratic processes and face-to-face interview procedures described by Gumperz and Cook-Gumperz in Chapter 1 of this volume. At interviews in social security benefit offices, in careers offices, in job centres, and with training agencies, workers are constantly evaluated by the officials of these agencies on the basis of how they project themselves – that is how they communicate linguistically. For example, recent research into ethnic minorities and unemployment concludes that South Asian workers with unskilled manual work experience and perceived poor communication skills are less well served by the employment services (Smith 1981). At the same time, employers are becoming more selective and are introducing more formal recruitment procedures which also depend on linguistic evaluation.

Jobs in categories (d) and (e) are different from (a), (b) and (c) in the sense that employment of this type requires recognized educational or vocational/professional qualifications. Nevertheless, the employment patterns of South Asians in these categories indicate patterns of marginality and low status within the organization or profession. Our own work in three Civil Service departments has shown that many clerical officers of South Asian origin are overqualified for their positions, and some have had work experience in East Africa at much more senior levels. Amongst doctors, 11% of general practitioners and 21% of hospital doctors first qualified in the Indian subcontinent (Smith 1980). Smith found that overseas hospital doctors were heavily concentrated in the more junior grades, and, to a lesser extent, within the less popular or 'shortage' specialities such as geriatrics, anaesthetics and psychiatry. The jobs held by South Asians in government departments, the public services, and in schools, while usually having a relatively low status within the particular organization, often provide an important point of contact between the organization and the general public.

Competence in English of educated and professional South

Asians has been increasingly and publicly questioned although such people usually have high levels of lexical and grammatical knowledge. In 1976, language tests were introduced for overseas-qualified doctors from many countries who wish to practice in Britain. In the field of Civil Service employment, research into equal opportunities (Civil Service Department 1978) has shown that many minority ethnic group applicants for jobs or promotion are judged as having insufficient ability to communicate in English on imprecise grounds which provide many opportunities for prejudice. For example, in the selection procedure for one particular Civil Service section (the Insolvency Service), 55% of rejected minority ethnic group candidates were classified as having "some difficulty in communication." The question of language has also arisen in relation to the competence of some South Asian teachers with substantial service in Britain. For example, a South Asian maths primary teacher was dismissed in 1980 after five years of service with a local education authority mainly on grounds of insufficient English (Industrial Tribunal Case Number 19252/79 between Mohammed Haseen and Walsall Metropolitan Borough Council held at Birmingham October and December 1979, January and February 1980. Decision entered in register 14 March 1980). So, as we have described with reference to unemployment and unskilled South Asian workers, language is also increasingly arising as an obstacle for white-collar and professional workers in a way which underlines their marginal status at a time of increasing unemployment and racial tension.

We have described how a negative cycle of social class and ethnicity has operated to create low social power for South Asians. This is reflected in all five categories of employment we have described by the way in which ethnic divisions largely coincide with lines of power and control. Promotion, job flexibility, successful training, and full-time trade union posts have not been achieved by South Asians on a scale that is anything like proportional to their numbers (Smith 1977). At the same time, South Asians have been disproportionately affected by the massive rise in unemployment since the late 1970s. We shall now examine how, within this social position, a social identity of lesser competence is created in the eyes of majority group people by the actual process of day-to-day interaction and communication with South Asians.

Language and social identity

Language use creates a social identity for the user, as Gumperz and Cook-Gumperz have explored theoretically in Chapter 1. The process is a reflexive one. Language as speaking practice creates and identifies social group membership. Through shared communicative conventions, individuals treat each other as part of their own social group. It is this that enables them to acquire knowledge and experience which reinforce the social group and sharedness. The process of understanding which forms the interactive use of language in social contexts depends upon a meaning system which recognizes the complexity of communication through the several channels which make up the act of speaking. Social and cultural differences which affect the signalling in all of these channels are many and subtle, so that small linguistic differences may have much bigger social-interactional consequences. Members of the white majority group in the workplace, sharing a linguistic and meaning system as a result of shared interactive experience, are immediately alerted to and focus on differences in speaking practices between themselves and South Asian workers. These differences are assumed by them to be broad cultural differences relating to language, behavior, and attitude. Since South Asian workers, even if they are good speakers of English, exemplify some of the differences in speaking practices with which their group is now identified and stereotyped, their style of speaking will trigger fixed assumptions about their competence and attitudes.

It is assumed by the white majority that South Asian workers either know English or do not. Any evidence that they do not may be used to reinforce assumptions about their ability or their unwillingness to integrate. The following interaction was recorded as part of a survey on communication practices in a textile mill (Etherton 1975). A South Asian man was interviewed by a supervisor for a job. The applicant had been speaking fluent English for some time, then the supervisor had to fill in a record form:

Supervisor: Can you speak English?
Applicant: No. (ironically)
Supervisor: (addressing observer) Oh, you see, he can't speak English.
Applicant: If I can't speak English, what am I speaking to you now?

In this case, differences in communicative style and the supervisor's experience with other Asian workers, caused the supervisor to ignore the evidence of actual interaction.

It is the two factors, the assumptions of poor language use and of weak communicative power on the one hand, and the low-status job position on the other which, in interaction with each other, make up the socially created identity of incompetence or lesser competence and uncooperative behavior and attitudes. This identity of the South Asian worker as less competent or in other ways inadequate is then used to warrant the maintenance of the lower status of this group. These factors operate to reinforce each other. So, through actual practices of speaking in social encounters, the lower status identity of the immigrant worker is reproduced.

This process begins with the apparently most trivial of social contacts such as greetings or simple requests, instructions or passing comments. Although the worker's performance is not being explicitly judged, s/he is evaluated on the basis of communicative intent as interpreted by the English supervisor or worker. These evaluations are openly expressed as negative behavior and attitude. The following is an extract from a tape-recorded interview with Mrs J, a middle-aged English supervisor in the packing department of a large food-processing company (Gubbay 1978). She describes a South Asian operator, Mrs K:

Well Mrs K you see, she came on the afternoon shift. I've never interviewed her, whatsoever, so I knew nothing about her, I'm just told on Friday afternoon, "You'll have Mrs K Monday morning, she's on the afternoon shift. She's alright." Oh well of course I done a few days with Mrs K I thought to myself "Ooh I don't know, I think they've told me a fast one here," you know. I used to go up and tell her things, she used to laugh at me . . . never look at me, if I was to say something, she'd laugh, head down and laugh. So "Oh dear, she couldn't care less, couldn't care less about me," you know. And this went on for a long while. "I mustn't get wild, I mustn't get wild, I must play it cool, I've got to play it cool" I thought, "Oh dear, they've really pulled the wool over my eyes, they've put her on my shift, you know, but she's like this."

An interview with a South Asian worker from the same shift, talking about the same supervisor, illustrates how the workers perceive their low social power and reinforce their marginal position by their ways of interacting or avoidance of interaction with the supervisor:

We never mix up English ladies and Asian ladies. We didn't bother to each other . . . we are going in the factory, we are working, we're getting our money and come back. Our supervisor, she don't want to talk to us. She prefer English lady to us – we thought she don't like us . . . we are not like friend with her. We respect her like in our country we respect our boss and we have to listen them . . . if they talk to us we are happy, if they don't bother we don't bother . . . If we want anything from G [the supervisor] we didn't say, because we are frightened that if we say she will refuse . . . we thought G, she upset very quick – we feel it – we never look on her face.

Without a minimal level of cooperation through routine social contact, no context is created within which fixed attitudes of the participants can be challenged. Everyday problems and difficulties rapidly escalate into situations of stress and discipline procedures are invoked. Recent changes in working practices, in the make-up of the workforce and in production techniques serve to create situations which, far from creating opportunities for the South Asian worker to renegotiate his/her social identity, tend to shore up his/her low social position.

For example, the introduction of new technologies can create environments which are even more isolating for individual workers than more traditional workplace environments. In a survey conducted in a plastics factory to examine the effects on communication of the introduction of the new technologies (Walsall ILT Unit 1980), the following situation was recorded: At the end of the day shift, an entire batch had to be scrapped because the South Asian worker had not been using a disk which ensures that an accurate hole can be drilled through the plastic product. It was established that the man knew the correct procedure and so was disciplined. What was not established was whether the worker understood why the use of the disk was necessary, whether the complexity and fiddly nature of the job had been explained and why the only explanation the worker was able to give was that the machine was too fast. All these matters could easily have been covered as part of the routine social exchanges between supervisor and operator if opportunities for interaction had been created and pursued on both sides and had resulted in shared knowledge and experience. The consequence, however, was the penalization of an individual and the reinforcement of a stereotype about 'the lackadaisical attitude of these people.'

This labelling of South Asian workers with negative characteristics firmly places the responsibility for any breakdown in the supervisory system or in communications in general on the minority group. The following are comments frequently heard: "they understand when they want to," "they are rude," "they lack initiative and sense of humor," or, relating to specific ability or performance, "they get over-excited," "they don't understand our way of doing things," "they don't seem to come over as well." Yet most supervisors would strenuously deny they were being unfair or discriminatory in their treatment and attitudes towards ethnic minority group workers.

These attitudes arise from recurrent problems frequently cited in interviews with English management. In a review of fifty communication survey reports written by Industrial Language Training units from seven different manufacturing industries between 1975 and 1980 the following were the most frequent problems identified:

(i)   Never sure an instruction has been fully understood.
(ii) Difficulties in explaining about quality, faults, and breakdowns.
(iii) Uncertain about how far responsibilities regarding health and safety legislation can be fulfilled with workers who have limited English.
(iv) Difficulties in explaining or obtaining explanations in relation to personal problems, such as pay queries, and sickness and absence.
(v)   Lack of understanding or wrong attitudes in relation to company practice and procedure; for example, grievance procedures, holidays, and extended leave.
(vi) Difficulties in getting 'cooperation' from workers, particularly in relation to general flexibility, leading to discipline problems.
(vii) Clashes of interest on the shopfloor to do with wages, overtime, revised work schedules, and bonus schemes.

Many of these problems are common to any workplace. But within this list of recurrent problems there is a persistent *uncertainty* about the results of communication frequently commented upon as: "We're never sure if . . ." which is illogically matched by an *over-certainty* in making firm judgments about the attitudes and behavior of South Asian workers, based on their perceived intent. Discussions with South Asian workers, particularly on training courses, indicate that they also perceive the same recurrent problem situations, particularly items (iv)–(vii) in the above list.

For South Asian workers, these key situations relate to their fears and anxieties about their position and performance in the organization and the extent to which they are fairly treated. In a position of low social power, habits of caution develop related to a fear of being judged as inadequate, being criticized, and ultimately of losing a job. Attempts by South Asians to communicate may be treated with contempt or simply confirm the negative characteristics assigned to them. They cannot therefore create the opportunities of day-to-day interaction through which knowledge of workplace practices and procedures are informally learnt. On the one hand, this makes South Asians even more cautious and isolated and, on the other, it can make them suspicious and uncertain. Apparently 'neutral' attempts by English supervisors to establish facts are interpreted as ways of "catching you out" or the first reaction of South Asian workers to changes in work practice may be to view them as a form of unfair treatment or discrimination, whether they are discriminatory or not.

Assumptions by South Asians about their own language use – that they already speak English adequately, or that speaking English is not important, or that, although correct English is a significant goal, it has no bearing on potential areas of discrimination – means that like the white supervisors, they will not locate judgments of attitude and behavior in issues of communicative power. As we have suggested, anxiety and uncertainty may also make South Asians apparently over-concerned with what are the rules, what is fixed, what are their rights. These concerns may involve them in more stressful communication which, in turn, can provide further examples of miscommunication and misinterpretation.

Attitudes based on the type of communicative difficulties described are, therefore, often glossed over as ethnic or race discrimination, but as such are hard to counteract or to change. The charges seem either justified or nebulous, since the small irritating differences that arise in interaction and can cause annoyance or misunderstanding do not appear to provide sufficient conditions for the failure of individuals to achieve goals or receive fair treatment. It is because of this apparent lack of clear causal connection between breakdowns in communication and continued disadvantage that we refer to the process as a hidden one. The three factors of class position, ethnicity, and speaking practices create a social identity for ethnic minority group workers which cannot be characterized as mere cultural difference, because the interactive effect of this position feeds into its own evaluation and tends continually to reproduce it.

Adult language socialization
In order to consider ways in which this mutually reinforcing negative cycle can be breached, it is important to understand the process whereby minority ethnic group adults can become and can be seen to be competent communicators in English settings. This process is not merely one of language acquisition, but is a process of language socialization. By language socialization, we mean the learning of speaking practices which construct and guide social interaction within specific social contexts. The question of how language is learnt cannot be considered independently of the social context in which learning is available and which provides the social grounds necessary for talk.

Research in first language development has recognized that, as children learn a language, they learn to be socialized into the particular culture in which they are brought up (Halliday 1975). However, the process of adult language socialization for South Asians in Britain cannot be compared with that of first language development, because the social contexts are so different. We shall examine later why this is so and ways in which appropriate social contexts can be created so that people can develop their communicative power in interaction.

Traditionally, adult language teaching has been based on acquiring the linguistic system through models of language use and rule giving. This is a unilateral form of learning which assumes that no changes have to be made to the communicative environment with which the second language speaker has to cope. In other words, it assumes a deficit model. When the deficiencies are overcome, it is argued, communications will be effective and people can talk their way through to opportunities and to more social power. The

Chart 2. *Ethnic background of workers on evening packing shift, instant coffee processing plant*

India		*East Africa*	
Punjab:	15	Kenya:	4
	(Sikhs 12, Hindus 3)		
Other:	4	Uganda:	3
		Tanzania:	1
British Isles		*Elsewhere*	
Local:	3	Italy:	3
England:	4	Portugal:	2
Ireland:	3	Ukraine:	1
		Pakistan:	2
Caribbean		Singapore (Sikh):	1
Jamaica:	3	Iraq (Christian):	1
Barbados:	2	Guyana (Muslim):	1

Source: National Centre for Industrial Language Training 1977

communicative environment which provides most adult minority ethnic workers with the opportunity to use English is the workplace. And the workplace is both too complex and too rigid to be changed solely by those individuals with the least communicative and social power.

The structural conditions of the workplace mean that, typically, there is little or no opportunity for the kind of unstressed peer-group interaction within which language socialization most readily takes place. We have already described the kinds of situations in which South Asian workers have an urgent need to communicate. These are usually stressful situations, involving significant status differential with white management, supervisors, and stewards communicating downwards to minority ethnic group operatives. The fact that there are few social contexts in which unstressed peer-group interaction can develop is well illustrated by Chart 2 which sets out the ethnic background of a group of 53 women workers on an evening shift in a food processing plant in West London. This is an example of category (a) jobs in Chart 1.

In such workplace contexts, contact between majority and minority groups is often minimal. Frequently a minority ethnic group worker will only communicate with an English supervisor over an important personal issue such as pay. This type of communicative task does not provide the minority group workers with an opportunity to learn, from gradually accumulated experience, how to use language either to get things done or to maintain social relationships in their second culture. Workers, therefore, with little language or education acquire only limited and instrumental English, which reinforces white majority stereotypes of them and serves to inhibit further any possible learning contexts. South Asian workers who have learnt English before coming to Britain and have used it previously for academic or professional purposes also lack the appropriate social contexts for language socialization with the white majority groups and this reinforces their use of an ethnically specific style of speaking English (see Chapter 2 in this volume).

These differences in speaking practices, and so in the perceptions of what is going on in the interaction, are interpreted by the white majority as deliberate behavior or are attributed to personal characteristics of the individual or the group. Neither side recognizes the complexity and subtlety of interaction in constructing a reality of shared knowledge and experience through which goals are negotiated and people evaluated. Neither side recognizes that the differences in speaking and perceptions put them in fundamentally new situations and that this means that both sides need to learn.

We consider below the learning needs of certain key members of the white majority group. But here the discussion of how shared knowledge and experience is created in interaction returns us to the question of first language (L1) acquisition. As already noted, the conditions under which L1 acquisition takes place are in marked contrast to the conditions under which South Asian workers are expected to develop a second language. L1 acquisition usually takes place in small group interaction with family and peers, in an encouraging and relaxed environment. Breaches of the social norms by unexpected or unacceptable language behavior provide an opportunity for children to learn from adults within their group without the unpleasant consequences that can affect the adult learner.

Parents assume that children are being socialized through language into their particular shared cultural group. This process includes explicit teaching and correcting and the creation of social contexts in which learning will naturally take place. Critical also to this process is the assumption that, whatever the day-to-day frustrations and irritations in communicating with a child, negative evaluations will be suspended when a matter of real importance to a child arises. For minority ethnic group workers, there are no such assumptions. They are expected to learn and behave appropriately without any of the conditions offered to children. The adult recognizes and adjusts to the child's attempts at interaction. But the white majority group does not accept the differences in speaking practices of the minority groups. Nor does the white majority recognize or accept the fact that in a multiethnic society there are no interactive norms. This lack of both recognition and acceptance of linguistic diversity has been and remains the single greatest barrier to language socialization for South Asians, and when applied to judgments about people is a significant source of indirect discrimination.

We have described how limited are the opportunities for adult language socialization in multiracial workplaces. We have also suggested that neither traditional approaches to adult language teaching nor models based upon child language acquisition are helpful in developing the communicative power of South Asian workers. What is needed is a change in awareness and perception which can influence both language use and language inference and so serve to create new contexts for language socialization. These changes in people's awareness and perception require a level of direction, opportunities for discussion, and an amount of time which can only be provided through a systematic training approach. We shall now, therefore, describe some of the training approaches which we have developed for this purpose.

Breaking the negative cycle through training

Breaking the negative cycle through training requires creating social contexts in which both sides can interpret and evaluate an interaction not just on the basis of their own language and social conventions, but with the knowledge and appreciation of the other's goals and conventions, which may be markedly different. Breaking the cycle means helping trainees to understand the hidden process whereby language differences feed into negative categorization of groups. Because this is a hidden process, the only way the training can have real impact is by endeavoring to reproduce the actual process for trainees and to examine its various stages with them.

In order to reproduce this hidden process, it is vital to have real interactive material to work on. This requirement means it is necessary for the trainers to participate in the workplace and gain the commitment of individuals to help with data gathering and analysis. These individuals then become both informants and interpreters. The experience of collecting and analysing data, in this way, becomes part of the training project itself. Trainees examine interethnic communication for differences in goals and style and for evidence of how these differences can lead to awkward moments, misinterpretation and real communication breakdown. Through this analysis, people can begin to recognize that the personal perceptions present in interaction are the result of an interplay of received cultural knowledge, of observation, and of inference from the linguistic data in actual interaction.

This type of training approach is very difficult to manage because white majority group participants tend to note clear ethnic and cultural differences without being willing to examine the subtle processes and momentary reactions out of which their evaluation of the other person is made. These processes and reactions are difficult both to record and to recall in detail so most individuals are unaware of them and often reluctant to recognize their real significance.

The research described in the earlier chapters of this volume has provided insights and analytic tools for examining with people these processes of inference in interethnic conversation. Differences in the linguistic conventions used by one speaker, for example, to establish context, maintain thematic cohesion, or to control the speaker's contribution to the conversation, can be explicitly related to perceptions by the other person about the speaker's intent, attitude, or competence. The subtle and usually unconscious ways in which syntax, prosody, and lexicon work together to signal such features as old and new information, speaker perspective and the connections between topics can be analyzed in training sessions through using specific pieces of data that are both familiar and authentic to the participants.

This analysis can then be related to stereotypical comments made about communications with minorities such as "they never seem to come to the point," "they understand when they want to," "they don't show up as well as the English fellows." The cumulative effect of miscommunication on minority group perceptions and attitudes can then be explored to help the white majority group to recognize how an inability to assess the adequacy and quality of minority ethnic group speakers' contributions in interethnic encounters can feed much broader stereotypes and prejudices.

Data of interethnic exchanges suitable for use in training is very difficult to collect even with cooperation. Much of the language concerned with an immediate job is routine, brief, and infrequent. Longer and naturally occurring exchanges can be recorded in such formal settings as departmental meetings or training sessions, but minority ethnic group workers are often low contributors or the situations require the giving or exchange of routine or technical information in familiar contexts where both the experience of the job, the shared lexical field, and well-established relationships of the participants mean that there is little potential for important personal negotiation or critical information loss. There are, of course, many such interethnic exchanges which are successful for just these reasons.

However, there are certain recurrent problem situations for communication in the workplace of the types we have described earlier in this chapter. Another very important type of interaction is when an evaluation of such things as the other person's competence, motivation, worthiness, and personality will decide whether the individual should have access to opportunities, resources, or facilities. In these 'gatekeeping' encounters (Erickson 1975), it is, typically, a member of the white majority group who makes the decision about a job, about promotion, about a training course, or about social security payments.

Data from both these types of communication can most clearly exemplify to the white majority group how ethnic differences in communicative style can create contexts in which indirect discrimination takes place. Such data are particularly useful for training purposes because the slow, cumulative processes of misevaluation and stereotyping are in effect 'speeded up.' Interactions of these types tend to display a low level of sharedness and a high level of negotiation. Significant characteristics of the interactions are that both sides have a specific and important communicative goal which is not identical, that power and status relations are unequal and that the conversation is likely to be extended. Conversations of this kind will tend to highlight most clearly the subtle processes of inference and interpretation of which people are generally unaware. But a problem confronting the trainer is that the very factors which make these interactions significant and interesting for training are often of a personal, confidential, and highly charged nature. Open recording is therefore difficult or impossible and for ethical reasons such interactions cannot be either openly recorded or secretly recorded. However, worthwhile data of this type can be created with cooperation for training purposes as we describe below.

The job interview: an example of training material
The selection and level of analysis of texts to develop awareness among both majority and minority groups must take account of the trainees' existing levels of perception and analytical skills. What follows, therefore, is not a comprehensive piece of discourse analysis for research purposes, but an example of an analysis of a job interview – a key 'gatekeeping' situation – made for the purpose of modifying the trainees' awareness and perception, but drawing on insights and analytic tools from this volume.

The job interview discussed here was specially made for training purposes (Gumperz, Jupp, and Roberts 1979). Since it would be impossible to protect individuals in a real job interview if the resulting video-taped material was used, a typical job interview was recreated by a South Asian job applicant with native English speakers whose background and experience was typical of such interviewers. In recreating such situations, the contextualization phenomena (described in Chapter 1) which arise in real interaction are found to be present. The recreation of such stressful situations entails a high level of involvement on the part of the speakers so that language use and interpretation will tend to operate below the level of conscious awareness.

The interview was for a post of librarian in a college of further education. The applicant was a South Asian graduate with a professional qualification recently obtained in Britain. Previous to taking this qualification, he had worked for fifteen years in manual and service industries jobs in Britain. The interviewers were two senior college staff members with wide job interviewing experience and a college registrar. A job description was drawn up, and the candidate filled in an application form and was able to discuss this and the interview with a friend. One interviewer knew the candi-

Chart 3. *Summary of the job interview*

1.   *Candidate's Application Form*
     (a) Education and previous employment
     (b) Librarianship Course
     (c) Present job

2.   *Professional questions*
     (a) Candidate's views on professional course
     (b) Experience in present job relevant to this application
     (c) Dealing with and getting on with people in the course of the job
     (d) Special professional interest in this post

3.   *Practical details*
     (a) Transport to work
     (b) Evening work
     (c) Housing
     (d) Present contract

date, the other two had not met him. The interviewers planned the structure of the interview and discussed the candidate's form before the actual interview. Although the situation was not real, it was very carefully set up and the people involved found they asked questions and reacted as they had done in previous situations. Discussions were held with the participants after the interview to establish intention and point-of-view, and to compare the differences in interpretation and in inferential processes of the participants. Such discussion is an essential part of the analysis of breakdowns and depends upon a real acceptance by both sides that self-examination and honest appraisal of an interaction is worthwhile.

In structuring the interview, we used the usual formula for this type of professional public service job. A detailed discussion of the structure and conventions of such interviews is contained in Chapter 8 of this volume (Akinnaso and Seabrook Ajirotutu). Chart 3 contains a summary of the structure and content of this library job interview.

The entire interview, although raising significant issues in every exchange, cannot be considered here. We will discuss only the section of the interview arising from the last question under Section 2, question (d). This was the last important question of the interview and was planned to deal with the candidate's special professional interest in the post in the college library. The question was, "Why are you applying for this particular type of job in a college?" There is an assumption in a job interview that all questions, however indirect, are related to the job the candidate has applied for. The degree of indirectness in questioning seems to have no limits. The higher level the job, the more likely it is that questions will be very indirect and the interviewee may have to search the question to find out the interviewer's real intention.

Interviewer 2:   One last question, Mr Sandhu, why are you applying for this particular type of job in a college – a librarian's job in a college?
Applicant: Well, in fact, I have, up till now – um – previous to my – this job which I'm at present doing, I did send about 150 applications and my present job that was the only interview I got and I was accepted there and I was given that job doing and that is a temporary job as you know. Job is going to finish next December – so I desperately need another job – I've already sent about 50 applications but this is my second interview.
Interviewer 2:   I see, thanks very much. Thanks, Mary.

Anyone familiar with this type of interview process in Britain would recognize such a question. The candidate needs to be able to infer from it the message, "What is there about this job which you are interested in professionally and which you think you could do well?" Mr Sandhu fails to respond to the implied question and in discussion afterwards confirmed that he was puzzled and some-what insulted by being asked a question which he interpreted as meaning, "Why do you want a job?" To test the generality of Mr Sandhu's reaction, other South Asian people were asked for their interpretation of the question. The resulting responses confirmed that Mr Sandhu's inference is quite typical of South Asian reactions whereas English people were immediately alerted to the inter-viewer's actual intent.

There are three factors which can be examined in relation to this short exchange. Firstly, the candidate seems to be unfamiliar with or unwilling to comply with the English convention of inviting candidates to 'sell' themselves on the basis of motivation towards a job. Second, the notions of directness and indirectness as under-stood in English convention for asking leading questions are not shared. However, if the candidate was not prepared for this use of indirectness, there was a clue in the interviewer's use of prosody.

This is the third factor. The interviewer raises pitch and increases amplitude on the word "college," implying a contrast between a librarian's job in a college and other librarian jobs. But, as has been described in Chapter 2 of this volume, a South Asian speaker of English is unlikely to interpret the meaning implied by using these prosodic features.

The candidate answered the question literally and introduced what was for him a very important subject, the issue of racial discrimination. But because his answer appeared to be irrelevant, the interviewers failed to listen carefully or to respond to a matter which was central to the candidate's experience of looking for work. This part of the interaction was as unsuccessful for the interviewers as for the interviewee. By failing, also, to convey explicitly, dissatisfaction with Mr Sandhu's reply, the interviewer withheld any direct feedback that might have helped the candidate to recognize that a different type of answer was expected from him. This lack of explicit feedback illustrates the general point that when people feel there has been a misunderstanding they generally become even more indirect.

Because Mr Sandhu's response was unsatisfactory to the question, "Why are you applying for this particular type of job in a college?", another of the interviewers asked a further set of questions on the same point. The original question is pursued by rewording it.

Interviewer 3: What attracts you to this particular librarian job and, in particular, why do you want to come to Middleton College?

Applicant: Well, as I have said, I have already applied for 50 other jobs, you know, sent 50 applications and – er – this is my second interview. I'm not particularly interested in this particular job. I'm interested in a job maybe in an academic library maybe in a public library – any job in this field, you know – I'm qualified for this and I desperately need one.

Interviewer 3: Um – well, we, I think, perhaps might be looking for someone who's really committed to working for the college for the next at least three or four years.

The rephrasing of the first question did not help the candidate at all. He gave an apparently plain answer which has all the lexical repetition and rhythmic features which signal a really relevant and firm response to an English listener: "I'm not particularly interested in this particular job." But this apparent direct response, which suggests the candidate had no interest in the job at all, was only a linking prologue to his main point that he was desperately keen to get *any* job for which he was qualified. Coming at the end of his answer and after an apparent dismissal of the job in question, the seriousness of his application, which for him was extremely serious, was quite overlooked by the interviewers.

We analyzed eighteen significant breakdowns in communication occurring during the whole interview. These arose for a variety of reasons and a significant portion of the interview (about 33% of the time) was spent in trying to resolve or clarify difficulties between interviewee and interviewer but largely without success. The following were some general conclusions arising from the analysis.

(i)   The candidate did not know about the planned overall structure of the interview, and many of the interviewers' key questions were indirect questions. That is, they relied upon the candidate being able to infer the type of answer wanted on the basis of his sharing their assumptions about what is considered relevant at a job interview of this type.

(ii) The candidate frequently made wrong inferences about these indirect questions. However, equally the interviewers made wrong inferences from the candidate's replies. This happened because the candidate's answers were often judged irrelevant, for two particular reasons:
— His way of speaking was not synchronized to the questions in terms of rhythm, key words and other features which indicate to an English ear that the reply is a real response to the question.
— He quite often structured his information so that the most relevant points were at the end of the reply.
For both these reasons, the interviewers were switching off or drawing conclusions unfavorable to the candidate early on in his reply. They failed to register important information which came later in his replies.

(iii) When the candidate failed to answer the indirect question about his professional interest in the post, the interviewers followed up. However, they indicated the previous replies were unsatisfactory by tone of voice and emphasis. Their attempts did not clarify the question but led to serious misunderstanding, to later irrelevant questions, and to some friction.

(iv) The interview in its entirety was judged unsatisfactory by both sides afterwards. The candidate felt he had not been properly questioned on his professional qualities and experience; the interviewers felt he had been unforthcoming and they had learned too little about him. Yet the interview was conducted in such a way that only someone who shared the interviewers' cultural and professional assumptions in the situation, and shared exactly the same means of communication could have done well.

The type of material and analysis which we have illustrated from this particular job interview indicates how data from key types of interaction can be used in training. Such material and discussion of it can be immediately relevant to both majority and minority groups. For example, everyone can agree on what a job interview is and participants will all have been through the experience themselves. But using this type of data and approach, trainees can relate to and analyze the event at a level which challenges their assumptions of shared knowledge about the communicative tasks involved in the interview. The two groups can discover together how apparently uncontroversial and straightforward moments in the interview or in other contexts are in fact problematic and create unexpected misunderstanding and stress which swings the pendulum of power even further over to the interviewer's side.

By working in detail on small pieces of data, the training can examine the involuntary processes of context-creation and inference in key situations of evaluation and negotiation, and through this examination can establish that these processes are culture-specific phenomena which are real only to those socialized into that culture. Selection and use of material such as our example of a job interview provides a concentrated or speeded up experience of how the involuntary processes act on existing assumptions to create a potential for misinterpretation and misunderstanding. The use of audio or video tape also allows momentary reactions and perceptions to be 'frozen,' and analyzed and located within the shared conventions recognized by a particular linguistic group. It is essential later for training to go beyond the analysis of 'outside' data, and for trainees to reach a stage at which they are collecting or creating and then analyzing their own data.

Through the training approach we have described, the presuppositions which enter into interethnic communication and which give rise to the kind of stereotyping described, can be examined using an analytic language, free of psychological overtones. Trainees can be taken through a process of analyzing even subtle and complex communication breakdowns and can use this analysis to question their judgments about behavior and attitude built up in cross-cultural contact.

NOTE

This paper draws upon the field work of the Industrial Language Training (ILT) Service in Britain. ILT is a government-funded training service which exists to help people learn the skills and acquire the awareness and self-confidence to communicate effectively in English in multiethnic workplaces and training workshops. This training is mainly provided at the workplace itself during working hours. The workplace, not the classroom, is taken as the communicative context and training has to be perceived by the learners and by others as actually effective on the shopfloor, in the office or while under instruction. This, in turn, requires that the initial phase of any project is one of observation, involvement with the people working in the environment, participant observation, and analysis. Observations are recorded of the physical and social environment, of how people work together, of their communication networks, of opportunities, and of avoidance strategies which are used. The aim of this phase is to build up an understanding of cross-cultural communication in the specific workplace.

The ILT service recognizes that native speakers of English need training as well as speakers of English as a second language and that an examination of cultural values and norms is an essential component of training for both sorts of language speaker. A wide range of training has been developed for speakers of English as a second language with only basic skills, with advanced skills, for bilingual speakers, and for speakers of English as a first language, particularly in key jobs; for example, supervisors, personnel officers, and trade union shop stewards. Training has also been developed for people in community and service jobs where they meet South Asians as clients; for example, employment services officers, community health workers, and housing officers.

Since 1975, the ILT Service has operated in about 500 workplaces, including manufacturing industry, service industries such as hotels and catering, public transport authorities, civil service departments, health authorities (for ancillary workers and for nurses and doctors), and in skill centres.

Bibliography

Abrahams, R. D. 1963. The "Catch" in negro Philadelphia. *Keystone Folklore Quarterly* 8(3):107–11.

Abrahams, R. D. 1975. Negotiating respect: patterns of presentation among black women. In *Women in Folklore*. C. R. Farrar, ed. Austin: University of Texas Press.

Abrahams, R. D. 1976. *Talking Black*. Rowley, Mass.: Newbury House.

Agar, M. 1973. *Ripping and Running*. New York: Academic Press.

Bauman, R. 1972. The La Have Island General Store: sociability and verbal art in a Nova Scotia community. *Journal of American Folklore* 85:330–43.

Becker, A. L. 1980. Person in Kawi. Typescript.

Berman, A. and Szamosi, M. 1972. Observations on sentential stress. *Language* 48:304–25.

Birdwhistell, R. 1970. *Kinesics and Context: Essays on Body Motion Communication*. Philadelphia: University of Pennsylvania Press.

Blu, K. I. 1977. Varieties of ethnic identity: Anglo-Saxons, blacks and Jews in a Southern county. *Ethnicity* 4:263–86.

Bolinger, D. L. 1958. A theory of pitch accent in English. *Word* 14:109–49.

Bolinger, D. L. 1972. *Intonation*. Harmondsworth, Middx: Penguin Books.

Bourdieu, P. 1973. Cultural reproduction and social reproduction. In *Knowledge, Education and Cultural Change*. R. Brown, ed. London: Tavistock.

Brazil, D. 1975. *Discourse Intonation*. University of Birmingham, English Language Research.

Bresnahan, M. 1981. "Why would I have a syringe?" Linguistic and cultural inference in the testimony of a non-native English speaking defendant. Typescript.

Bronner, S. J. 1978. A Re-examining of white dozens. *Western Folklore* 37(2):118–28.

Brooks-Gunn, J. and Matthews, W. S. 1979. *He and She: How Children Develop their Sex-Role Identity*. Englewood Cliffs, NJ: Prentice-Hall.

Brown, P. and Levinson, S. 1978. Universals in language usage: politeness phenomena. In *Questions and Politeness*. E. N. Goody, ed. Cambridge: Cambridge University Press.

Brown, R. and Gilman, A. 1972. Pronouns of power and solidarity. In *Readings in the Sociology of Language*. J. A. Fishman, ed. The Hague: Mouton.

Burns, T. 1969. On the plurality of social systems. In *Industrial Man*. T. Burns, ed. Harmondsworth, Middx: Penguin Books.

Cappon, P. 1974. *Conflit entre le néo-canadiens et les francophones de Montréal*. Centre Internationale de Recherche sur le Bilingualisme, Quebec: Les Presses de L'Université Laval.

Castles, S. and Kosack, G. 1973. *Immigrant Workers and the Class Structure in Western Europe*. London: Oxford University Press and Institute of Race Relations.

Cazden, C. and Hymes, D. 1978. Narrative thinking and storytelling rights: a folklorist's clue to a critique of education. *Keystone Folklore Quarterly* 22:21–36.

Chafe, W. 1976. Givenness, contrastiveness, definiteness, subjects, topics and point of view. In *Subject and Topic*. C. Li, ed. New York: Academic Press.

Chafe, W. 1980. The deployment of consciousness in the production of a narrative. In *The Pear Stories*. W. Chafe, ed. Norwood, NJ: Ablex.

Chao, Y. R. 1968. *A Grammar of Modern Spoken Chinese*. Berkeley and Los Angeles: University of California Press.

Civil Service Department 1978. *Application of race relations policy in the Civil Service*. London: Her Majesty's Stationery Office. Study undertaken by the Tavistock Institute of Human Relations.

Cole, P. and Morgan, J. L. (eds) 1975. *Syntax and Semantics*, vol. 3: *Speech Acts*. New York: Academic Press.

Condon, J. C. and Ogsten, D. 1969. Speech and body motion. In *Perception of Language*. P. Kjeldergaard, ed. Columbus, Ohio: Charles Merrill.

Covelli, L. H. and Murray, S. O. 1980. Accomplishing topic change. *Anthropological Linguistics* 22:382–9.

Crystal, D. 1969. *Prosodic Systems and Intonation in English*. Cambridge: Cambridge University Press.

Crystal, D. 1975. *The English Tone of Voice*. London: Edward Arnold.

Danet, B. 1980. Language in the legal process. In *Law and Society Review*. Special Issue on Contemporary Issues in Law and Social Sciences. R. A. Able, ed.

Denzin, N. 1970. *The Research Act in Sociology*. London: Duckworth.

Department of Employment, Unit of Manpower Studies 1974. *The Role of Immigrants in the Labour Market*. London: Department of Employment.

Dillard, J. L. 1972. *Black English*. New York: Random House.

Doeringer, P. and Piore, M. 1971. *International Labor Markets and Manpower Analysis*. Lexington, Mass.: Heath.

Eder, D. and Hallinan, M. T. 1978. Sex differences in children's friendships. *American Sociological Review* 43:237–50.

Ekman, P. and Friesen, W. 1969. The repertoire of non-verbal behavior: origins, usage, coding and categories. *Semiotica* 1: 49–98.

Emmeneau, M. 1964. India as a linguistic area. In *Language in Culture and Society*. D. Hymes, ed. New York: Harper and Row.

Erickson, F. 1975. Gatekeeping and the melting pot: interaction in counseling encounters. *Harvard Educational Review* 45(1): 44–70.

Erickson, F. and Schultz, J. J. 1982. *The Counselor as Gatekeeper*. New York: Academic Press.

Ervin-Tripp, S. 1970. Structure and process in language acquisition. In *21st Annual Roundtable Monograph Series on Language and Linguistics*. J. E. Alatis, ed. Washington DC: Georgetown University Press.

Ervin-Tripp, S. 1972. On sociolinguistic rules: alternation and co-occurrence. In *Directions in Sociolinguistics*. J. J. Gumperz and D. Hymes, eds. New York: Holt, Rinehart and Winston.

Ervin-Tripp, S. 1976. Is Sybil there? The structure of some American English directives. *Language in Society* 5:25–66.

Etherton, P. 1975. The language of supervisors and operatives in a spinning mill. MA dissertation. University of Lancaster.

Faris, J. C. 1966. The dynamics of verbal exchange: a Newfoundland example. *Anthropologica* (Ottawa) 8(2):235–48.

Fishman, P. M. 1978. Interaction: the work women do. *Social Problems* 25(4):397–406.

Foley, W. A. 1980. Towards a universal typology of grammar. *Studies in Language* 4(2):171–99.

Frake, C. 1969. The ethnographic study of cognitive systems. In *Cognitive Anthropology*. S. A. Tyler, ed. New York: Holt, Rinehart and Winston.

Frake, C. 1975. How to enter a Yakan house. In *Sociocultural Dimensions of Language Use*. M. Sanches and B. Blount, eds. New York: Academic Press.

Garfinkel, H. 1967. *Studies in Ethnomethodology*. Englewood Cliffs, NJ: Prentice-Hall.

Geoghegan, W. 1981. Samal personal pronouns. Typescript.

Giles, H. and Powesland, P. F. 1975. *Speech Style and Social Evaluation*. New York: Academic Press.

Glazer, N. and Moynihan, D. P. 1975. *Beyond the Melting Pot*. Chicago: University of Chicago Press.

Goffman, E. 1959. *The presentation of self in everyday life*. Garden City, NY: Doubleday.

Goffman, E. 1961. *Encounters*. Indianapolis: Bobbs Merrill.

Goffman, E. 1963. *Stigma: Notes on the Management of Spoiled Identity*. Englewood Cliffs, NJ: Prentice-Hall.

Goffman, E. 1967. *Interaction Ritual: Essays on Face-to-Face Behavior*. Garden City, NY: Anchor Books, Doubleday and Co., Inc.

Goffman, E. 1981. *Forms of Talk*. Philadelphia: University of Pennsylvania Press.

Goodwin, M. 1978. Conversational practices in a peer group of urban black children. Doctoral dissertation. University of Pennsylvania, Philadelphia.

Goodwin, M. 1980a. Directive-response speech sequences in girls' and boys' task activities. In *Women and Language in Literature and Society*. S. McConnell-Ginet, R. Borker, and N. Furman, eds. New York: Praeger.

Goodwin, M. 1980b. He-said-she-said: formal cultural procedures for the construction of a gossip dispute activity. *American Ethnologist* 7(4):674–95.

Goody, E. N. 1978. Towards a theory of questions, In *Questions and Politeness*. E. N. Goody, ed. Cambridge: Cambridge University Press.

Grice, H. P. 1975. Logic and conversation. In *Syntax and Semantics*, vol. 3: *Speech Acts*. P. Cole and J. P. Morgan, eds. New York: Academic Press.

Gubbay, D. 1978. Personal audio-taped interviews. Unpublished.

Gumperz, J. J. 1975. Language, communication and public negotiation. In *Anthropology and the Public Interest: Fieldwork and Theory*. P. Sanday, ed. New York: Academic Press.

Gumperz, J. J. 1977. Sociocultural knowledge in conversational inference. In *Linguistics and Anthropology*. M. Saville-Troike, ed. Washington DC: Georgetown University Press (Georgetown University Round Table on Languages and Linguistics, 1977).

Gumperz, J. J. 1978a. The conversational analysis of interethnic communication. In *Interethnic Communication*. E. Lamar Ross, ed. Athens, Ga.: University of Georgia Press.

Gumperz, J. J. 1978b. Dialect and conversational inference in urban communication. *Language in Society* 7(3):393–409.

Gumperz, J. J. 1979. The sociolinguistic basis of speech act theory. In *Speech Act Ten Years After*. J. Boyd and S. Ferrara, eds. Milan: Versus.

Gumperz, J. J. 1982. *Discourse Strategies*. Cambridge: Cambridge University Press.

Gumperz, J. J. and Cook-Gumperz, J. 1976. Context in children's speech. Language Behavior Research Laboratory, Working Paper No. 46. University of California, Berkeley.

Gumperz, J. J. and Tannen, D. 1979. Individual and social differences in language use. In *Individual Differences in Language Ability and Language Behavior*. W. Wang and C. Fillmore, eds. New York: Academic Press.

Gumperz, J. J. and Roberts, C. 1980. Developing awareness skills for inter-ethnic communication. Occasional Paper No. 12. Seameo Regional Language Centre, Singapore.

Gumperz, J. J., Agrawal, A., and Aulakh, G. 1977. Prosody, paralinguistics and contextualization in Indian English. Language Behavior Research Laboratory, typescript. University of California, Berkeley.

Gumperz, J. J., Jupp, T. C., and Roberts, C. 1979. *Crosstalk: a study of cross-cultural communication*. London: National Centre for Industrial Language Training in association with the BBC.

Guthrie, G. M. and Azores, F. M. 1961. Philippine interpersonal behavior patterns. In *Modernization, its Impact in the Philippines III*. Walden F. Bells and A. deGuzmand, eds. IPC Papers, No. 6, Atteneo de Manila. Quezon City: University Press.

Haas, A. 1979. The acquisition of genderlect. In Language, Sex and Gender: Does La Différence make a Difference? J. Orasnu, M. Slater, and L. Adler, eds. *Annals of the New York Academy of Sciences* 327:101–13.

Hall, E. T. 1959. *The Silent Language*. New York: Doubleday.

Halliday, M. A. K. 1967. *Intonation and Grammar in British English*. The Hague: Mouton.

Halliday, M. A. K. 1975. *Learning How to Mean*. London: Edward Arnold.

Halliday, M. A. K. and Hasan, R. 1976. *Cohesion in English*. London: Longmans.

Hannerz, U. 1969. *Soulside*. New York: Columbia University Press.

Harding, S. 1975. Women and words in a Spanish village. In *Towards an Anthropology of Women*. R. Reiter, ed. New York: Monthly Review Press.

Hechter, M. 1978. Considerations on Western European ethnoregionalism. Paper presented at conference on Ethnicity and Economic Development. University of Michigan, Ann Arbor. October 1978.

Heller, A. F. n.d. Recent innovations in ambulatory health services. Department of Sociology, McGill University, Montreal.

Heller, A. F. and Solomon, D. N. 1976. Innovation and personal strategies: a study of work in a new out-patient clinic. Department of Sociology, McGill University, Montreal.

Hirschman, L. 1973. Female–male differences in conversational interaction. Paper presented at Linguistic Society of America, San Diego.

Hymes, D. 1974. *Foundations in Sociolinguistics*. Philadelphia: University of Pennsylvania Press.

Jakobson, R. 1971. Boas' view of grammatical meaning. In *Selected Papers*, vol. 2. R. Jakobson. The Hague: Mouton.

Jefferson, G. 1978. Sequential aspects of storytelling in conversation. In *Studies in the Organisation of Conversation Interaction*. J. Schenker, ed. New York: Academic Press.

Johnson, J. L. 1980. Questions and role responsibility in four professional meetings. *Anthropological Linguistics* 22:66–76.

Jones, W. E. 1971a. Syllables and word-stress in Hindi. *Journal of the International Phonetics Association*: 47–78.

Jones, W. E. 1971b. A reading transcription for Hindi. *Journal of the International Phonetics Association*: 88–97.

Jupp, T. C. 1981. *Evidence given to House of Commons Home Affairs Committee, Race Relations and Immigration Sub-Committee Session 1980–81 22 January 1981*. London: Her Majesty's Stationery Office.

Kachru, B. 1970. Some style features of South Asian English. In *National Identity*. K. L. Goodwin, ed. London and Melbourne: Heinemann Educational Books.

Kalčik, S. 1975. ". . . Like Anne's gynecologist or the time I was almost raped": personal narratives in women's rap groups. In *Women and Folklore*. C. R. Farrar, ed. Austin: University of Texas Press.

Kalin, R. and Rayko, D. 1980. The social significance of speech in the job interview. In *The Social and Psychological Contexts of Language*. Robert N. St. Clair and Howard Giles, eds. Cambridge: Cambridge University Press.

Kaplan, R. B. 1966. Cultural thought patterns in inter-cultural education. *Language Learning* 16:1–20.

Kendon, A. 1970. Movement coordination in social action. *Psychologica* 32:100–24.

Kochman, T. 1971. Cross-cultural communication: contrasting perspectives, conflicting sensibilities. *Florida F1 Reporter* Spring–Fall: 3–16.

Kress, G. and Fowler, R. 1979. Interviews. In *Language and Control*. R. Fowler, B. Hodge, G. Kress, and T. Trew, eds. Boston, Mass.: Routledge and Kegan Paul.

Labov, W. 1972. Ritual insults. In *Language in the Inner City*. Philadelphia: University of Pennsylvania Press.

Labov, W. 1973. *Language in the Inner City*. Philadelphia: University of Pennsylvania Press.

Labov, W. and Fanshel, D. 1977. *Therapeutic Discourse: Psychotherapy as Conversation*. New York: Academic Press.

Lada, R. D. 1976. Intonation, main clause phenomena, and point of view. Typescript.

Lakoff, R. 1973. The logic of politeness; or, minding your p's and q's. *CLS* 10: Chicago Linguistics Society.

Lakoff, R. 1975. *Language and Women's Place*. New York: Harper and Row.

Lakoff, R. 1979. Stylistic strategies within a grammar of style. In *Language, Sex, and Gender*. J. Orasanu, M. Slater, and L. Loeb Adler, eds. *Annals of the New York Academy of Sciences* 327: 53–78.

Laver, R. 1972. Voice quality and indexical information. In *Face to Face Interaction*. R. Laver and J. Hutchinson, eds. Harmondsworth, Middx: Penguin.

LeMasters, E. E. 1975. *Blue Collar Aristocrats: Life-Styles at a Working-Class Tavern*. Madison: University of Wisconsin Press.

Lever, J. 1976. Sex differences in the games children play. *Social Problems* 23:478–83.

Lever, J. 1978. Sex differences in the complexity of children's play and games. *American Sociological Review* 43-471–83.

Li, C. and Thompson, S. 1976. Subject and topic: A new typology of language. In *Subject and Topic*. Charles Li, ed. New York: Academic Press.

Liberman, M. and Sag, I. A. 1974. Prosodic Form and Discourse Function. *CLS* 10: Chicago Linguistic Society.

Lynch, F. 1973. Social acceptance reconsidered. In *Four Readings on Philippine Values*. IPC Papers No. 2, Atteneo de Manila. Quezon City: University Press.

Maltz, D. N. and Borker, R. A. 1980. 'Boy talk'/'girl talk': gender-based differences in friendly conversation. Paper presented at the Annual Meeting of the Knoeber Anthropological Society and Berkeley Sociolinguistics Group.

McGuire, M. T. and Lorch, S. 1968. Natural language and conversation modes. *Journal of Nervous and Mental Diseases* 146:239–48.

Meditch, A. 1975. The development of sex-specific speech patterns in young children. *Anthropological Linguistics* 17:421–33.

Mitchell-Kernan, C. 1972. Signifying and marking: two Afro American speech acts. In *Directions in Sociolinguistics*. J. J. Gumperz and D. Hymes, eds. New York: Holt. Rinehart and Winston.

Moore, R. 1975. Migrants and the class structure of Western Europe. In *Industrial Society; Class Cleavage and Control*. R. Scase, ed. New York: St. Martin's Press.

National Centre for Industrial Language Training 1977. *Annual Report 1976*. London: National Centre for Industrial Language Training.

Naylor, P. B. 1980. Legal testimony and the non-native speaker of English. Typescript.

O'Connor, J. D. and Arnold, G. F. 1961. *The Intonation of Colloquial English*. London: Longmans.

Ogbu, J. 1978. *Minority Education and Caste: The American System in Cross-Cultural Perspective*. New York: Academic Press.

Ohala, M. 1977. Stress in Hindi. In *Stressfest*. L. Hyman, ed. Southern California: Occasional Papers in Linguistics.

Pacana, H. C. 1958. Notes on a Filipino rule of conduct: non-interference. *Philippine Sociological Review* 6(1):29–30.

Pawley, A. and Syder, F. 1978. Sentence formulation in spontaneous speech: the one-clause-at-a-time hypothesis. Typescript.

Peach, C. 1968. *West Indian Migration to Britain*. London: Oxford University Press.

Philipsen, G. 1975. Speaking 'like a man' in Teamsterville: cultural patterns of role enactment in an urban neighborhood. *Quarterly Journal of Speech* 61:13–22.

Pike, K. L. 1945. *The Intonation of American English*. Ann Arbor: University of Michigan Press.

Pollner, M. 1979. Explicative transactions: making and managing meaning in traffic court. In *Everyday Language*. G. Psathas ed. New York: Irvington, Publishers, Inc.

Propp, V. 1958. *Morphology of the Folktale*. Ed. with an introduction by S. Pirkova-Jacobson. Trans. L. Scott. Bloomington: Indiana University Research Center in Anthropology, Folklore and Linguistics, No. 10.

Rapport de la Commission (Gendron)d'Enquête (1972) sur la situation de la langue francaise et sur les droits linguistiques au Québec. Livre I: *La Langue de travail*. Livre II: *Les Groupes ethniques*. Québec: Gouvernement du Québec.

Rex, J. and Tomlinson, S. 1979. *Colonial Immigrants in a British City*. London: Routledge and Kegan Paul.

Rey, A. 1977. Accent and employability. *Language Sciences* October 1977:7–12.

Richler, M. 1977. Oh Canada! Lament for a divided country. *The Atlantic Monthly*. December: 41–55.

Robinson, J. A. 1981. Personal narratives reconsidered. *Journal of American Folklore* 94:58–85.

Rothstein, M. and Jackson, D. N. 1980. Decision-making in the employment interview: an experimental approach. *Journal of Applied Psychology* 65:271–83.

Sacks, H. 1974. An analysis of the course of a joke's telling in conversation. In *Explorations in the Ethnography of Speaking*. R. Bauman and J. Scherzer, eds. Cambridge: Cambridge University Press.

Sacks, H. and Schegloff, E. 1974. Opening up closings. In *Ethnomethodology*. R. Turner, ed. Harmondsworth, Middx: Penguin.

Sacks, H., Schegloff, E., and Jefferson, G. 1974. A simplest systematics for the organization of turn-taking in conversation. *Language* 50(4):696–735.

Sag, I. A. and Liberman, M. 1975. The intonational disambiguation of indirect speech acts. *CLS* 11: Chicago Linguistic Society.

Sanches, M. 1975. Falling words: An analysis of a Japanese Rakugo performance. In *Sociocultural Dimensions of Language Use*. B. Blount and M. Sanches, eds. New York: Academic Press.

Savin-Williams, R. C. 1976. The ethological study of dominance formation and maintenance in a group of human adolescents. *Child Development* 47:972–9.

Schachter, P. and Otanes, F. T. 1972. *Tagalog Reference Grammar*. Berkeley: University of California Press.

Schegloff, E. 1972. Sequencing in conversational openings. In *Directions in Sociolinguistics*. J. J. Gumperz and D. Hymes, eds. New York: Holt, Rinehart and Winston.

Schutz, A. 1970. *On Phenomenology and Social Relations*. Chicago: University of Chicago Press.

Scollon, R. Forthcoming. The machine stops: silence in the metaphor of malfunction. In *The Uses of Silence* D. Tannen and M. Saville-Troike.

Seaman, P. D. 1972. *Modern Greek and American English in contact*. The Hague: Mouton, 1972.

Searle, J. 1975. Indirect speech acts. In *Syntax and Semantics* Vol. 3: *Speech Acts*. P. Cole and J. L. Morgan, eds. New York: Academic Press.

Selltiz, C. et al. 1964. *Research Methods in Social Relations*. New York: Holt, Rinehart and Winston.

Shuy, R. 1974. Problems of communication in the cross-cultural medical interview. *Working Papers in Sociolinguistics* 19. Austin, Texas: Southwest Educational Development Laboratory.

Silverman, D. 1973. Interview talk: bringing off a research instrument. *Sociology* 7:31–48.

Slobin, D. I. 1975. Language change in childhood and in history. Language Behavior Research Laboratory, Working Paper No. 41. University of California, Berkeley.

Smeall, C. 1976. Intonation. Special Field Exam. University of California, Berkeley.

Smith, D. J. 1977. *Racial Disadvantage in Britain*, The PEP Report, Harmondsworth, Middx: Penguin Books.

Smith, D. J. 1980. *Overseas Doctors in the National Health Service*. London: Heinemann Educational Books.

Smith D. J. 1981. *Unemployment and Racial Minorities*. The Policy Studies Institute, Castle Lane, London SW1.

Smitherman, G. 1977. *Talkin and Testifyin*. Boston: Houghton Mifflin.

Solomon, R. H. 1971. *Mao's Revolution and the Chinese Political Culture*. Berkeley: University of California Press.

Soskin, W. F. and John, V. P. 1963. The study of spontaneous talk. In *The Stream of Behavior*. R. G. Barker, ed. New York: Appleton-Century-Croft.

Strodbeck, F. L. and Mann, R. D. 1956. Sex role differentiation in jury deliberations. *Sociometry* 19:3–11.

Tannen, D. 1976. An indirect/direct look at misunderstanding. Master's thesis. University of California, Berkeley.

Tannen, D. 1979. Processes and consequences of conversational style. Ph.D. dissertation. University of California, Berkeley.

Tannen, D. 1981. New York Jewish conversational style. *International Journal of the Sociology of Language* 30:133–49.

Taylor, S. 1967. A preliminary study of the stress system in Indian English. Unpublished paper. University of Illinois, Urbana, Ill.

Trager, G. L. and Smith, H. L. 1951. An outline of English structure. *Studies in Linguistics*: Occasional Paper No. 1.

Traugott, E. C. 1979. From referential to discourse meaning. Paper presented at Colloquium of the Berkeley Sociolinguistics Group, University of California, Berkeley.

Trim, J. 1976. English Intonation. Typescript. Department of Linguistics, University of Cambridge.

US Department of Labor 1973. *The role of local governments under CETA*. Washington DC.

Van Dijk, T. A. 1977. *Text and Context*. London: Longmans.

Varma, M. K. 1971. The particles *hi* and *bhi* in Hindi. Typescript.

Vassiliou, V., Triandis, H., Vassiliou, G., and McGuire, H. 1972. Interpersonal contact and sterotyping. In *The Analysis of Subjective Culture*. H. Triandis, ed. New York: Wiley.

Wallace, A. 1970, *Culture and Personality*. New York: Random House.

Walsall ILT Unit. 1980. Assessment of communications training needs. Walsall: Industrial Language Training Unit.

Weiser, A. 1975. How not to answer a question: purposive devices in conversational strategy. *CLS* 11: Chicago Linguistic Society.

West, C. 1979. Against our will: male interruptions of females in cross-sex conversation. In Language, Sex and Gender: Does La Différence make a Difference?. J. Oransanu, M. Slater and L. Adler, eds. *Annals of the New York Academy of Sciences* 327:81–100.

West, C. and Zimmerman, D. H. 1977. Women's place in everyday talk: reflections on parent–child interaction. *Social Problems* 24(5):521–9.

Zimmerman, D. H. 1974. Fact as practical accomplishment. In *Ethnomethodology*. R. Turner, ed. Harmondsworth, Middx: Penguin Books.

Zimmerman, D. H. and West, C. 1975. Sex roles, interruptions, and silences in conversation. In *Language and Sex: Differences and Dominance*. B. Thorne and N. Henley, eds. Rowley, Mass. Newbury House.

Subject index

Tagalog 163, 173, 179, 181–6, 191,
  193; *see also* Filipinos in USA
  verb aspect 185–6, 193
  verb tense 174–5, 186, 193
temporal ordering in discourse 64–71
thematic structure in discourse 22–56,
  60–1, 64–71, 171, 183; *see also*
  information structuring
topic, discourse 25–6, 33, 41, 48, 56
topicalization 27, 28, 33, 41, 42, 192
topic–comment relationship 73–5,
  77

Urdu 32; *see also* North Indian
  languages

West Indian English 148–9, 154–6; *see
  also* Black English in USA
  prosody of 159–62
Western English *see* Indian English vs.
  Western English
word order in Hindi and Indian
  English 32–6

yes and *no* 46

Author index

272 *Author index*